RURAL PUBLIC POLICY DEBATES IN INDIA

About the Editors

Prof. (Dr.) M.R. Biju, currently working as Dean, School of Social Sciences and Professor of Public Administration and Policy Studies, Central University of Kerala, Kasaragod. He has served the full term as Dean, School of Social Sciences (2017-2020), School of Legal Studies (2019-2022) and also a short span as Dean, Academic (2020). Prof. M.R. Biju is one of the widely cited writers in the field of Social Sciences with 161 citations and H-index of 6 and i10 index of 3.

Prof. Biju is the Editor of *South Asian Journal of Socio-Political Studies* (*SAJOSPS*), a UGC Listed Journal (No. 34425 dated 11.01.2017 with an impact factor of 3.1028). He is also serving as Editor-in-Chief of *International Journal of Political Science* (*IJOPS*). He is a prolific writer on socio-political and developmental issues.

He has published Thirty five (35) books, One hundred and Seventy-Five (175) research papers, Seventeen (17) book chapters and 11 (Eleven) Seminar Proceedings. All the books were published by leading publishing houses in New Dehi. He has delivered 78 (Seventy-Eight) Invited Lectures, 16 (Sixteen) Key note addresses and reviewed over Nine Hundred books for *South Asian Journal of Socio-Political Studies.*

His teaching and research experience, spanning over three decades, includes several achievements such as completion of three major research projects funded by Ministry of Panchayati Raj, Government of India and University Grants Commission, New Delhi and the post-doctoral fellowship awarded by the UGC in 2004-07. He has also successfully guided doctoral students of the University of Kerala. Seven students are currently pursuing their doctoral studies under his supervision at CUK. He is consistently making professional academic contributions in the capacity of an Associate Board Member of *Economics and Management*, a prestigious journal published by the Technical University of Liberce, Czech Republic; as the Director and Member Secretary of the Asian Institute of Development Research (AIDR); and as a life Member of several Academic and Professional Bodies.

M.R.B. Anantha Padmanabha is currently serving as Deputy Editor of *South Asian Journal of Socio-Political Studies.* He has to his credit a sizeable number of publications in reputed research journals and he has presented papers in National Seminars and Conferences. He is a Doctoral Student in International Relations and Politics at Central University of Kerala, Kasaragod.

RURAL PUBLIC POLICY DEBATES IN INDIA

Edited by
M.R. Biju
M.R.B. Anantha Padmanabha

CONCEPT PUBLISHING COMPANY PVT. LTD.
NEW DELHI - 110059

ISBN: 978-93-5594-669-0

First Published 2025

Published and Printed by

Concept
Since 1974

Concept Publishing Company Pvt. Ltd.
A/15-16, Commercial Block, Mohan Garden
New Delhi-110059 (India)
T: +91-11-41101460
E: publishing@conceptpub.com, *W*: www.conceptpub.com

Cataloging in Publication--Courtesy: D.K. Agencies (P) Ltd. <docinfo@dkagencies.com>

Rural public policy debates in India / edited by M.R. Biju, M.R.B. Anantha Padmanabha.
pages cm
Contributed articles.
Includes bibliographical references and index.
ISBN 9789355946690

1. Rural development--India. 2. Rural development--Government policy--India. I. Biju, M. R., 1965- editor. II. Anantha Padmanabha, M. R. B., editor.

LCC HN690.Z9C6 2025 | DDC 307.14120954 23

Preface and Acknowledgements

Rural Public Policy Debates in India encompass a wide range of critical issues and reflect the complex challenges faced by rural communities. Agriculture and rural development, poverty alleviation, education and skill development, healthcare and sanitation, infrastructure development, natural resource management, and governance and decentralization are key areas of contention and deliberation. These debates underline the need for comprehensive and integrated approaches to rural development that address the multidimensional aspects of rural life. To navigate these challenges, policymakers must adopt evidence-based approaches and engage in inclusive and participatory decision-making processes. It is crucial to involve diverse stakeholders, including rural communities, civil society organizations, academia, and experts, in policy formulation and implementation. This ensures that policies are grounded in local realities and take into account the needs and aspirations of rural populations.

Furthermore, addressing the interlinkages between different policy areas is essential. For instance, improving agricultural productivity and ensuring food security can contribute to poverty reduction, while investments in rural infrastructure can enhance access to education, healthcare, and markets. Adopting a holistic perspective that recognizes the interconnectedness of rural issues is key to achieving sustainable development outcomes. In addition to policy formulation, effective implementation and monitoring mechanisms are crucial for translating policies into tangible outcomes on the ground. This requires building institutional capacity at various levels, ensuring adequate financial resources, promoting accountability, and leveraging technology for efficient service delivery and data-driven decision-making.

Rural Public Policy Debates in India also need to take into account the diverse socio-cultural contexts and regional variations that exist within the country. Solutions cannot be one-size-fits-all, and policies must be tailored to address the specific challenges and opportunities unique to each region. It is important to note that rural public policy debates are not static, but evolve over time in response to changing socio-economic and environmental dynamics. Continuous dialogue, research, and evaluation are essential to adapt policies to emerging challenges and leverage new opportunities. Ultimately, rural public policy debates in India reflect the aspirations of creating inclusive, sustainable, and prosperous rural communities. By addressing the challenges in agriculture, poverty, education, healthcare, infrastructure, natural resource management, and governance, policymakers can contribute to transforming rural India and unlocking its immense potential for growth and development. Thus, rural public policy debates in India encompass a broad spectrum of issues, requiring comprehensive and integrated approaches to address the multifaceted challenges faced by rural communities. By fostering inclusive and participatory processes, adopting evidence-based approaches, and recognizing the interconnectedness of rural issues, policymakers can drive sustainable rural development and create a more equitable and prosperous India. Against this backdrop, this volume presents sixteen chapters on varied aspects and issues connected with rural public policy in India, viz. nature of rural public policy issues connected with unemployed youth, matters related to global goals and local actions, involvement of private sector in public health care system, public policy debates pertaining to child care, child parents relations, general issues in rural public health, *Swachh Bharat* mission, deprivations and vulnerabilities of the child bride, gender and development in rural areas, food security among the socially excluded communities, health status of STs, inclusive development in rural areas, financial literacy, political empowerment at the grassroots etc.

Before concluding, the volume editors, would like to add that through these research papers and articles from the academics and researchers, they have tried to explore and examine a few fundamental issues confronted with the management of COVID-19 during the pandemic days. Apart from their presentations, the contributors have submitted solid and practical suggestions to revitalise the system, which may be useful for the students, researchers, practitioners and policymakers in the field. These prefatory remarks remain incomplete without expressing our gratitude to those who have been kind enough to help us in the preparation of this volume. First of all, we would like to thank our esteemed contributors to this anthology of articles. Similarly, we are extremely thankful to Shri Ashok Kumar Mittal, Managing Director of Concept Publishing Company Pvt. Ltd., New Delhi, who brought out the volume in an elegant form.

M.R. Biju
M.R.B. Anantha Padmanabha

Introduction

Rural Public Policy Debates in India encompass a wide range of critical issues and reflect the complex challenges faced by rural communities. Agriculture and rural development, poverty alleviation, education and skill development, healthcare and sanitation, infrastructure development, natural resource management, and governance and decentralization are key areas of contention and deliberation. These debates underline the need for comprehensive and integrated approaches to rural development that address the multidimensional aspects of rural life. To navigate these challenges, policymakers must adopt evidence-based approaches and engage in inclusive and participatory decision-making processes. It is crucial to involve diverse stakeholders, including rural communities, civil society organizations, academia, and experts, in policy formulation and implementation. This ensures that policies are grounded in local realities and take into account the needs and aspirations of rural populations.

Furthermore, addressing the interlinkages between different policy areas is essential. For instance, improving agricultural productivity and ensuring food security can contribute to poverty reduction, while investments in rural infrastructure can enhance access to education, healthcare, and markets. Adopting a holistic perspective that recognizes the interconnectedness of rural issues is key to achieving sustainable development outcomes. In addition to policy formulation, effective implementation and monitoring mechanisms are crucial for translating policies into tangible outcomes on the ground. This requires building institutional capacity at various levels, ensuring adequate financial resources, promoting accountability, and leveraging technology for efficient service delivery and data-driven decision-making.

Rural Public Policy Debates in India also needs to take into account the diverse socio-cultural contexts and regional variations that exist within the country. Solutions cannot be one-size-fits-all, and policies must be tailored to address the specific challenges and opportunities unique to each region. It is important to note that rural public policy debates are not static, but evolve over time in response to changing socio-economic and environmental dynamics. Continuous dialogue, research, and evaluation are essential to adapt policies to emerging challenges and leverage new opportunities. Ultimately, rural public policy debates in India reflect the aspirations of creating inclusive, sustainable, and prosperous rural communities. By addressing the challenges in agriculture, poverty, education, healthcare, infrastructure, natural resource management, and governance, policymakers can contribute to transforming rural India and unlocking its immense potential for growth and development. Thus, rural public policy debates in India encompass a broad spectrum of issues, requiring comprehensive and integrated approaches to address the multifaceted challenges faced by rural communities. By fostering inclusive and participatory processes, adopting evidence-based approaches, and recognizing the interconnectedness of rural issues, policymakers can drive sustainable rural development and create a more equitable and prosperous India. Against this backdrop, this volume presents sixteen chapters on varied aspects and issues connected with rural public policy in India, viz. nature of rural public policy issues connected with unemployed youth, matters related to global goals and local actions, involvement of private sector in public healthcare system, public policy debates pertaining to childcare, child-parents relations, general issues in rural public health, *Swachh Bharat* mission, deprivations and vulnerabilities of the child bride, gender and development in rural areas, food security among the socially excluded communities, health status of STs, inclusive development in rural areas, financial literacy, political empowerment at the grassroots etc.

Content of the Volume

In the inaugural chapter **Md. Ayub Mallick** presents a detailed enquiry on the nature of rural public policy in India based on his studies from the state of West Bengal. According to the researcher, public is a group or a programme of action intended to fulfil certain common goals with certain course within a certain environment, both intra-societal and extra-societal. Public policies are the purposive actions on the part of the government (Presthus, 1975 and Anderson, 1975). Public policies are formulated by authorities and these are authoritative allocation of values (Easton, 1965). The policies provided by the political system produce new demands as inputs through feedback mechanism within particular environment. But, how decisions are made within the 'black box' that converts mass demands into policies? Elite theorists regard policies come from upward to downwards, masses are passive receivers. There is mass-elite gap. The elites try to share the basic values and norms of the society and try to maintain the social system—they influence and dominate masses producing mass culture through mass culture industry suitable for neo-market liberal society. In public policy process, there are few steps—identification, formulation of policy, implementation of policy, necessary outcomes and evaluation of policy, necessary outcomes and evaluation of policy in pursuance of the present environment and situation. It is a continuous process —a 'feedback' linkage—'evaluations of current policy identify new problems and set in motion the policy-making process once again' (Dye, 1992: 16-17). Planning-Programming-Budgeting System (PPBS) is to regularize and legitimize decision-making in bureaucracy by and through defining the programme objectives, measuring the project outcomes and the cost-benefit analysis. Demands made by the civil society are legitimized through 'passive revolution of capital'.

The author further adds that rural public policy formulation and rural development in India is in the process of transition and in the phase of prismatic society. The development paradigm is within and between fused and diffracted. The basic problems faced by the Indian populace is service delivery of basic needs. All the policies taken in the globalized world are essentially oriented to neo-liberal market set up and to continue the process of passive revolution of capital. Rural development policies in the spheres of health, education and employment are at stake. There are many provisions for social welfare in rural areas, but there is rank and rivalry. Due to contestations and political marketing rural development is not conducive to the needs of the rural down-troddens. Socio-economic development in terms of equality, capacity and differentiation is very poor. Mobilization is poor. Globalization, mobilization and development—all these are not synchronized due to loopholes of 'agraria-industria' transition. The social attitudes of non-participation and non-satisfaction, aspiration-satisfaction gap are growing day by day. The need is the change from 'passive revolution' of Gramsci to 'democratic herd' of Nietzschian paradigm, participation, dialogue, representation, mass politics, mass culture, public education and counter-revolution on the part of the underprivileged.

Shankar Chatterjee *et al.* in chapter two examine Impact of DDU-GKY among Rural Unemployed Youth. It is a case study from Five States of India. The authors by citing a statistics of Centre for Monitoring Indian Economy states that India's labour market is under pressure mainly because of a fall in the employment rate in rural India and continued low employment rate in urban India. Employment generation is need of the hour in India both in rural and urban areas. In India, two major employment programmes for rural youth are—RSETI and DDUGKY. RSETIs mean Rural Self-Employment Training Institutes, an initiative of the Ministry of Rural Development (MoRD) to have dedicated infrastructure in each district of the country to impart training and skill upgradation of rural youth geared towards entrepreneurship development. And the Deen Dayal Upadhyaya Grameen Kaushal Yojana (DDU-GKY) was launched on 25 September, 2014 with the dual objectives of adding diversity to the incomes of rural poor families and caters to the career aspirations of rural youth with wage employment. DDU-GKY is exclusively focused on rural youth between the ages of 15 and 35 years from Below Poverty Line (BPL) families. In this chapter, a few lines about DDU-GKY with successful cases across India and Amritsar, Punjab (in Amritsar study was carried by Shankar Chatterjee in August 2017) are presented. Also the authors feel that academicians, researchers and others can take up extensive research on DDU-GKY. And educated persons should inform rural youth about the *Yojana* so that rural youth can take the advantage.

In chapter three, **S. Nagabhushana Rao** presents a chapter titled Global Goals: Local Action No One is Left Behind: A Case of Jorand Jharia. According to Rao, global goals, known as Sustainable Development Goals (SDGs) are a new global development vision to create a better world by 2030. The global goals were adopted by the 193 countries and India is a visionary to the document. The global goals or Sustainable Development Goals (SDGs) are universally set goals to create a better and sustainable future for all by transforming our world. It is the agenda for 2030 for sustainable development. The countries are expected to frame their agenda and policies over the next 15 years. Already, 5 years have elapsed and remaining 10 years, the countries are expected to transform the world by framing and implementing the policies, to end poverty, to fight inequality, to protect the plant, to enjoy peace and to ensure prosperity for all. This is to create equitable society and providing social and economic justice for all in the world. Aims of the global goals are 'define the world we want in future and to ensure that no one is left behind'.

The author further adds that the SDG were build on success of the Millennium Development Goals (MDGs) and complete what they did not achieve. India has moved ahead on implementation of the SDGs and initiated preparation of the Vision Document 2030 with National Institution for Transforming India (NITI) Aayog in the lead. Based on the guidance from NITI Aayog, the state governments have begun the process of SDGs implementation. In addition to the state level (provincial) there is a need to take SDGs to the grassroots level. Here lies the importance of local governments, especially the Gram Panchayat/Gram Sabha, the institutions at grassroots level.

The main lacuna in development process was failure to develop the leadership among the villagers and institutionalisation of development process. The civil servants will be transferred after 3 years and elevated to higher positions. After Mr. Deepak Soni's withdrawal from the development process, the development may be weakened in the village and the village may go back to the underdeveloped stage. Dr. G. Narendra Kumar, Director General, National Institute of Rural Development and Panchayati Raj aptly puts it by saying "In any village, developing leadership and strengthening of local institutions is vital in sustainable development process." To sum up, to implement global goals or to transform village, the leadership building and strengthening local institutions is a must for local action and is an essential element in sustainable development process.

Strategies to Enroll Private Sector in Public Health Care: An Indian Experience is the topic of discussion in chapter four. According to **Madhu Thawani**, the chapter contributor, the Constitution of India under healthcare allocates various services to the Central or State Governments based on 3 lists, viz. (a) Central List includes research, establishment of tertiary level institutes etc., (b) State List includes provision and regulation of basic preventive, promotion and curative services, establishment of public health and sanitation services, hospitals and dispensaries etc., and (c) Concurrent List includes programmes like population control, family planning, medical education, registration of births and deaths etc. The Central Government provides guidelines and the respective State governments implement them. On the whole, provision of majority of health services is States' responsibility. Due to the limited capabilities of the Public Health Sector in providing healthcare service to all and the public expenditure on health being less than 1 per cent of GDP, the need of Public-Private Partnership in healthcare system was emphasized. The private sector today provides nearly 80 per cent of outpatient care and about 60 per cent of inpatient care. To reap the benefits of private sector in healthcare industry private healthcare sector is recognized as an integral part of the Indian Healthcare by the National Health Policy 1983 and thereafter National Health Policy 2002, National Population Policy 2001 and National Rural Health. Private healthcare in its own way is complementing and supplementing efforts of public healthcare system. However, the results are not encouraging as private sector is a profit making institution which is not ready to work with public sector unless they get profits. In this chapter, we will examine the reasons why the private sector is not ready to enroll itself in government programmes and what can be done to overcome this situation.

In chapter five **Nafeesath Sabida S.M.** and **A. Shahin Sultana**, examine the issues pertaining to Snakebite Envenoming in India and Public Health Issues connected with the theme. According to contributors, WHO officially listed snakebite envenoming as a highest priority neglected tropical disease in June 2017. Nearly 5.4 million snakebites take place each year, resulting in 1.8 to 2.7 million cases of envenoming. Extensive community-level research on snakebite deaths in India was estimated at 45,900 deaths in 2005. Annual snakebite deaths were most significant in the state of Uttar Pradesh (8,700), Andhra Pradesh (5,200), and Bihar (4,500). The literature on snakebite in India indicates that snakebite envenoming has failed to draw requisite attention for public health policy inclusion and investment for dynamic, sustainable efforts to reduce the medical and societal burden. This chapter draws a narrative review of the economic, socio-cultural and ecological aspects of snakebite in India along with its public health importance. Suggestions for improving the mitigation and management of snakebite by actively engaging the members of society is put forward, focusing on WHO's identified objective of empowering and engaging local communities in halving snakebite mortality and morbidity by 2030.

Public Policy Debates in Childcare: The Case of Odisha is the theme of discussion in chapter six, which is presented by **Swapna S. Prabhu**. According to her, the Government of Odisha has introduced various child-centric strategies and schemes since 1975 emphasising mainly on expectant and nursing mothers, maternal mortality rate, and women nutritional deficiency, however, ignoring the aspect of 'assess to childcare' for women workers. This deprives the nursing mothers and their children of their basic right to good health and nutrition. By analysing the existing social security measures introduced by the State towards childcare, the chapter argues that in order to promote the health and welfare of mothers and children, strong legislations are needed that treat maternity and childcare services as one, besides generating awareness amongst the people about the rights of the child to family environment and maternal care.

Deepa Awasthi, in chapter seven presents a study titled Impact of Child-Parents Relations on Child Development: A Comparative Study of Students of Lucknow City of Uttar Pradesh. According to Deepa every child is a potential citizen of nation and development of child lies on whole society. Any nation cannot be expected to develop and compete with the rest of the world for long time without a mass of good progressive children and they become more important in the case of country like India having largest population of young and adolescents. They are the only ray of hope for country. Family, friends, school, society contributes to development of children; out of this family is most important. Family include mother, father, siblings, and grandparents. It is necessary that relations among them should be healthy for their all-round development. Safety, unconditional love, mutual respect, acceptance and flexibility in relations are the few important factors for strong parent-child relationship. Whole personality of child depends upon the parents-child relations. Odd relations among both parents and parents-child relations have adverse impact on child development. Now-a-days it is seen that relation between children and parent reaches to a state where their lies no communication between them. This research chapter is based on a comparative study of students of secondary level (class 9th) of government and private schools of Lucknow city. The aim of the study was to compare the parent-child relationship between male and female students of government and private schools. Sample of the study was comprised 120 students. Random and incidental sampling techniques have been used to select the sample. Data has been gathered through Personal data schedule and Parents-Child Relationship Scale, constructed by Dr. Nalini Rao. Findings can be summarized as—(1) No significant difference in parent-child relationship has been found between male and female students of government schools. Mean scores have shown that female students of government schools have better parent-child relationship with their parents than male students. (2) Significant difference in parent-child relationship has been noticed between male and female students of private schools in favour of female students. (3) Significant difference in parent-child relationship has been found between students of government and private schools in favour of students of government schools.

Mapping the Vulnerabilities and Deprivations of the Child Bride: Critical Pathways and Policy Imperatives is the subject of discussion in chapter eight, which is presented by **Moushumi Pattnaik**. According to her, solemnization of marriage is an important socio-cultural practice of invariably in all communities. Each community approves its specific norms and rituals relating to marriage. Marriage is often lauded as a 'holy ordinance', 'holy sacrament' and an important '*sanskara*'. Although the formal legal systems define and govern the age at marriage but customary rules associated with puberty and purity of the girl child sanction and readily allow marriage before the legal age. Though there are other socio-cultural and structural factors underpinning this practice, whatsoever, child marriage unleashes menacing effects on the girl child in myriad ways—from mental health issues to a lack of access to education and career opportunities and also adverse health effects as a result of early pregnancy and childbirth. The study aims to explore the critical pathways and nuances relating to child marriage and its inter-sectionality with other manifestations of gender inequality and oppression through a perusal of significant literatures so as to open up broad avenues for research in this field. The study intends to scan through policy imperatives to curb this practice. It is a work not only of diagnosing the problem but envisaging measures on how to respond.

In chapter nine **Padmalaya Mahapatra** submits a study titled Gender & Development—A Study of Maternal and Child Health Care Policies in Odisha. According to the author gender discourse within the field of development has come a long way from building a case of 'inclusive' growth which prevents the marginalization of women to questioning of the predominant notions of development itself. The body of feminist critique continues to traverse new terrains and posit new challenges. The neo-liberal vision of society with a strong undercurrent of economic determinism often celebrates the atomistic, unconnected, self-maximizing individual—a conception which largely inhibits the space of both culture and development. Women's limited access to and control of material resources and limited decision-making power within the household can produce high fertility rates, underinvestment in aspects of family welfare such as child nutrition and education, and sub-optimal allocations of human capital in the economy. Maternal morbidity and mortality along with infant mortality rate is universally considered as human development indicators in a country and determines the health status of the people. In spite of very good plans and programmes, the reduction in MMR & IMR is much below the target set in Odisha. The present study is based on both primary and secondary sources of data. The chapter attempts to analyse the impact of maternal healthcare policies on women's health status in Odisha. It mainly focuses on maternal mortality relating to socio-economic characteristics of deceased, status of antenatal care, major causes that led to maternal death, major steps taken through various policies and programmes initiated by Government of India/Government of Odisha and their achievement.

Food security among the socially excluded communities in India is the study presented by **Arun Kumar Nayak** and **Padmalaya Mahapatra** in chapter ten. In their study they have presented policy options to revamp and restructure food security among the socially excluded communities. They further state that, the right to food and freedom from hunger reemerged during the 1990s. The historical World Food Summit was held in Rome in 1996, in which 185 countries participated and signed the 'Rome Declaration on World Food Security' which reaffirmed the right of everyone to have access to safe and nutritious food. Consequently, the right to adequate food is recognized as a fundamental human right. It is reiterated by the UN's one of the Millennium Development Goals (MDGs), viz. "Eradicate poverty and hunger", by 2015 and subsequently it is the foremost priority in the Sustainable Development Goals (SDGs) to achieve by 2030. Food security is an important means to realize the right to food. It means assured access to adequate food for all members of the household throughout the year. India has been witnessing the phenomenon of erratic monsoon consistently. It has serious implications on the food sufficiency and food security of the country. Poor monsoons also affect the welfare of people in terms of the availability of drinking water and employment opportunities. Food security addresses the inherent issues like nutrition, health, education, economic access to nutritious food and safe drinking water, and livelihood security of the marginalized communities. Food insecurity being the result of social, economic, and livelihood backwardness, the most affected are the socially and economically vulnerable sections of the communities—SCs, STs, and Muslims. The insecurity will be more among the landless labourers, female-headed households and women, widows, the aged persons and households with more children (especially the girl children), and casual workers who formed the core of the vulnerable sections of the total population and consequently constitute the poorest communities.

Cheruku Jeevan Kumar and **Rahul Kumar** have made a study on *Swachh Bharat* Mission in Rajasthan: A Case Study of Chirawa

Block in Jhunjhunu District in *chapter eleven*. The study focused on the problem of open defecation and the implementation of SBM-Gramin in the study area. The analysis focused on some major components of the SBM-G like open defecation, financial subsidy provision for toilet construction, and availability of the CSC facility. Researchers adopted interview schedules and observations. Though SBM was implemented in the study area by following SBM guidelines, there is still scope for effective implementation. The data shows that approximately 79 per cent of households have access to toilet facilities and left the OD practice. But there are still some households lacking the facility of the toilet and compel to practice OD. There is a question on the sustainability of the official declaration of ODF status. One of the fifth households or members was practising OD despite having toilet facilities due to old habits and other reasons. There is the scope of complete ODF if we include those who prefer OD practice due to lack of a toilet. There is an immediate need to make aware and provide a toilet facility. The facility of CSC is not available at the community level; people lack sanitation and toilets facilities. In the case of households that lack the facility of toilets could access the toilet at the community level. The CSC must follow an ideal structure designed by MDW&S. In case of lack of space to construct a toilet at the household level, and it is a better alternative to access the toilet facility. It helps to curb the problem of OD and sustainability of the ODF more viable. The most important is maintaining the sustainability of ODF. If awareness is created among the people about personal hygiene and sanitation practice, it is possible to leave the OD practice and achieve ODF status at the grassroots level.

In chapter twelve **D. Pulla Rao** presents an interesting study on Demographic and Health Status of Scheduled Tribes in Andhra Pradesh. It is a comparative study of Visakhapatnam and Vizianagaram districts. According to Rao, the tribal areas constitute a very significant portion of backward areas of the country presenting a complex situation for both planners and administrators. The tribal communities predominately live in hilly and forest regions, which are comparatively inaccessible and isolated. This chapter analyses the demographic and health status of Scheduled Tribes in the study area. The sex ratio in Vizianagaram is less than Visakhapatnam District. In the study area more than 50 per cent of the women got married before they attained fifteen years of age. On an average, both the districts have more than 70 per cent of women have their first conception in the age group of 15-20 years. More than 70 per cent of the sample households are aware of AIDS. In every 100 females in the study area 29 are affected with diseases. Most of the Scheduled Tribes do not agree for modern medicine, and they are reluctant to accept it. Most of the sample households are approaching the private unqualified doctors when they are sick. So, the government should educate the tribals about the importance of the modern medicine.

In chapter thirteen **Manas Behera** presents a study titled Inclusive Development in Rural Areas through PRIs. It is a Comparative Study of Two Districts in Odisha. To her, the basic objective of inclusive development is to include the excluded in the process of development so that they will get the benefits of development. The rural areas suffer from multiple forms of inequalities like caste, class, gender etc. Without an effective, inclusive and democratic system of decentralised governance system, inclusive development is not possible. The present chapter is an empirical study of the role and capacity of the Panchayati Raj System in two districts; Sundergarh and Jajpur from a comparative perspective in bringing inclusive development, particularly for the marginalised and the excluded. The study was conducted through a combination of methods, comparative method, survey method and behavioural method through questionnaires, personal interviews etc. The variables of job, food security, housing, drinking water, education, poverty reduction programmes, transparency etc. were taken as minimum for inclusive development in rural areas. The opinions of both the elected representatives as well as of the beneficiaries were taken and analysed to develop an objective analysis regarding the capacity and role of the PRIs in inclusive development. These institutions have huge capacities and spaces for inclusive development. But the functioning of these institutions, their capacities, their governance structures and processes, the power structure and equations in rural areas, the shadow of the state over them and many factors are hindrances in their role for inclusive development. The democratic structures at the grassroots level need to be inclusive to achieve inclusive Development.

In chapter fourteen **Anjali C.M.** and **Dr. B. Johnson** make a critical study on the Financial Literacy and Personal Financial Decision among households. According to the researchers being technically independent and having financial security and financial freedom is a crucial factor of financial success. Rather than earning more money, managing the money in proper means creates more wealth. Now-a-days, tremendous of financial products and services are available in the market along with abundant of credit opportunities. A wise utilization of these opportunities can lead the individuals to the next level. However, the financial literacy level of individual are not significantly considered in our economy. Even the authorities are more concerned about financial inclusion whereas the low level of financial literacy itself is the reason for it. Financial literacy influences the personal lives in many ways. The level of financial literacy determines the level of success of their personal financial decisions. The present chapter attempts to highlight the issues related to financial literacy and personal financial decision among households.

In chapter fifteen **Anthony Rodrigues** and **Alok Kumar Chakrawal** present a Study on Thematic Plan for Youth in the Rural Economy. The chapter focuses on Skill Development and Employment at the rural level. According to the authors "Skill development is critical for economic growth and social development". The demographic transition of India makes it imperative to ensure employment opportunities for more than 12 million youth entering working age annually. It is estimated that during the seven-year period (2005-2012), only 2.7 million net additional jobs were created in the country. To enable employment ready workforce in the future, the youth need to be equipped with the necessary skills and education.

The authors further feel that the country presently faces a dual challenge of severe paucity of highly-trained, quality labour, as well as non-employability of large sections of the educated workforce that possess little or no job skills. The skill development issue in India is thus pertinent both at the demand and supply level. To meet the demand side challenge, consistent efforts are being made towards expansion of economic activities and creation of large employment opportunities. On the supply side, a simple look at the projected youth population provides a fair reason to believe that India has the strength to cater to this demand. However, the employability quotient is questionable and remains a major area of concern. Already huge gaps exist between the industry requirements and the level of skills of workers due to varied reasons including inadequate training infrastructures, inappropriate mix of skills and education, outdated curricula, limited industry interfaces, limited standards etc.

In the concluding chapter Sixteen **Kavya C.T.** and **Midatala Rani** highlight on Political Empowerment of Women through Self-Help Groups in Karnataka with special reference to Kodagu district. To them the concept of women development sought to include women at deeper of levels of inclusions in terms of political, social and economic empowerment, which needs to be implemented at the basement of the Social pyramid. The authors further feel that even today women development seems to have different connotations. The women development model is pondering upon either to seek collaborations or contradictions among the various stakeholders of the society. It may include women and development, women development and child welfare, gender studies or main streaming of women activism and movement. According to the UN declaration on women development noted that, the interlink ages between women development and its social, economic and political elements have been neglected with a serious discord and same needs to be re-established and monitored.

M.R. Biju
M.R.B. Anantha Padmanabha

Contents

List of Contributors

A. Shahin Sultana (Dr.), Professor, Department of Social Work, Pondicherry Central University, Kalapet, Puducherry. **Email:** shahin.samaroh@gmail.com

Alok Kumar Chakrawal (Dr.), Vice Chancellor, Guru Ghasidas Vishwavidyalaya (Central University), Bilaspur, Chattisgarh. **Email:** alochak69@gmail.com

Anjali C.M., PGP Finance, Indian Institute of Management, Kozhikode. **Email:** aafin3@iitmk.ac.in

Anthony Rodrigues (Dr.), Professor & Director, Research Centre, Department of Commerce, GOA University, Fr. Agnel College, Pilar, Goa. **Email:** anthony.rodrigues@unigoa.ac,in

Arjun Gope (Dr.), Assistant Professor, Department of Commerce, Ramthakur College, Tripura. **Email:** shankarjagu@gmail.com

Arun Kumar Nayak, Doctoral Scholar, P.G Department of Public Administration, Utkal University, Vanivihar, Bhubaneswar, Odisha. **Email:** padma2seema@gmail.com

B. Johnson (Dr.), Professor, Department of Commerce and Management Studies, University of Calicut, Malappuram, Kerala. **Email:** bensavier01@gmail.com

Cheruku Jeevan Kumar (Dr.), Assistant Professor, Department of Public Policy, Law and Governance, Central University of Rajasthan. **Email:** jeevan_pplg@curaj.ac.in

D. Pulla Rao (Dr.), Honorary Professor, Department of Economics, Andhra University, Visakhapatnam, Andhra Pradesh. **Email:** pullaraod_2003@yahoo.co.in

Deepa Awasthi (Dr.), Assistant Professor, A.N.D. Teacher's Training (P.G.) College, Sitapur, U.P. **Email:** dawasthi.india@gmail.com

Gautam Purkayastha (Dr.), Associate Professor and Academic Coordinator, Margherita College, Margherita, Assam. **Email:** gautameconomics@gmail.com

Kavya C.T., Research Scholar, Department of Studies in Political Science, University of Mysore, Manasagangothri, Mysore. **Email:** mallirani@yahoo.co.in

Madhu Thawani (Dr.), Associate Professor, Department of Public Administration, South Gujarat University, Rajkot, Gujarat. **Email:** madhuthawani.2008@rediffmail.com

Manas Behera (Dr.), Head of the Department of Political Science, R.D. Women's University, Bhubaneswar, Odisha. **Email:** manasbehera1964@gmail.com

Md. Ayub Mallick (Dr.), Professor, Department of Political Science, Kazi Nazrul University, Kalla Bypass More, Asansol, Paschim Barddaman, West Bengal. **Email:** ayubbdu2008@gmail.com

Midatala Rani (Dr.), Formerly Professor, Department of Studies in Political Science, University of Mysore, Manasagangothri, Mysore. **Email:** mallirani@yahoo.co.in

Moushumi Pattnaik (Dr.), Assistant Professor, Shailabala Women's Autonomous College, Cuttack, Odisha. **Email:** pattnaikmoushumi@gmail.com

Nafeesath Sabida S.M. (Dr.), Doctoral Scholar, Department of Social Work, Pondicherry Central University, Kalapet, Puducherry. **Email:** nafeesathsabida@gmail.com

Padmalaya Mahapatra (Dr.), Associate Professor, P.G. Department of Public Administration, Utkal University, Vanivihar, Bhubaneswar, Odisha. **Email:** padma2seema@gmail.com

Rahul Kumar, Doctoral Scholar, Department of Public Policy, Law and Governance, Central University of Rajasthan. **Email:** rahulsingh@nls.ac.in

S. Nagabhushana Rao (Dr.), Associate Professor and Head, Centre for Equity and the Social Development, NIRD & PR, Hyderabad. **Email:** snrao2001@gmail.com

Shankar Chatterjee (Dr.), Former Professor & Head (CPME), NIRD & PR, Hyderabad. **Email:** shankarjagu@gmail.com

Swapna S. Prabhu (Dr.), Asst. Professor, Department of Political Science, Utkal University, Bhuveneswar.
Email: swapna_p3@yahoo.co.in

1

Nature of Rural Public Policy in India

Examples from West Bengal

Md. Ayub Mallick

Public is a group or a programme of action intended to fulfil certain common goals with certain course within a certain environment, both intra-societal and extra-societal. Public policies are the purposive actions on the part of the government (Presthus, 1975 and Anderson, 1975). Public policies are formulated by authorities and these are authoritative allocation of values (Easton, 1965). The policies provided by the political system produces new demands as inputs through feedback mechanism within particular environment. But, how decisions are made within the 'black box' that converts mass demands into policies? Elite theorists regard policies come from upward to downwards, masses are passive receivers. There is mass-elite gap. The elites try to share the basic values and norms of the society and try to maintain the social system—they influence and dominate masses producing mass culture through mass culture industry suitable for neo-market liberal society. In public policy process there are few steps—identification, formulation of policy, implementation of policy, necessary outcomes and evaluation of policy, necessary outcomes and evaluation of policy in pursuance of the present environment and situation. It is a continuous process—a 'feedback' linkage—"evaluation of current policy, identify new problems and set in motion the policy-making process once again" (Dye, 1992: 16-17). Planning-Programming-Budgeting System (PPBS) is to regularize and legitimize decision-making in bureaucracy by and through defining the programme objectives, measuring the project outcomes and the cost-benefit analysis. Demands made by the civil society are legitimized through 'passive revolution of capital'.

Earlier, I have mentioned the neo-liberal market aspect of public policy. The onset of NEP and globalization and the rolling back of the state—this conjectural juncture has made possible to re-adjust the delivery of public goods and market interests through public policy. The success of this adjustment has been pointed out by Jean Dreze and Amartya Sen (1997). The role of public action in public policy formulation is important in this respect. They have pointed out that with regard to ill health, illiteracy and poverty Kerala's performance is better than that of other states. The basic reasons behind the Kerala's success are active public organizations, mass movements and state actions. Public action, and not the policies of globalization and liberalization was the core of Kerala's progress. There were more markets, but we have to go beyond markets. Not only deregulation and reform, but positive initiatives on the part of the state and civil society should be taken for public policy formulation and development. There is co-ordination and complementarity between capitalism, state and globalization. "Capitalism needs the state is not independent from capital; elites of both work together in the globalization process because it serves both" (Ali, 2007: 9). Public policy in the market economy not only provides inputs for smooth functioning of the market economy, but legitimizes the operation of the market within the society in addition to human face of social services.

The Planning Commission of India formulated policies with regard to top-down approach and trickle-down method. The policy agenda was state-controlled and hegemonic. After New Economic Policy of 1991 and later on NITI Aayog in 2015 in the age of globalization, the dimensions of policy agendas changed to decentralized service delivery and participatory development from rights-based social provisions and redistribution of national resources. The growing importance of civil society under the grab of the hegemonic control of the elites of both the market and the state. The state has become the actor for creating a balance between the market and civil society. Before liberalization planning and public policy were both the anticipation of power and anticipation of concrete forms through which power was exercised through state control and hegemony by means of accumulation, legitimization and rationality, the cost-benefit analysis. The post-colonial public policy is connected with representation, participation, redistribution of national income and accumulation of capital with legitimization. In its legitimizing process, planning has become the instrument of politics. Politics, we know, comprises (1) scarcity of resources, (2) multiple interests, (3) conflict of interests, and (4) resolution of conflict.

I think, planning is the embodiment of rational calculations of physical and human resources, the capacities and capabilities. The policy approach in the early 1950s was basically on 'commodity', on accumulation that could not be legitimized through representative politics. The policy approach during this period was essentially based on original accumulation followed by classical Marxism (Chatterjee, 1997).

Actually, it was like—original accumulation—forms of expropriation that could not be legitimized through representative politics—'unnecessary rigours' of industrial transition in the policy process.

The post-colonial development policy is necessarily to avoid the unnecessary rigours, to bring the masses to accept the same and to keep behind the bitter taste of exploitation. The policy approach was accumulation with legitimization. Planned capitalist development is a "part of a process of what may be called the passive revolution of capital" (Chatterjee, 1997: 286). Antonio Gramsci has talked about 'passive revolution' as one in which the new claimants to power, lacking the social strength to launch a full-scale assault on the old dominant classes, opt for a path in which the demands of a new society are "satisfied by small doses, legally in a reformist manner"... "The object of the strategy of 'passive revolution' was to contain class conflicts within manageable dimensions, to control and manipulate the many diversed power relations in society to further as best as possible the thrust towards accumulation" (Chatterjee, 1997: 286, 287, 290).

Earlier, I have said that planning and policy issues and the embodiment of rational calculation of physical and human resources, capacities and capabilities. Health and education are important social opportunities that can help in the development of human resources. Sen (1995) has defined that health and education have some 'intrinsic' and 'instrumental' roles and 'empowerment and distributive' roles. Education and health have some intrinsic, instrumental and distributive roles. Education and health can perform the role of inculcating the values within the persons themselves, the role of getting and using economic benefits and social opportunities. I agree with Sen (1995) that an appropriate public policy and its implementation at the grassroots level, especially at the rural level are lacking. Expansion of health and education that can go beyond immediate personal effects, that is the Bazar-Canteen Model of Riggsian paradigm. Public action in the sphere of public formulation and implementation, such as health, education, social security, environmental protection and rural infrastructural development etc. Non-implementation of public policy formulation is the result of biased political activism and undue political pressures from which results social inequality, i.e. inequality in terms of health, education, income and social security etc. and capacities to influence others, i.e. that is power. Distributive public policies are interfering with market transactions (Sen, 1995). Alternative measures for redistribution of resources and more equitable allocation mechanism may be more effective to reduce the costs of Hobbesian market transaction of buying and selling and Weberian rational economy. However, market transactions have some effects of liberation for the downtrodden sections of the society by giving an opportunity to sell their labour in the market. But, there should be a redistributive public focus on rural public policy. I think, there should be a proper balance between market transaction and public action. The groundwork of public policy formulation was to make a balance between political marketing, market transaction and public action. "Promoting the socio-economic life of people in rural areas should become a priority item even on purely selfish grounds. The political parties in general and the ruling party in particular have to approach the villagers to seek their votes, and unless there is an appreciable record of work done by the party in power, it is bound to face rejection at their hands. Besides, new markets will have to be developed for what is being produced in the country. Otherwise, there will be hardly any incentive for raising and diversifying production. The purchasing power of the rural sector must appreciably improve so the demand of goods and services increases. Roads will have to be constructed and the communication system must be improved so as to link rural areas to commercial and business centres. It is, therefore, in the interest of business and industry that rural areas be developed" (Maheswari, 1985: 15-16).

Rural public policy is oriented to neo-liberal market economy. I have tried to relate the aspect of political marketing with public policy formulation and its implementation and market economy. Actually, marketing "is the analysis, planning, implementation and control of carefully formulated programmes designed to bring about voluntary exchanges of values with target markets for the purpose of achieving organizational objectives. It relies heavily on designing the organizations offering in terms of markets' needs and desires, and on using effective pricing, inform, motivate and service the markets" (Kotler, n.f.: 6). "I can relate political marketing with public policy formulation and implementation in diagrammatic format. Market oriented reforms and policy formulation not only produce social divisions and inequalities, but also produce an improvement in per capita income that enhances the expansion of the market. The distributional aspect of public policy will reduce the negative

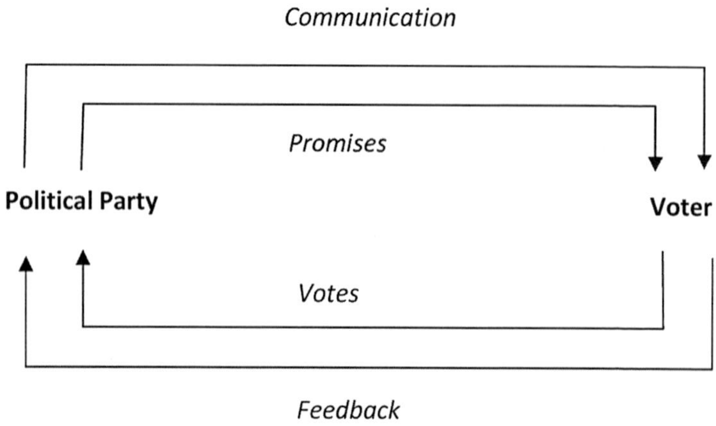

Fig. 1.1

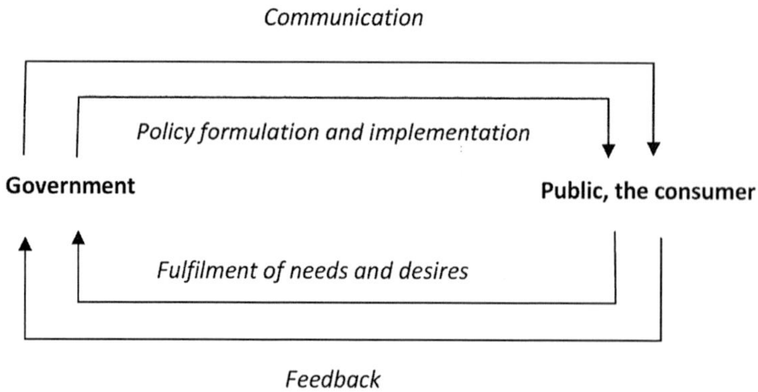

Fig. 1.2

consequences of market orientation, such as unemployment benefits, old age pension, health insurance, healthcare facilities, land entitlements, public distribution, water supply, infrastructural facilities etc. All these have positive role in addressing social security problem. The public interventionalist action is the way to dilute or so to say neutralize the negative consequences of market orientation of neo-liberal tradition in a distributive fashion. The distributional aspect is oriented to reduce the gap between higher income groups and lower income groups. It tends to be qualitative, where production is equal to accumulation and consumption is linked with stock of capital goods" (Chakravarty, 1987).

Various rural development programmes and policies, land reform policies were taken during the plan periods to reduce the gap between higher income groups and lower income groups and the tensions between the rural haves and have nots, respectively. Few rural development policies during the plan period are mentioned below:

Plan Periods	**Programmes (Policies)**
First Five Year Plan	Community Development Programme National Extension Service
Second Five Year Plan	Khadi and Village Industries programme Multi-purpose Tribal Development Blocks Programme
Third Five Year Plan	Applied Nutrition Programme Rural Industries Projects Intensive Agricultural Areas Programme High-Yielding Variety Programme
Annual Plans, 1966-69	Farmers' Training and Education Programme Rural Works Programme Tribal Development Block Rural Manpower Programme
Fourth Five Year Plan	Cash Scheme for Rural Employment Small Farmers' Development Agency Tribal Area Development Programme Rural Employment Programme Basic Needs Programme
Fifth Five Year Plan	Hill Areas Development Programme Food for Work Programme Desert Development Programme Integrated Rural Development Programme
Sixth Five Year Plan	National Rural Employment Programme Development of Women and Children in Rural Areas
Seventh Five Year Plan	Rural Landless Employment Programme National Rural Employment Programme Indira Awas Yojana
Eighth Five Year Plan	Indira Awas Yojana Development of Women and Children in Rural Areas

Source: Maheswari, 1985, pp. 37-38.

Planning Commission (1969) states that in "the agricultural sector, the Fourth Plan has two main objectives. The first objective is to provide the conditions necessary for a sustained increase of about 5 per cent per annum over the next decade. The second objective is to enable as large a section of the rural population as possible, including the small cultivator, the farmer in dry areas and the agricultural labourer, to participate in development and share its benefits. Accordingly, the priority programmes of development in agriculture fall broadly in two categories, namely those which aim at maximizing production and those which aim at remedying imbalances" (Planning Commission, 1969: 120). But, improved agricultural practices are needed for remedying the imbalances between different regions and different sections of cultivators. Reserve Bank of India (RBI) reports that—"If the fruits of development continue to be denied to large sections of the rural community while prosperity accrues to some, the resulting tensions, social and economic, may not only upset the process of orderly and peaceful change in the rural economy but even frustrate the national effort to keep up agricultural production" (RBI, 1969: 579). In another report, RBI (1954) says that the agricultural credit supplied to cultivators falls short of right quantity and the large share of credit goes to big cultivators. RBI (1954) observes, "Large holdings are relatively few and are to be fewer as a result of land policies which governments have adopted in pursuit of social ends. If only in the numerical aspect, therefore, the medium and small cultivator,..., will become increasingly important as a person whose needs have to be studied and borne in mind in the formation of policies of agricultural credit and development. Medium and small holdings now account for about two-fifths of agricultural produce of the country" (RBI,1954: 371).

The aspect of rural public policy can be analysed with reference to West Bengal during the Left Front regime as an example. However, during that period agrarian reform has not been outstanding compared to the other states and the previous Congress regime and power has been shifted from pro-Congress elite to a new middle landed class. The Left Front Government with the aim of neutralizing bureaucracy provided wide powers to the Panchayats for implementing the Integrated Rural Development Programme (IRDP). But, the village Panchayats lacked administrative expertise and did not take decisions with regard to policy implementation, and hence, Food-for-Work Programme, IRDP and other schemes remained unimplemented and were at stake. Undue political pressures vested interests were responsible for this. Though the poor were benefited, the CPI(M) controlled Panchayats provided the benefits to consolidate their political and economic control over the villages (Mallick, 1993). In fact, the leftist leaders were connected with the rural power structure, where the '*jotedars*' and affluent farmers, had to give economic assistance to the rural poor in terms of loans for consumption; the power structure tended to maintain *status quo* through the conditions of scarcity, rich-poor disparity and indebtedness without making an agricultural breakthrough. There was no free competition among the labourers for work and employers for cheapest labour and profit (Gupta, 1972). The struggle between the Rural Power Structure and the State Power Structure has been going in West Bengal, until now in favour of the *jotedars* and the rich peasants. The masses of the pauperised peasantry vote for those candidates as per the instructions of the "Rural Economic and Power Elite" (Gupta, 1972: 45). The village middle class rural elites control the local system of Panchayats. The transfer often took place either from highest aristocrat elite castes to the landowning dominant castes or from one faction of the dominant caste to another. The lower castes, SCs, STs were mobilized by the dominant elites and guided by the personal motivations of these leaders only to raise them against their landlords and make secure their own leadership position. The lower castes could not achieve political power and village headmanship (Chattopadhyay, 1964). The lower and middle classes formed dominant alliance in terms of "mutual understanding and accommodation of interests" (Dasgupta, 1984: A-146). In fact, the leftist leaders used 'class' as a currency to buy panchayat votes, which had nothing to do with lower class emancipation. The socio-economic background of the Gram Panchayat members reveal the class-caste composition of leaders, their orientation to leadership and the nature of the Rural Power Structure (Mallick, 1993).

The Left Front Government was not able to remove totally the shackles of feudalism as its leadership in West Bengal came from the middle class intellectuals. Rural land policy implementation was at stake. "The only thing that was real about it was the quest for power... was sought to be derived from the ballot box" (Mohan, 1972: 86). But, while pursuing revolutionary aims within the parliamentary framework, the left parties of the Front only implemented the laws enacted by the Congress Government and supplemented parliamentary actions with non-parliamentary or extra-parliamentary ones. Land reforms or land policy implementation within the framework of legality and distribution of surplus lands were merely the tactics, but not the strategies with long-term goals of socialist transformation, but the appeasement of land hunger of as many people as possible. The point is that "there was not enough land to distribute.... It was hoped that temporary whetting of their appetite for land would bring the landless labourers to the side of the party. The CPI(M) Kisan Sabha took the charge of distributing land on the ground that the party was the vanguard for the proletariat. Also, in order to maximize the number of party supporters, the workers tried to distribute land to as many peasants as possible" (Mitter 1986: 598). The rural land policy implementation under the Left Front regime was at stake. The CPI(M)-led Front had incorporated the small and middle peasants into its organization than that of the lower ones, provided security of tenure to the share-cropper and sought to identify areas with concentration of share-croppers; to politicize them through Panchayats outmanoeuvring bureaucrats; and to register them illegally "aimed at the limited goal of recording the tenancy right of the bargadars" (Khasnabis, 1986: 178). "... since barga recording depends much on the oral evidence of the bargadars concerned instead of a broad-based programme for identification of the real bargadars and the land cultivated, partisan outlook and malpractice may easily creep in... beggars and farm hands have been provoked by some people to record their names" (Bakshi, 1980: 24). However, compared with the past performance of the Congress, the Left Front made a spectacular success with regard to the recording of the share-croppers. But in 1982, it was recorded as 11,98,000 which reached 13,29,087 by September 1985. It showed that the programme had virtually come to a halt, experiencing "an average landholding of 0.97 acres under barga cultivation" (Mallick, 1993: 56). Besides, the bargadars were evicted from possession of their lands for maintaining order and safeguarding the existing property relations. In this respect, Ross Mallick (1993) has said, "11.25 per cent of recorded bargadars have thrown out of possession by one way or the other" (Mallick, 1993: 58).

Therefore, Operation Barga Programme was not able to recuperate the share-croppers from the "grip in which the rich farmers hold the village community" (Rudra, 1981: A-65) and the "authority of big landholders" (Khasnabis, 1981: A-147). "Those who had to own <5 acres of land were placed in a position to control the rural economy; and lease transactions were made mostly among small and medium sized holders rather than >10 acres jotedars who accounted for 25 per cent of the area leased out" (Bandyopadhyay, 1983). Ajit Kumar Ghosh has pointed out that "about 36 per cent share-cropper households, each owning between 1.0 and 5.0 acres of land, account for about 58 per cent of the total share-cropped area. Operation Barga thus serves to strengthen the economic position of the group of households operating between 2.5 and 7.5 acres" (Ghosh, 1983: 120).

Big farmers and landholders still continued to provide credit and input facilities to bargadars. Most of institutional credit and input facilities are pocketed by rich farmers, when non-institutional credits offered to the poorer sections of the society. Pradip Kr. Bose (1984) has presented few statistical data favouring rural indebtedness of the poor peasants and labourers and middle peasants to the private money-lenders mostly for consumption and ceremonies rather than for production and cultivation, which would divert their production initiatives and incentives into consumptive thirst and convert their income to the repayment of cumulative indebtedness (Bose, 1984: 127-28).

The implementation of rural development policies through Panchayati Raj System in West Bengal is not so promising. Few examples may be cited here. A significant decentralization of power and functions took place in West Bengal under the leadership of CPI(M). The decentralized power was grabbed by the Leftists. Having a rural strongholds since 1977, the Left Front Government has given security to the tenant-farmers and land to the landless, but not to the sizeable extent. However, "production has begun to rise; and consequent to the programme of rural electrification in the eighties, food production in West Bengal has increased at a rate comparable with that of Punjab, the home of the Green Revolution. It is also true that the biggest beneficiaries of the recently provided irrigation facilities in West Bengal are the larger farmers. These have joined the Communist Party (Marxist) and have come even to control the panchayats" (Maheswari, 1985: 85).

Following the above we can proceed further with the implementation of rural development policies perpetuated through Panchayats in West Bengal during the Left Front Government. A survey result with special reference to the most weaker sections, that is the Scheduled Tribes may be cited as an example of the implementation of rural public policy and rural development programmes.

The 'red panchayats' (Sen Gupta, 1979), however, have not been able to mobilize the rural people along class political lines and for development purposes. With the help of Panchayats, the party represents two interlinked patterns of political change, i.e. the organizational penetration of party 'centre' into 'periphery' and simultaneous shift in the class basis of institutional power. Though, it is a party of lower middle income group, the party is electorally supported by the poor, and in turn they do get benefits from the government policies (Kohli, 1990). The poverty alleviation programmes remain a narrow management subject to manipulation by those who enjoy the monopoly of social knowledge and power (Rahman, 1984). I am saying that the rural power structure has changed to some extent with the reorganization and institutionalization of Panchayats. The rural elites stand as nets between the poorer people and the well-to-do sections. The Panchayats act as buffers so that no collision takes place between the poorer classes and the rural elites. For improving the economic conditions, especially the STs in the Block area concerned, different types of small scale industries should be set up, so that they may utilize their leisure time in productive works. Their participation in Panchayati Raj Institutions and rural development is meagre and insignificant in the area surveyed. No active woman leader was found in *Kanksa* block of Burdwan district, West Bengal during the survey period.

"The Scheduled Tribes live mostly in well defined areas; these areas are relatively underdeveloped and poorly integrated with the rest of the economy.... Redistributive policies must pay special attention to these and other backward classes if it is to be successful" (Government of India, 1963: 36). The development efforts through industry, mining, forest exploitation, agricultural extension, cottage industries, co-operative and marketing societies, institutions of laws, public health programmes and general administrative system have effects on the socio-economic life process of the tribals. At the implementation and operation levels, emphasis should be on the socio-economic life process, community and individual needs: (a) food, clothing, housing and basic consumer goods including social necessities, (b) services like education, water supply, health, environmental situation, communication and infrastructure, (c) productive employment so as to meet basic personal consumption needs, (d) human and physical infrastructure to produce the goods and services required and garnering surpluses for building basic community services required and for investment, and (e) people's participation in the making of all decisions. "It has been recommended by people with long experience of working with tribals that the officials should hold frequent general open meetings with the tribals and convey important information through this medium. This modality assures direct and accurate communication..." (Sharma and Krishnayya, 1975: 157). The outcomes of development through various rural development programmes should be decentralized and dispersed, not concentrated in core areas. This disequilibrium position can be corrected through the following stages:

Stage A : Stage of conflict of interests of migrant and tribal groups.

Stage B: Disequilibrium in the assimilation of developmental benefits among these two groups.

Stage C: Measures for correcting disequilibrium—tribals' involvement in the development process; countering migrant groups' command over the resources of the tribal areas; effective administration of Panchayats; proper institutionalization of Panchayati Raj in tribal areas; development of economy, education and health among the tribals; utilization of tribal skill and promotion of their self-confidence.

Stage D: Wait and See Measures.

Stage E:

(1) Co-operative farming and institutional credit facility,
(2) Integration of various development projects to make a total development,
(3) Distribution of sizeable portion of surplus arable land,
(4) Establishment and promotion of forest-based small and cottage industries, and
(5) Promotion of tribal skill and their actual utilization.

Stage F: Development in tribals' life situation—the impact of development measures.

Stage G: Confrontation or Direct Conflict for Command Over Resources Ceases to Exit.

Stage H: Tribal groups become free to share with the larger community.

Stage I: Gradual Process of Development.

Suitable administrative setup should be formulated and constituted according to the conditions and problems of different tribal areas. Government should take into account local conditions, utilize the existing administrative set up for the development of local conditions, reconstitute the administrative set up, if necessary and necessary corrective measures for the solution of local problems. There is the need for the review of works of various development organizations and institutions—their working co-ordination and interrelationships. Administrative and institutional lacunae would have to be identified and necessary corrective measures would have to be seriously taken in order to solve the dilemma: "the present quality of life of the tribal community is not satisfactory and the quality of our lives or that of those who are non-tribals is much more satisfactory" (Zaheer, 1975: 47). Further, "it is proposed to prepare a comprehensive long-term plan highlighting various aspects like production, consumption, investment, employment, manpower development, trading, self-sufficiency and technology to be used, and so on and so forth.... The plan will start from the target of the desired consumption/expenditure of various agricultural, industrial and service items...consumption will be given preferences over exports till the region is able to meet its own needs; and investments in a year should be sufficient to ensure the achievement of a higher level of consumption targets for the future as per the long-term and Five Year Plan targets" (Dasgupta and Dhar, 1975: 83-85).

In post-Independent India, four phases can be identified with regard to the development policies involving the tribals. They are:

(a) provision of immediate relief in providing amenities and building up the productive infrastructure for future growth;
(b) emphasis on resource mobilization and development of social service infrastructure;
(c) protection from social injustice and all forms of exploitation;
(d) participatory development, self-management, harnessing of productive forces for meeting the basic needs as well as self-reliant growth. For self-reliant growth and meeting the

> basic needs of the tribal people, emphasis has been laid on commercialization of productive forces and formulation of various poverty alleviation and development programmes.

In fact, the planning is considered to be rational and scientific endeavour and it is supported to follow a given procedure, that is identification of problems →scenario building for problem solving →identification of projects →prioritization → inter-sectoral co-ordination→plan finalization→ implementation→monitoring and evaluation (United Nations Centre for Rural Development, 1977).

In West Bengal, the tribal population live interpersed with the general population. Only 11 per cent of the total tribal population in the district falls under the purview of the ITDP project. Tribal population in the Sub-Plan areas of Burdwan district is dependent on agriculture and their problems loom around agriculture. The Scheduled Castes and Scheduled Tribes Welfare Department has introduced a new scheme for the purchase of tribal lands and redistribution of such lands among the tribals. The West Bengal Tribal Development Co-operative Corporation Ltd. and LAMPS are now enjoying the monopoly right of collecting forest produce. The Corporation has taken the scheme to provide consumption loans to tribal members for the purpose of children's education, marriage and other consumption needs. Besides, the Corporation is mainly responsible for looking into the non-credit functions of LAMPS providing financial support to LAMPS for marketing minor forest produce and industrial and processing operation, organizing collection and marketing of minor forest produce through LAMPS for fair payment to the tribal collectors, organizing *sal* leaf plate preparation and *biri* making, arranging supply of cloths and other essential commodities. The credit function includes consumption loan, short-term loan for seri-culture and other purposes.

In the First Plan, the main emphasis was on health, housing and communication, but in the Second Plan the emphasis was shifted to development in agriculture, cottage and small-scale industries, co-operative societies and setting up of multi-purpose tribal blocks. In this Second Plan, development orientation was more clearly introduced. The Third Plan renamed these blocks as Tribal Development Blocks with the priorities for economic uplift, housing, communication, health and education. In the Fourth and Fifth Plans further importance was given to 'Area and Regional Approach' and 'Integrated Area Development Approach', respectively. In the Sixth Plan emphasis was laid on protective measures for the programmes of employment, health and education. The Seventh Plan approach took into account the wide gap between different tribal communities and development areas in the fields of education and economy leading to the lack of occupational diversities and disproportionate sharing of benefits among them.

A number of special provisions have been enumerated in the Constitution for protecting the rights and interests of the tribals and weaker sections of the society. Article 46 of the Constitution states that the State with special care shall promote the economic and educational interests of the weaker sections of the society in general and of the Scheduled Castes and Scheduled Tribes in particular, protect them from all forms of exploitation and injustice. For development and welfare of the weaker sections, SCs and STs, the 73rd Constitution Amendment Bill focuses on the political structures and processes of rural India and participation of these disadvantaged groups in these structures and leadership and decision-making processes. The Panchayati Raj Administration is aimed at restructuring of land distribution, choice of appropriate technology and application of appropriate knowledge, development of cottage and small-scale industries, and better co-ordination of planning and programmes (Basu, 1984). In addition to land reform measures, detection of *benami* land and distribution of these among the disadvantaged and the recording of *bargadars*, implementation of Food-for-Work, NREP, RLEGP, IRDP by the panchayats in identification of beneficiaries, selection of schemes and monitoring, the Drought Prone Area Programme (DPAP), schemes relating to 'minikit' distribution in agriculture, small irrigation, social forestry, rural water supply, housing and several important schemes on Scheduled Castes and Scheduled Tribes and on cottage and small-scale industries have been under the direct responsibility of the Panchayats.

Apart from these Swarna Jayanti Swarozgar Yojana (SJSY) is a combination of IRDP, TRYSEM, SITRA and DWCRA. The implementation procedures point out the importance of Panchayats in tribal development or more clearly in rural development. Further, the bank-linked schemes like Prime Minister's Rojgar Yojana (PMRY), Khadi and Village Industry (KVI) and National Scheduled Castes and Scheduled Tribes Finance and Development Corporation Linked Scheme (NSFDC) are directly and indirectly related with Panchayati Raj so far the implementation procedures are concerned. Besides, the non-bank schemes, which are important in rural development, are cited below and their implementation procedures do not need any further explanation. Examples may be cited as the following:

(1) Swarna Jayanti Swarozgar Yojana (SJSY)—Fund from Zilla Parishad,
(2) Employment Assurance Scheme (EAS)—Fund from Zilla Parishad,
(3) Indira Awas Yojana (IAY)—Fund from Zilla Parishad,
(4) Million Wells Scheme (MWS)—Fund from Zilla Parishad,
(5) District Plan Fund (DPF)—Fund from Zilla Parishad or District Magistrate,
(6) MP Local Area Development Fund—Central Fund through DM,
(7) Bidhayak Elaka Unnayan Parishad—State fund through DM,
(8) Tenth Finance Commission—Central fund through DM, and
(9) Special Tribal Area Development and Paschimanchal Unnayan Parishad—Central and State fund through Zilla Parishad.

During the field level data collection, I have identified two types of schemes initially, i.e. directly benefiting the tribes and schemes indirectly benefiting the tribes. I have identified so far Special Component Plan (SCP), Tribal Sub Plan (TSP), Special Tribal Area Development (STAD), Community Development Scheme under Integrated Tribal Development (ITDP) in the first category and Employment Assurance Scheme (EAS), Individual Beneficiary Scheme (IBS), Basic Minimum Service Scheme (BMSS), Integrated Child Development Scheme (ICDS) etc. in the second category at the initial stage of field level data collection.

The development programmes under EAS, STAD, JRY, SJSY, IAY, IRDP and TSP throughout Kanksa block are non-entrepreneurial, distributive and time consuming. Development efforts start with a single dosage and end with no long-run and trickle-down effects. A slight dosage of input might produce a deadlock in development. The development efforts within this block may be presented through a diagram (Fig. 1.3). There is no feedback between input and output. All the efforts are scattered and isolated.

Kanksa Panchayat Samity has sanctioned various projects like fishery, goatery, poultry, bullocks and cart, carpentry, *sal* leaf plate

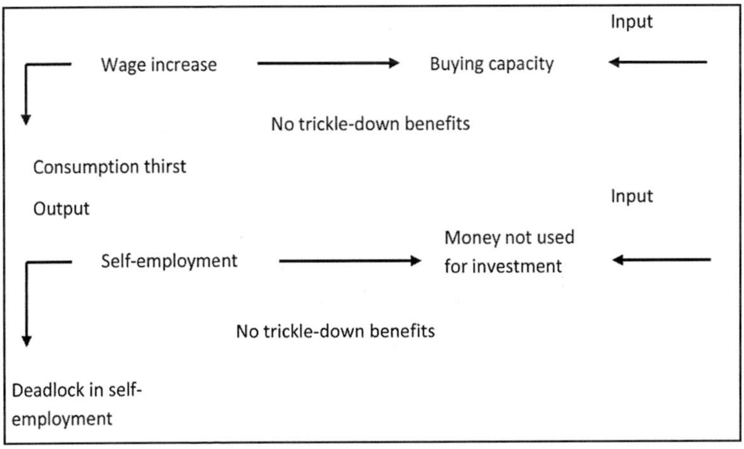

Fig. 1.3: Stagnation in investment and development

making, paddy processing etc. through individual beneficiary schemes like IRDP, TSP. The projects have failed due to economic hardship, indebtedness, lack of adequate infrastructural facilities etc. Lack of power facility, absence of co-operative farming and lack of subsidiary sources of income—all these have made the projects unsuccessful. Land remains the main source of income. Very few of the tribes in this block are owner cultivators. Most of the *pattadars* are from SC categories. *Pattadars* are mostly illiterate and below the poverty line. The conditions of the *bargadars* are much more improved than the mere *patta* holders. Distribution of *patta* lands is only the instrument to catch vote, but not intended to improve the conditions of the poor *patta* holders. Administration is subservient to the interests of the party leaders and party dictates. Programmes like land distribution among the tribal people, recording the names of *bargadars*, resettlement of landless agricultural labourers providing house sites and housing loans, extension of employment, generation of self-employment have made a very little impact on their pressing problems and urgent needs.

In fact, development centres round a high rate of economic growth with social justice, priority investment, political decentralization and moulding of tradition with modernization. Popular participation should be treated as the basic policy in national development. Active participation of all individuals in the development process is the *sine qua non* of development. Participation provides the beneficiaries of development an opportunity for opinion building, helps the planners in setting the goals and objectives, formulating policies, implementing plans and programmes, organizing and evaluating the target community, the less privileged. Participation makes the people aware of their problems relating to development and empowerment. To find out the extent of participation, I interviewed 175 respondents in this block area. 38.75 per cent respondents said that they were regular in attending *Gram Sansad* meetings, 42.00 per cent were regularly casual, 43 per cent and 46 per cent were non-participatory when needed and occasionally, respectively. Only 1 per cent was never non-participatory. It seems crystal clear that the participation of the tribals in development programmes was mainly through labour, moral support and benefits sharing, but very poor through decision-making process, which remained only within 6.24 per cent while 93.76 per cent of the tribal people did not participate in the making of decisions at all as to who would get the benefits, how the benefits should be provided, and how much the beneficiary would get. The leaders themselves made decisions, took the decisions and justified the decisions. The tribal people only heard about decisions and participated the meetings only to raise hands and voices in favour of the decisions, but did not say anything to counteract the decisions and muddle the decision-making process. The respondents who had secondary education, ran business, had more than three acres of land, and were from higher economic category said that participation was satisfactory and that in the selection of beneficiaries they discussed the matter with all. Most of the respondents who were from the lower to middle category did not know the objectives of various development programmes. 3 per cent of the total was silent. 25 per cent answered in favour of self-employment and 12.25 per cent for poverty alleviation. In terms of perception and perceptive capacity they are deficient. What may be the reasons behind that? Poor economic access is the basic reason. They are not aware about the guidelines of development programmes like IRDP, TSP, JRY etc. 72 per cent of the respondents said that they did not know the guidelines required for IRDP, TSP, JRY and the like. They took money as governmental help and for self-employment and poverty alleviation. Only 28 per cent knew about the guidelines. They received the information from Gram Panchayat officials and party-panchayat leaders of their locality.

It is to be noted that ignorance has made them more oriented to consumption pattern rather than investment. Among the respondents only 12 per cent were interested in investment. 1.28 per cent said that banks should be liberal in terms of loan. An environment of investment has not been created among the tribals. Most of the respondents were not satisfied with the selection of beneficiaries. They said that the depressed and poor families were least benefited. Selection through Beneficiary Committee and meetings convened for this selection were procedurally defunct. Selection was based more on good understanding with party-panchayat leaders and members of the Committee than on economic background. The former scored 75 per cent, the latter 25 per cent only. This does not mean that the beneficiaries are from higher economic background. In response to the present economic hardships, an old tribal of Tilakchandrapur Gram Panchayat lamented with great despair—"We had to live a happy communitarian life based on forest and forest produce. We are deprived by the *baboos* and now we are also depressed. We depend on daily labour. I have no land. Few of us have. When we have no work we move from one area to another for work. Women collect *sal* leaf, knit them with stick and dry them up in sunlight for final supply to the factory during this hour of seasonal unemployment. Economic hardship is a regular phenomenon. Fishing is for mere consumption. Hunting is an old age story, in general. Though sometimes we practice this for mere recreation. Governments do provide meagre help to us. Party workers and men having good relations with them get more benefits than others do. We worship forests as gods. We do not destroy it due to tradition and religious practices. Some Hindu low castes are destroying the forests for their own economic benefits. We are against it" (Field Survey). They are at the margin of survival and in struggle to achieve a level of consumption just enough to survive. They have been absorbed in the national and local economy and techno-economic fold of settled peasantry. Basically, they can be divided into two categories —those who own, work and hire-out themselves and those who do not own and hire-out themselves. For them, class-consciousness signifies that they are an organized force struggling for survival, and they are autonomous. The determinants of their consciousness about the class position are inequalities, trend in occupational diversification and mobilization. The proletarianization of the tribal peasants is not different from the proletarianization of the non-tribal peasants. They are differentiated in terms of production relations, place in the society in relation to other classes, and forces of production like land, irrigation, seeds and fertilizers. When the immediate problems before the tribal labourers are with adequate wage rates, food and clothing, the problems before the share-croppers and those who own a few plots of land are with better prices for agricultural produce, better credit and loan facilities and irrigation facility. Formation of class consciousness among the former is at the rudimentary stage. The latter in alliance with its non-tribal counterparts have subdued their class-consciousness at a low level. They are mobilized on tribal development and techno-economic pursuits of development programmes. Politicization of the poor by the left parties is a legacy of the past. The politicization among the tribals by the CPI(M) is a noteworthy phenomenon in this area. The left parties have had capitalized tribals' discontent during the 60s and 70s and made of it as their support base. CPI(M)-dominated *Krishak Sabha* had a number of followers in several villages of *Jungle Mahal* who had experience of restlessness among the landless labourers and share-croppers. In 1969, the tribal and Scheduled Caste *bargadars* demanded 60 per cent crop-sharing from the landowners, who resisted the move. The CPI(M) tried to ensure a bargaining and compromise formula to make a peaceful settlement. The restless share-croppers did not accept the move. Clashes between landowners and *bargadars* occurred in Rakshitpur and Hariki as a result of this. Finally, the CPI(M) leaders could not effectively intervene in the disputes, and for that the area was left open to the influence of the extremists. Dissidents of the CPI(M)-dominated *Krishak Sabha* in Chua, Rakshitpur and adjacent villages supported the extremists. Due to police action and harassment, the extremists favoured underground activities and this created apathy in the minds of a large number of supporters. The extremists did not achieve much except expediting the registration of a handful of *bargadars*. The CPI(M) capitalised the situation. It made strong organizational base in this area. The party has institutionalized the discontents through Panchayats. Panchayats have taken various measures to improve the economic conditions of the tribal, such as direct benefits like providing pump sets, IRDP loans for better cultivation, and animal husbandry and fisheries. Their children are taking educational facilities. They are more conscious about their own interests. But, the institutionalization of Panchayats with regard to tribals' participation in Panchayats and various development programmes is not quite satisfactory. Tribals' discontent has been institutionalized within the Panchayati Raj Institutions and various development programmes through it. It is like Ralf Dahrendorf's 'institutionalization of conflict'.

The rural society in India is hegemonized by political and local power elites and the benefits of rural development programmes are capitalized by them. Marx and classical economists agree that the economy provides the substance of the political. A distinct domain has developed from determinism of economy to new potentialities of the power of 'culture'. The cultural domains challenge the domains of the economy, liberal politics, state administration and revolution as popular movement. There is the democratizing role of technology and dissemination of culture. Nietzschian theory has no destiny, no conception of a just society. To him, intellect is the mode of continuous provocation and production. Nietzschian paradigm is suitable for our time. There is the need for public space to make grand success for the implementation of rural public policies. Nietzsche's politics is rarely pre-occupied with state structure, rule of law, justice etc., rather it is pre-occupied with thought deeds, forms of social morality and aesthetics. There is the need for the triumph of the will-to-power of the weak. Political element of cultural values lies in generality. The idea of the 'good' is the expression of herd morality and the sign of the power of the 'masses'. There is the need for external politics, i.e. cultural politics outside the state, society, laws, parliamentary institutions as the main concerns. Unlike Marx, Nietzche identified the crisis of modern world with the Few, in the cultured elites, not in contradiction between the forces of production. Nietzche identified the crisis of the modern world in the cultured elites. He called for counter-revolution on the part of the 'underprivileged'. The 'democratic herd' has made politics for itself, politics for mass parties, election, representation, political and civil liberties, constitutional restraints as well as supporting culture of popular culture, literature, arts and crafts, civic culture, public education etc. (Wolin, 2004).

Rural public policy formulation and rural development in India is in the process of transition and in the phase of prismatic society. The development paradigm is within and between fused and diffracted. The basic problems faced by the Indian populace is service delivery of basic needs. All the policies taken in the globalized world are essentially oriented to neo-liberal market set up and to continue the process of passive revolution of capital. Rural development policies in the spheres of health, education and employment are at stake. There are many provisions for social welfare in rural areas, but there is rank and rivalry. Due to contestations and political marketing rural development is not conducive to the needs of the rural downtroddens. Socio-economic development in terms of equality, capacity and differentiation is very poor. Mobilization is poor. Globalization, mobilization and development—all these are not synchronized due to loopholes of 'agraria-industria' transition. The social attitudes of non-participation and non-satisfaction, aspiration-satisfaction gap are growing day by day. The need is the change from 'passive revolution' of Gramsci to 'democratic herd' of Nietzschian paradigm, participation, dialogue, representation, mass politics, mass culture, public education and counter-revolution on the part of the underprivileged.

References

Ali, Farazmand (2007). "Globalization : A Theoretical Analysis with Implication for Governance and Public Administration" in F. Ali and J. Pinkowski (eds.) *Handbook of Globalization, Governance and Public Administration*, London: Francis and Taylor.

Anderson, James E. (1975). *Public Policy Making*, London: Thomas Nelson and Sons.

Bakshi, Manas (1980). "Land Reforms in West Bengal", *Frontier* (October 18).

Bandyopadhyay, Nripen (1983). *Evaluation of Land Reform Measures in West Bengal*, Calcutta; Centre for Studies in Social Sciences.

Bose, Pradip Kr. (1984). *Changes in a Rural Society*, New Delhi; Ajanta Publications.

Chakravarty, Sukhamoy (1987). *Development Planning*, New Delhi: Oxford University Press.

Chatterjee, Partha (1997). "Development Planning and the Indian State" in Partha Chatterjee (ed.) *State and Politics in India*, New Delhi: OUP.

Chattopadhyay, Gouranga (1964). *Ranjana: A Village in West Bengal*, Calcutta: Bookland Private Ltd.

Dasgupta, Biplab (1984). "Agricultural labour under colonial, semi-capitalist and capitalist conditions", *EPW* (September 29, 1984).

Dasgupta, S. and R. Dhar (1975). "An Approach to Development of Santhal Pargana Tribal Area" in NICD, *Integrated Tribal Development Planning*, Papers and proceedings of seminar held at National Institute of Community Development, May 2-4.

Dreze, Jean and Sen, Amartya (1997). *Indian Development.* New Delhi: OUP.

Dye, Thomas (1992). *Understanding Public Policy*, Englewood Cliffs: Prentice-Hall.

Easton, David (1965). *A Systems Analysis of Political Life.* New York: Wiley.

Ghosh, Ajit Kr. (1983). *Agrarian Reform in Contemporary Developing Countries*, New York: Martin's Press.

Government of India (1963). *Report of the Commission for Scheduled Castes and Scheduled Tribes, 1962-63.*

Gupta, Ranjit K. (1972). *Agrarian West Bengal*, Calcutta: Institute of Social Research and Applied Anthropology.

Khasnabis, Ratan (1981). "Operation Barga: Limits to Social Democratic Reformism", *EPW*, Vol. XVI, Nos. 25/26.

Khasnabis, Ratan (1986), "More on West Bengal Tenancy Reforms", *EPW*, Vol. XXI, No. 4.

Kohli, Atul (1990). "From Elite Activism to Democratic Consolidation" in F.R. Frankel and M.S.A. Rao (eds.) *Dominance and State Power in Modern India*, Vol. II, New Delhi: OUP.

Kotlar, Philip (n.f.). *Marketing for Non-profit Organizations*, New Delhi: Prentice-Hall.

Maheswari, S.R. (1985). *Rural Public Policy in India*, New Delhi: Sage.

Mallick, Ross (1993). *Development Policy of a Communist Government*, Cambridge: Cambridge University.

Mitter, Swasti (1986). "Peasant Movements in Sonarpur" in A.R. Desai (ed.) *Agrarian Struggles in India after Independence*, New Delhi: OUP.

Mohan, Ananda (1972). "Reviving the Sick Child" in Dhires Bhattacharya (ed.) *Focus on West Bengal*, Calcutta: Oxford Book and Stationery Company.

Planning Commission (1969). *Fourth Five Year Plan*, New Delhi: Planning Commission.

Presthus, Robert (1975), *Public Administration*, New York: The Ronald Press.

Rahman, Anisur (1984), *Grassroots Participation and Self-reliance,* New Delhi: OUP.

RBI (1954). *All India Rural Credit Survey*, Bombay: RBI.

RBI (1969). *Report of the All-India Rural Credit Review Committee* (Bombay: RBI).

Rudra, Ashok (1981). "One Step Forward, Two Steps Backward', *EPW*, Vol. XVI, Nos. 25/26.

Sen Gupta, Bhabani (1979). *CPI(M): Promises, Prospects and Problems*, New Delhi: Young Asia Publications.

Sen, A. and Dreze, J. (1995), *India: Economic Development and Social Opportunity*, Oxford: Clarendon Press.

Sharma, S.K. and J.G. Krishnayya (1975). "The Role of Informatics in Tribal Development" in NICD, *Integrated Tribal Development Planning* (Hyderabad: NICD).

United Nations Centre for Rural Development (1977). *Methods of Comprehensive Regional Development*, Nagoya: Japan.

Wolin, Sheldon S. (2004). *Politics and Vision: Continuity and Innovation in Western Political Thought*, Princeton: Princeton University Press.

Zaheer, M. (1975). "Policy for Planning and Development in Tribal Areas" in NICD, *Integrated Tribal Development Planning*, Papers and proceedings of seminar held at National Institute of Community Development, Hyderabad, May 2-4.

2
Impact of DDU-GKY among Rural Unemployed Youth

Cases from Five States of India

Shankar Chatterjee, Arjun Gope and *Gautam Purkayastha*

Introduction

For the survival of human beings, employment is *sine qua non*. In this regard, Food and Agriculture Organisation (FAO) can be mentioned as according to them, "Decent rural employment refers to any activity, occupation, work, business or service performed by women and men, adults and youth, in rural areas that:

(i) Respects the core labour standards as defined in ILO Conventions, and therefore:
   (a) Is not child labour;
   (b) Is not forced labour;
   (c) Guarantees freedom of association and the right to collective bargaining and promotes organization of rural workers;
   (d) Does not entail discrimination at work on the basis of race, colour, sex, religion, political opinion, national extraction, social origin or other.

(ii) Provides an adequate living income;

(iii) Entails an adequate degree of employment security and stability;
(iv) Adopts minimum occupational safety and health (OSH) measures, which are adapted to address sector-specific risks and hazards;
(v) Avoids excessive working hours and allows sufficient time for rest; and
(vi) Promotes access to adapted technical and vocational training" (FAO, Applied definition of decent rural employment (DRE) (15/09/2014).

Unemployment Scenario and Youth: According to the Centre for Monitoring Indian Economy, India's labour market is under pressure mainly because of a fall in the employment rate in rural India and continued low employment rate in urban India. Employment generation is need of the hour in India both in rural and urban areas. In India, two major employment programmes for rural youth are—RSETI and DDU-GKY. RSETIs mean Rural Self-Employment Training Institutes, an initiative of the Ministry of Rural Development (MoRD) to have dedicated infrastructure in each district of the country to impart training and skill upgradation of rural youth geared towards entrepreneurship development. And the Deen Dayal Upadhyaya Grameen Kaushalya Yojana (DDU-GKY) was launched on 25 September, 2014 with the dual objectives of adding diversity to the incomes of rural poor families and caters to the career aspirations of rural youth with wage employment. DDU-GKY is exclusively focused on rural youth between the ages of 15 and 35 years from Below Poverty Line (BPL) families. DDU-GKY is for the youth and the National Youth Policy 2014 defines 'youth' as persons between the ages of 15-29 years. Regarding unemployment rate National Sample Survey Organisation (NSSO) may be mentioned—rural male and female youth unemployment rates were 17.4 per cent and 13.6 per cent respectively in 2017-18 (indiaapprenticeshipforum.org). It is also evident from NSSO data that "unemployment rates increased sharply overall in India among educated youth. Youth with degrees seek aspirational jobs and when unable to get one, prefer to sit it out, or are forced to take up any available work. This predicament deepens in rural India where opportunities are fewer."

It is pertinent to mention that more than 180 million or 69 per cent of the country's youth population between the ages of 18 and 34 years live in its rural areas of India. Of them, the youth from poor families with no or marginal employment were about 55 million. It is pertinent to mention that the National Policy for Skill Development & Entrepreneurship 2015 has identified a skills-gap of 109.73 million in 24 key sectors by the year 2022. This number cannot be achieved without addressing 55 million from rural India who are from the BPL families. Also, a FICCI and Ernst-Young study published in 2013 identified a shortage of over 47 million skilled workers across the globe by 2020. This presents an unprecedented opportunity for India to train its poor youth population and place them in jobs across the world and realize its demographic dividend. Under DDU-GKY, skill training at the Training Centre is fully free. There are no fees also there are no registration charges. There are no examination or certification charges also. There are no placement charges. So, rural youth should take the full advantage of DDU-GKY and youth should know that no one is doing a favour to them by recommending his/her name for training. Also the World Youth Report reveals that in India, the unemployment rate for youth remains at about 10 per cent, but there are concern that this will increase if India's high economic growth rate of 7 per cent per year fails to boost employment at the rates needed to generate sufficient work for the country's growing youth population (UN, World Youth Report, 2018).

About DDU-GKY: DDU-GKY is in implementation in 28 States and UTs, across 689 districts, impacting youth from over 7,426 blocks. It presently has more than 1,575 projects being implemented by over 717 partners, in more than 502 trades from 50 industrial sectors. Little more than 9.9 lakh youth have been trained and more than 5.3 lakh youth have been placed in jobs as on 1st April, 2020. From 2012, DDU-GKY has so far committed an investment of more than Rs. 5,600 crore, impacting rural youth pan-India (ddugky.gov.in/content/about-us-0). The data reveals that till March 2022, the cumulative target of youth to be trained are little more than 28.9 lakh and I request the Union Government and all the State Governments utmost action should be taken to achieve the target and placement should also go up. After COVID lot of youth have lost jobs so through DDU-GKY if employment is created many will get jobs and the economy will develop because of the 'Multiplier Effect'.

It is pertinent to mention that sometimes some youth are not interested to work as wage earners, instead prefer to start self-employment and also girls after marriage may not continue to work so by carrying the study reasons may be known.

DDY-GKY Cases: In this chapter, four cases collected from secondary sources from four states of India are presented. Shankar Chatterjee also has done a primary study at Amritsar district of Punjab in August 2017 so based on his study few cases are also highlighted.

Case 1: Gagandeep Kaur (female) was from Jharon, Punjab working as retail associate at Kapsons, Sangrur. Her parents through seasonal farming were earning around Rs. 34,000 yearly which is very low for survival of a family. After completion of Intermediate, she was trained on selling of goods under DDU-GKY by Centum Learning Limited and later on she was placed at Kapsons Sangrur in December 2017 and according to 2020 information she was earning Rs. 11,000 per month.

Case 2: Pabitra Buragohain (Male) of Dhemaji, Assam was trained as a hospitality assistant by JIS Foundation, Satmile, and Guwahati. Through his Gram Panchayat he came to know about DDU-GKY training courses and accordingly joined a 3-month hospitality assistant course. After completion of Higher Secondary course he could not continue as his father was a marginal farmer and he has four children. So Pabitra underwent DDU-GKY training and after training, he joined Mountain Trail Foods Private Limited (Chai Point), Hyderabad in March 2017. According to him, as manager he was earning a monthly salary of Rs. 29,681 in 2020.

Case 3: Rekha (female) of Nelamangala, Karnataka belonged to below poverty line (BPL) family. The parents have two children—she and her brother, and mother had serious health issues so whatever father saved was spent on treatment of mother (although later on she passed away). She was trained under DDU-GKY, a course in retail sales associate from Wazir Advisors Private Limited (Bengaluru centre). After training she was placed as customer sales associate with Hypercity, Bengaluru and as wage was paid Rs. 15,000 per month.

Case 4: Ruhi Praveen (female) from Ranchi of Jharkhand belongs to minority community completed a course in sewing machine operator from Wazir Advisors Private Limited (Ranchi centre) under DDU-GKY in 2017. Her father was a hawker used to sell clothes door to door in a cycle earning a low income. She after completion of her training was placed as operator with Jay Jay Mills (India) Private Limited in Erode, Tamil Nadu. While income data was collected in 2020, she informed that her income was little more than Rs. 11,000 per month.

DDU-GKY Case from Amritsar district, Punjab: In this part two centres were studied in Amritsar district of Punjab where DDU-GKY trainings were going on. In both the centres, Shankar Chatterjee in 2017 (August) studied DDU-GKY. Based on the study few cases are presented as these are primary study.

First Case: Under DDU-GKY, in Amritsar district—Orion Edutech is one of the PIAs functioning in the following places:

- Government Senior Secondary School, Ramdass, Ajnala,
- Government High School Preetnagar, Block Chogawan,
- Government Senior Secondary School Tapiala,Block Chogawan,
- Government High School Cheema Bath, Block Rayya, and
- Government Senior Secondary School, Harsha Chhinna, Block Harsha Chhinna.

It may be mentioned that Orion Edutech Private Limited has been relentlessly working to develop the skill of the rural youth of India with the assistance of the Ministry of Rural Development under DDU-GKY. A Few cases collected by Orion Edutech Private Ltd. are presented below:

(a) *Hardev Singh* (male) was trained in the 'Customer Care Executive' programme in 2017. After successful completion of training, he was posted at *Mohali* in a private company, namely 'Competent Company' as customer support representative (CSR). His job was taking customers' calls *vis-à-vis* resolving the issues; promoting new products into the market. In addition to free lodging and two meals an amount of Rs. 12,475 was paid to him as monthly wage.

(b) *Ruby Sharma* (female) was trained in Food and Beverages service and after successful completion of training she joined *Sodexo*, Noida as steward, at the salary of Rs. 8,000 per month with free lodging and two times free meals. It is pertinent to mention that the job of steward was serving food, arranging utensils, serving to the customers, helping in the catering services etc.

(c) Like *Ruby Sharma* six others were given employment after successful completion of training at *Sodexo,* Noida with the same terms and conditions with a monthly wage of Rs. 8,000. The names of the youth are: (a) Prabhdial Singh, (b) Gagandeep Kaur, (c) Gurpreet Kaur, (d) Money, (e) Palwinder Kaur, and (f) Navjot Kaur. All were trained at Government Senior Secondary School Tapiala Center of DDU-GKY in Amritsar district of Punjab (Chatterjee, 2017).

Second DDU-GKY Case from Amritsar district Punjab: In addition one more Centre was visited in Amritsar district by Shankar Chatterjee for research study. The study was conducted at *Sahid Captain Amar Singh* Government Secondary School, *Majitha* Block, *Majitha.* During the course of study, it was reported by the officials of the Centre mainly by *Manohar Randhawa* that 93 days training consisting of 756 hours would be covered by imparting two types of training, viz. Documentation Assistant and Warehouse packer. The training programmes were started on 22 May, 2017 and would complete on 19 September, 2017 (Chatterjee visited in August 2017). It was reported that in each batch 35 youth were undergoing training totalling to 70—25 were females and 45 males. The timing of the training was 8.15 AM to 5 PM with half an hour lunch break. Two trainers—one specialized in Information Technology (IT) and other one on English and Soft skills—were imparting training to all the trainees' *inter alia* master trainers were also giving training. The in-charge of the Centre *Randhawa* further informed that "all would be absorbed in the *Safeducate Learning Private Limited* or would be provided employment by *Safeducate* as it is the PIA". To get an idea about the youth undergoing training, a few youth (both male and female) were contacted. Among them one was a person with disability (PwD) and another female trainee who had family issues as father and mother had separation so different types of youth were covered in this study. The cases are presented here (*ibid.*):

(a) *Puja* (20 years, unmarried, female) Higher Secondary School Leaving Certificate examination (HSSLC) passed was undergoing training as a Documentation Assistant as she could not continue her further study because of financial problems as father was earning through wage labour.
(b) *Ameen Preet Kaur* (23 years, female) could not complete her graduation because of financial issues (father was tailor). She was also one of the trainees of Documentation Assistant and expressed her happiness about the training.
(c) *Sandeep Kaur* (18 years, female) HSSLC pass and her training was on Warehouse packer and Lovepreet Kaur (22 years) commerce graduate was undergoing training in Documentation Assistant. Ms. *Laxmi* (26 years) hailing from below poverty line (BPL) family everyday after completion

of the training of Documentation Assistant teaches seven girls at free of cost in her village.

(d) Among the male persons who were undergoing training, one was *Willian Mattu* (30 years), a person with disability, married. He worked as compounder (medical assistant) in his village but his income was not sufficient, so he expected that after completion of training as Warehouse packer, he would earn substantial income for sustenance of the family.

(e) *Manjinder Singh* (20 years, male) HSSLC pass also completed his diploma in Electrical Engineering from local polytechnic was one of the participants as job is assured. The other persons who were interviewed were Gurpreet Singh (24 years) HSSLC pass; Arun (19 years) father was brick-kiln worker and Vikash Sharma (22 years), Diploma in Civil Engineering.

Conclusion

It is evident from the above cases that DDU-GKY has created an impact among the youth in rural areas of India. So DDU-GKY is having enormous scope to usher a ray of hope to rural youth of India. I suggest to the Government of India after studying technical feasibility and economic viability in the district where population is huge at sub-divisional level DDU-GKY centres may be opened.

References

Chatterjee Shankar (2017). "Impact of DDU-GKY among Rural Unemployed Youth in Punjab: A Case from Amritsar District", *Journal for Studies in Management and Planning*, e-ISSN: 2395-0463, Vol. 3, Issue 9, August 2017.

Chatterjee Shankar (2017). "Unemployment a serious issue in developed Punjab: A study focusing on DDU-GKY", *International Journal of Applied Research* (ISSN Print: 2394- 7500, ISSN Online: 2394-5869) Vol. 3, Issue 8, 2017.

http://ddugky.gov.in/

http://www.fao.org/fileadmin/user_upload/fao_ilo/pdf/DRE_Applied_Definition.pdf

https://kaushalpragati.nic.in/login/landingReport.do?methodName=mapTCReport&reqtrack=L4nHhDptt21NpTL6raIfLhcZ3

United Nations, (2018). "World Youth Report: Youth and the 2030 Agenda for Sustainable Development", United Nations Department of Economic and Social Affairs.

www.indiaapprenticeshipforum.org/skilling-rural-india-challenges-and-opportunities

3
Global Goals: Local Action No one is left behind

A Case of Joranda Jharia

S. Nagabhushana Rao

Global Goals, known as sustainable development goals (SDGs) are a new global development vision to create a better world by 2030. The global goals were adopted by the 193 countries and India is a visionary to the document. The global goals or Sustainable Development Goals (SDGs) are universally set goals to create a better and sustainable future for all by transforming our world. It is the agenda for 2030 for sustainable development. The countries are expected to frame their agenda and policies over the next 15 years. Already, 5 years have elapsed and remaining 10 years, the countries are expected to transform the world by framing and implement the policies, to end poverty, to fight inequality, to protect the plant, to enjoy peace and to ensure prosperity for all. This is to create equitable society and providing social and economic justice for all in the world. Aims of the global goals are 'define the world we want in future and to ensure that no one is left behind'.

The SDG were built on success of the millennium development goals (MDGs) and complete what they did not achieve. India has moved ahead on implementation of the SDGs and initiated preparation of the Vision Document 2030 with National Institution for Transforming India (NITI) Aayog in the lead. Based on the guidance from NITI Aayog, the state governments have begun the process of SDGs implementation. In addition to the state level (provincial) there is a need to take SDGs to the grassroots level. Here lies the importance of local governments, especially the Gram Panchayat/Gram Sabha, the institutions at grassroots level.

In India, Gram Panchayat/Gram Sabha is identified as a grassroots level local institution. The SDGs are implemented at local level. So the phrase "Think globally and act locally" is the epitome and the process of implementation of Sustainable Development Goals (SDGs). There are 17 sustainable development goals (SDGs) with 169 targets. Gram Panchayats/Gram Sabha will have a crucial role to play in achieving the SDGs.

There are 17 Global Goals to create the new world of future. The global goals are: (1) No Poverty, (2) Zero Hunger, (3) Good Health and Well-being, (4) Quality Education, (5) Gender Equality, (6) Clean Water and Sanitation, (7) Affordable and Clean Energy, (8) Decent Work and Economic Growth, (9) Industry, Innovation and Infrastructure, (10) Reduced Inequalities, (11) Sustainable Cities and Communities, (12) Responsible Consumption and Production, (13) Climate Action, (14) Life Below Water, (15) Life on Land, (16) Peace, Justice and Strong Institutions, and (17) Partnerships for the Goals.

The global goals (SDGs) will be implemented through grassroots institutions at local level. The 'twin' objectives of the local institutions (Panchayati Raj system) are envisaged in the Constitution of India. These are: (1) to ensure local economic development and (2) social justice. Panchayats are expected to play an effective role in the planning and implementation of functions related to 29 subjects of rural development, enlisted in the Eleventh Schedule of the Constitution. Many Sustainable Development Goals are within purview of these 29 subjects. In fact, few Gram Panchayats like Hivre Bazar in Maharashtra Province, Gangdevpalli in Telangana Province and Punsari in Gujarat Province are being implementing the SDGs and have become a model villages in the country. Besides these gram panchayats, few unnoticed Gram Panchayats/Gram Sabhas are implementing the global goals to transform the world and no one is left behind in this development process.

India is celebrating 75 years of Independence and putting every effort to develop the nook and corner of the county and to reach the last person in development process. The federal government and provincial governments are employing different strategies to develop the areas and to reach the last person. The Government of India is insisting to implement the Sustainable Development Goals (SDGs) in more than six lakh villages.

The Government has adopted multi-pronged approach to implement the SDGs in rural areas: (i) Developing a wage employment policy (MGNREGA), (ii) Developing a technical skills to empower the youth (DDU-GKY), (iii) Providing entrepreneur skills to the women by creating livelihood options (NRLM), (iv) By laying roads in every part of the county for better transport (PMGSY), (v) Saving every drop of water and providing water to the agriculture and to every rural households through water mission, (vi) Helping the age old people, single headed families and disabled people through social security measures like National Social Assistance Programmes etc. This multi-pronged approach is to develop every part of the country and to reach the last man.

The Government of India has adopted 'two' strategies to implement global goals in rural India. These are: (i) People's planning campaign, and (ii) Preparation of Gram Panchayat Development Plans (GPDPs)/Village Development Plan (VDP).

People's Planning Campaign—Kerala's Experiment: People's plan campaign was initiated in the Kerala Province in 1996. It was a new approach in development planning. People's participation was the epitome of development process. Kerala Province has adopted 'three' pronged strategy of people's planning campaign. These are: (i) Administrative decentralization, i.e. local government institutions in both rural and urban areas were given new functions and powers in decision making. Officials of several line departments were brought under the authority of local governments, (ii) Fiscal decentralization, i.e. 40 per cent of the State's Annual Plan budget was allocated directly to the local government institutions, and (iii) Decentralisation of political power, i.e. elected representatives were given the autonomy to design policies, implement and fund development projects at local level. The crux of people's plan campaign is people's right to participate in the planning process through Gram Sabha.[1]

People's Plan Campaign (PPC) was launched on 17th August, 1996. It was the auspicious day for the people of Kerala, i.e. celebration of Malayalam New Year Day. The Government of Kerala has empowered the local governments through people's planning campaign by rallying volunteers, experts, officials and the people. To prepare a people' plan, six rounds of cascading training programmes were done, at one time involving one lakh people. These training programmes have prepared the people to involve in planning process. As a result, local plans emerged through a bottom-up planning process. Since then, local governments in Kerala has been preparing its local plans and implementing them.[2]

People's Plan Campaign has created a new civic culture. It has nurtured a development culture among the local grassroots democratic institutions. This facilitated local level planning to address the problems at the local level. The campaign has brought an attitudinal change among the elected representatives, officials, experts, and the people towards development process.[3] People's plan campaign has given an opportunity for direct participation of the people in development process. A major achievement of the People's Plan Campaign was participation of people in their development. Another achievement of the campaign was gender dimension, i.e. women development was part of the campaign. The participation of women has made successful of people's planning campaign.

Kerala's achievement through people's planning process was praiseworthy. The gap between rural and urban was reduced. In 1993-94, the poverty ratio was 25.76 per cent and 24.59 per cent in rural and urban areas of Kerala state. According to the Rangarajan Committee Report on Poverty Estimation, in 2011-12, the poverty ratio in Kerala had declined to 7.3 per cent and 5.3 per cent respectively. The local roads under the Local Government's was doubled from 1,15,306 km in 1995-96 to 2,31,676 km in 2018-19. There was a lot of improvement in the condition of towns and country roads. The roads were evenly distributed across the districts and the regions. 5.7 lakh houses were constructed for the poor people. All the houses in Kerala have been electrified and have toilets.[4]

The best outcome of people's planning campaign and democratic decentralisation was the emergence and growth of women SHGs locally known as Kudumbasree Neighbourhood Groups (NHGs). The NHGs are basically a micro-finance network linked to Local Governments. The NHGs is a community organisation and a platform for convergence of anti-poverty programmes, for women empowerment. At present, there are 2.77 lakh NHGs with membership of 43 lakh households, each represented by a woman member. The NHGs have become the most accessible source of micro credit with a fund base of more than Rs. 11,000 crore.[5] Kerala's People's plan campaign and decentralisation approach has taught that people can participate in planning process at local level. The development was according to the people's priorities and needs.

After 24 years of people's planning campaign and decentralisation approach, the Government of India has adopted PPC to implement SDGs through decentralisation approach. People's participation is vital for action at local level.

Gram Panchayat Development Plan (GPDP): The second strategy by the Government of India, to implement SDGs are to prepare development plan at gram panchayat level, known as "Gram Panchayat Development Plan (GPDP)."

The Constitution of India defines that the objectives of local government is economic development and social justice at local level. 29 subjects related to rural development were enlisted in

Eleventh Schedule of the Constitution. The Gram Panchayats were expected to prepare a development plan through people's participation.

Pre-conditions for successful preparation of Gram Panchayat Develoment Plan (GPDP): People's Participation is an essential element of human development. Participation refers to "taking part or sharing." Participation means involvement of people in the economic, social, cultural and political processes that affect their lives. People may, in some cases, have complete and direct control over these processes. In other cases, the control may be partial or indirect. One important aspect of participation is that the people should have constant access to decision-making and power.

The concept of participation is understood differently in different contexts. Stan Burkey (1993) defines participation as "an essential part of human initiative, creativity, responsibility, pride and cooperation."[6] Burkey understands that "participation as a process by which people learn to take charge of their own lives and find solutions to their own problems."[7] People's participation is central to development in democratic systems. The operation of democracy results in innovations and provides opportunity for citizens to participate in the activities of democratic functioning and developing themselves.

Women's Participation: 'Women hold up half the sky'— Mao Zedong.[8] Development surrounds the women. Women's participation is essential to the success of development and plays a catalytic role towards achievement of transformational economic, environmental and social changes required for sustainable development.

The women are near equal to men in numbers (49.55%), but there exists a gender gap in access to education and finances. In India, the women were less literate compared to men. The women are 65.46 per cent literate and whereas the men are 82.14 per cent literate (Census, 2011). The women have limited access to credit, healthcare and education. These are further aggravated by the global food and economic crises and climate change. Empowering them is essential, not only for the well-being of individuals, families and rural communities, but also for overall economic productivity, given women's large presence in the agricultural workforce worldwide.[9] Empowering women with finances, education will change the society towards development.

Challenges of People's Participation: There are many challenges to the people's participation. There exists a wide gap between the people and the attitude of government officials. Superior attitude of the officials is a major hurdle for people's participation. The officials were not trusted by the people because of their superior attitude and when the officials were transferred, developmental projects were abruptly ended or not completed. Taking the trust of the people and building confidence is a major challenge. There exists a knowledge gap between the people, facilitators and government officials, who drives the development plan. Capacity building in terms of knowledge and skill orientation to the people and attitudinal changes among the government officials is vital for preparation of village development plan.

Glimpses of Rural India

India is largely Rural and a country of villages. At present (2019), India is having 2,69,250 Gram Panchayats[10] and there are 6,64,369 villages representing rural India.[11] India lives in villages and the village economy is the soul of Indian economy and provides food security to the country. If the villages fail to produce food grains, the country starves. Culturally, the villages are full of traditions and family values continue. It is a tradition of joint family and the human relations were unbroken. The human feelings and emotions expressed in villages are still a happy family. The rural India (villages) is vibrant with 68.84 per cent of human resources, fascinating culture and ethnic values but, often unemployed and underutilised.

The rural India suffers from innumerable problems. The widespread poverty, growing inequalities, rapid population growth, rising unemployment (65% of youth are in the age group of working) in rural areas is a concern. The problems of hunger, ignorance, ill health and high mortality are most acute. No schools. If the school exists, the teacher will not be available or one teacher headed schools and the buildings of the government schools are in dilapidated condition. The sanitation conditions in Government Schools are worst. The girls are afraid to attend the schools due to bad sanitation conditions in the schools.

In the villages, there is no infrastructure, like roads and drinking water. 67 per cent of villages do not have water for irrigation, depends upon the vagaries of monsoon. Liquor is the main enemy of the villagers and it is available and destroying the families. But for some bad elements it is a livelihood and profit making activity. Conflicts in the village have become common as politics divide the people. As a result many families were disturbed. Corruption has become a common feature affecting the poorest of the poor. Many people has lost livelihoods in rural areas and migrated to urban areas. The villages also face natural calamities like droughts, floods. The pandemic COVID-19 has wrecked the havoc in rural areas, as their health and livelihoods were threatened. Therefore, there is a dire necessity to develop the infrastructure and also to improve the quality of life in rural areas. The Government is initiating many schemes to develop rural India.

The development process in rural India has witnessed several changes and achieved a new dimension. The people have become the 'centre stage' in the process of participatory development. The journey of rural development has started from food security to Rural Livelihoods. In fact 'three' pronged strategy was adopted to alleviate poverty in rural areas. The first strategy is creation of employment and infrastructure through major schemes like MGNREGA, NRLM, DDU-GKY etc. The second strategy is area development through different schemes like PMKSY, MGNREGA etc. The third strategy is social security measures, i.e. special assistance to the differently disabled, under NSAP. Besides these strategies, there are many schemes which also target different individuals. Ministry of the Rural Development (MoRD) with the outlay of more than

Rs. 1,15,000 crore carries out various programmes of Rural Development, like MGNREGS, NRLM, DDU-GKY, PMGSY, NSAP, PMAY(R) etc.

Implementation of Global Goals (SDGs): A Case of Joranda Jharia: There are two important elements in implementation of global goals: (1) Resource Envelope, and (2) Process for preparation of Gram Panchayat Development Plan (GPDP)/Village Development Plan (VDP).

Resource Envelope to Implement SDGs

1. Funds from Central Rural Development schemes, such as the Mahatma Gandhi National Rural Employment Guarantee Scheme, Prime Minister Awas Yojana, Pradhan Mantri Gram Sadak Yojana etc.,
2. The Member of Parliament Local Area Development Scheme (MPLADS),
3. The gram panchayat's own source of revenue,
4. Central and State Finance Commission Grants,
5. Corporate Social Responsibility Funds, and
6. Fifteenth Finance (XV) Commission Funds, which directly reaches to the gram panchayats.

Process for Preparation of Gram Panchayat Development Plan (GPDP)

The following strategy was adopted to prepare village development plan:[12]

1. Rapport building with the people. It is the main element of participatory planning.
2. Entry point activities, which are useful for people will be done to take the confidence of the people. This will energize and mobilize the community towards positive common action.
3. Situation analysis will be done to know the status of development in the village.

4. Participatory planning exercise to identify peoples' needs and priorities in an integrated manner.
5. Converging Centrally Sponsored Schemes and Provincial Government Schemes.
6. Repairing and renovating existing infrastructure.
7. Strengthening the Gram Panchayats, peoples' institutions and promoting transparency and accountability.

Glimpse of Joranda Jharia

Joranda Jharia is a small tiny Gram Panchyat in Frasabahar block of Jashpur district of Chhattisgarh state. The majority of the population belongs to the tribes, i.e. Oraon/Kurunkh, Baiga and Munda. The GP is situated 25 km away from block headquarters of Farsabahar and 107 km away from district headquarter Jashpur. Joranda Jharia Gram Panchayat has a population of 1451 and 285 households. The GP falls under the Schedule V of the Constitution of India where PESA (Panchayat Extension in Scheduled Areas) is implemented. The Act provides special powers to the Gram Sabha to "safeguard and preserve the traditions and customs of people, their cultural identity, community resources and the customary mode of dispute resolution." The tribal community have a strong unity and ethnic binding. The Jashpur district is a left wing extremist (LWE) district bordering with the provinces of Jharkhand and Odisha. Joranda Jharia village is in remote location and have innumerable problems and a challenge for development. It is a Naxalite corridor, elephant corridor, snake corridor and have evils like liquor consumption and internal quarrel. The literacy rate was low.

Problems in Joranda Jharia

Naxalite Corridor: The Jashpur is a Left Wing Extremist (LWE) district bordering Jharkhand and Odisha. The Joranda Jharia is a border village of three states, namely, Chhattisgarh, Jharkhand and Odisha. In a thick forest, the village was under the cloud of naxalite corridor. After 5 pm, the people used to afraid to come out of the village, due to passage of naxalites through this village. If the people in the village provide the shelter to the naxalites, the police harass them. To avoid the problems, the people used to stay in the houses. Due to naxalite passage, the police used to visit the village frequently and harass the people whom they suspect of being naxalite sympathisers. As the naxalites are very active in this village, the officers were daring not to visit this village after 5 pm. The people were always sufferers in this passage and lived with the fear.

Elephant Corridor: Elephant corridors are narrow strips of land that allow elephants to move from one habitat patch to another. There are 88 identified elephant corridors in India. 12 are in north-western India, 20 in Central India, 14 in north-west Bengal, 22 in north-eastern India and 20 in southern India. Of the total, 77.3 per cent of the corridors are being regularly used by elephants.[13] Joranda Jharia falls in east and central India. In a thick forest, the elephants used to visit the village in day time and also in nights. Whenever the elephants visit the village, the people used to hide in their houses, fields and wherever they find a place to hide. The elephants used to destroy the crops and also houses. The peoples used to afraid of the elephants and will be vigilant about their visit to the village. The people were not able to control the menace of the elephants as it is a natural passage of the elephants. The people of the village are always afraid of elephant passage. Sometimes, the elephants become violent. This will threaten the fields and their lives are in jeopardy.

Snake Corridor: At the village entrance, the Health and Family Welfare Department has displayed big flexi board about the famous poisonous snakes moving in the village. The village is a part of Tapkara Region where a large variety of snakes are found. This region is referred as a *Naglok* (kingdom of snakes) due to the number of snakes that are moving in this region. The varieties of snakes are Indian Cobra, Common Krait and Common Cobra. Different poisonous snakes will be moving in day time and night time. In, all the houses, the people will keep anti-venom medicine. Sometimes, the people will carry anti-venom medicine in their pockets. But still, every year 4 to 5 people die of snake bite.

Liquor Consumption: Most of the people in the village belong to tribes. As a part of the tribal culture, the people consume local liquor (rice beer). It is a custom to consume the liquor. But it has become an addiction and women also used to consume the liquor. As a result, the people suffered with poverty, the break of families and internal quarrels were common. The liquor has destroyed the people's income, livelihoods and health. Sometimes, the people will quarrel. As a result, the people will go to the police station. It affects family life and children education. The Naxalites are very active in this village. The officers dare not to visit this village after 5 pm. Conflicts are common.

Joranda Jharia—Implementation of Global Goals (SDGs)

In India, development process is driven by the civil servants. The civil servants are enthusiastic, vibrant, receptive to challenges, adaptive to every situation and excel in their job. The civil servants frame the policies and also implement the policies at local level.

The village development process was facilitated by the officer, Mr. Deepak Soni, a young civil servant, (2011 batch). He was the Chief Executive Officer, Zilla Parishad, Jashpur district and took it as a challenge to develop this village. In a brief stint, he worked in Narayanpur district of Bastar region, a Naxalite Corridor. He made his mark and got awarded for successful implementation of MGNREGA in Naxalite region. After that he was posted to urban areas, i.e. Raipur (state headquarters). He was disappointed with the urban posting, that to state headquarters, he went to the Chief Secretary and requested him for posting in tribal and remote part of the region. The Chief Secretary was aghast about his desire to post in remote and tribal areas, because most of the officers request him for urban posting, mainly state headquarters. But, Mr. Deepak Soni has requested the Chief Secretary to post him in remote and tribal areas. He says that "I don't want urban posting. I want work in remote and tribal areas." He further says that "If I want, I should have become a Software Engineer and should have gone to USA. But I choose this career to help the poor tribals." The Chief

Secretary was aghast but posted him to Jashpur district, i.e. tribal and Naxalite area.

Rapport Building and Building the Confidence Among the People

The first strategy followed by Mr. Deepak Soni was rapport building with the people and putting the confidence that the administration can help them. Initially, the people have not cooperated with him because, the village falls under the Naxalite corridor and after 5 pm the Naxalites will be moving in this area. The people felt that there is a risk in talking to him. But, he kept on visiting this village and used to stay up to 8 pm talking to the people. He gradually reduced the gap between the people and the administration. Slowly, the people weaned from the Naxalites. He used to respond to phone calls and to SMS even in midnight. This made the people to accept him as a good administrator. He used to solve their problems immediately.

After acceptance by the people, he started his work of changing the attitude of the villagers. Mr. Deepak Soni says that "the most prominent issue to transform the village is to change the attitude of people towards development." In one of the meeting with the people he said that "I can make all roads as cement roads. I can make all houses *pucca* houses, construct more *anganwadi* centre and additional rooms for the school. But you should change your attitude towards development." The people trusted and promised him to be along with him to develop their village. His strength lies in transforming the problems into opportunities to develop the village.

SDG-1: No Poverty: First and foremost in Sustainable Development Goals is "End poverty in all its forms everywhere." According to 'World Poverty Clock' 8 per cent of the world population live in extreme poverty.[14] According to official estimates in India (2012) 22 per cent of its population is below poverty. It is said that in the country 190.7 million people in India will sleep hungry every night.[15] Although, the extreme poverty is decreasing, the poverty in the country is a concern. In India, 25.70 per cent of rural population is below poverty and 13.70 per cent is below poverty in urban areas.

The poverty means "a state or condition in which a person or community lacks the financial resources and essentials for a minimum standard of living."[16] It means lacking enough resources to provide the necessities of life like, food, clothes, shelter, water, education and health.[17] There are two kinds of poverty. These are: (1) Absolute poverty, i.e. lack of resources to maintain basic necessities of life, and (2) Relative poverty, i.e. income or resources in relation to the average. At present we are discussing about absolute poverty/extreme poverty, i.e. the people surviving on less than $1.90 a day.[18]

"When cruel poverty comes on it deprives one of it both the present and the future"—Thiruvalluvar.[19] Poverty is the worst form of deprivation. It deprives the basic necessity of human being, i.e. food, cloth, housing, education and health. At present 689 million people are in poverty.[20] The pandemic (COVID-19) has reversed the progress against global poverty and had driven more people into the poverty. Although, there was no accurate estimate of poverty rise in the world, the World Bank estimates that additional 97 million people were driven into poverty by the COVID-19. The pandemic has jeopardised the future of a generation of children.[21]

According to situational analysis, the village had 60 to 70 percentages of the people in poverty. Several factors contributed to the poverty in the village. One factor was liquor consumption. The first challenge is to make the village as a 'Liquor free Village'. The liquor consumption is a tradition of the tribals and it is a part of their culture. The women are also used to consume the liquor. It has become a challenge to the administration. To make the village as liquor free, a movement was created by involving the people. From each tribe, the leaders were selected and were made as the torchbearers of the movement. The tribals have a tradition of unity and listening to their leaders. The harm in consumption of liquor was printed on flexi boards and pasted on different places in the villages. The flexi boards clearly described the wife beating, children suffering of denial of education due to financial loss, internal quarrels and loss of health. At the same time, the benefits of the not consuming liquor were also depicted on flexi boards like the concept of happy family, children going to schools, financial improvement and construction of new houses and buying new vehicle and travel by the entire family on the vehicle. Besides, putting flexi boards, street plays were enacted about the bad and good about the stopping of liquor. The women were told not to allow the drunken husbands inside of the house. The SHG women have taken as a challenge to stop the liquor consumption.

The first step was a resolution passed by the Gram Sabha in which people unanimously decided:

- Not to make any liquor in homes.
- Stored liquor bottles may be destroyed in public view.
- No to buy or sell liquor in Panchayat area (special powers under PESA).
- Not to engage in drinking of liquor in, around and outside of the Panchayat.

Soon the people have formed 'Nasha Mukti Samiti', which included Self-Help Group (SHG) members in majority, with the objective to oversee the implementation of above passed resolution. Children added to the momentum by requesting their family members to continue abstinence and formed their own drama society. Teachers scripted plays for the society to present to the people. In successive gram sabhas people reviewed the situation, the liquor quitters were honoured and the defaulters were publically admonished. In one gram sabha, the people decided for the provision of penalty with a fine of Rs. 1,000 being imposed for every defaulting act and the informer to be rewarded with 50 per cent of the amount so collected. This led to collection of Rs. 3000. The people slowly stopped weaning away from the liquor.

Today, Joranda Jharia is a total addiction free panchayat with people taking pride in their achievement. This helped the amount spent on liquor was spent for family purpose. To remove the poverty in the village, all the families were given job cards under the MGNREGA to get minimum 100 days of employment for the villagers. The newly married couples were provided with separate job cards to avail the 100 days employment in lean season. Free houses were provided to the poor people under the Prime Minister Awas Yojana (PMAGY). Women were organised into Self-Help Groups and Livelihoods activities were provided to them. Youth were given technical skills to employ themselves in various activities. The government schemes were utilised to overcome the poverty in the village.

SDG-3: Good Health and Well-being: Good health refers to free from bodily or mental disease. This is to prevent and fight every disease to protect the health of the people of all ages. This means to promote healthy lifestyles and to provide efficient healthcare for everyone. To provide, good health to everyone in the village, Public Health Centre (PHC) was made active in the village. The doctor and nurses presence in the PHC was mandatory. Medicines were assured to take care of the people in the village. Small diseases like fever, cough, and cold were treated locally. If the diseases persist, the patients were referred to urban hospitals and the treatment is free.

The main problem in the Joranda Jharia was malnutrition of the children. Malnutrition is a complex aspect. It is defined as a lack of proper nutrition, caused by not having enough to eat, or not eating enough right kind of food to eat. There are various forms of nutrition deficient—stunted, (low height for age) wasted (low weight for height), anaemic (deficiency of haemoglobin in blood) and underweight (low weight for age). The joint study of Assocham-EY (2017) says that "India is home to the largest number of malnourished children in the world and 50 per cent children in India are undernourished."[22]

Although, there has been an overall reduction in the infant mortality rates and under-five mortality rate, the country is having about 50 per cent of undernourished children of the world.[23] The study reveals that at the end of 2015, about 40 per cent of the children were undernourished, about 37 per cent of under-five children are underweight, 39 per cent are stunted, 21 per cent are wasted and 8 per cent are severely acutely malnourished.

The prevalence of underweight children was higher (38%) in rural areas compared to urban cities (29%). Only about 10 per cent children under the age 6-23 months were reported to receive an adequate diet. Various forms of undernutrition are predominant in rural India. According to National Family Health Survey (NFHS)-4 (2015-16) to the Global Nutrition Report, 2016 and the Global Hunger Index (GHI) 2017, ranks India at 100 out of 119 countries.[24] According to GHI and NFHS reports, in India, less than 25 per cent children, less than 5 year of age are still malnourished.[25] Among the children less than 5 years, wasting (low weight for height), is 20 per cent in 1992 and 21 per cent in 2017. There has been a reduction in stunting (height for age) from 61.9 per cent in 1992 to 38.4 per cent in 2017. Mortality among children less than 5 years old has declined to around 5 per cent from 11 per cent during the same period.[26]

The Government is trying with at most care to bring down the malnourishment. Integrated Child Development Service (ICDS) with strong network of 1.4 million *Anganwadi* centres are reaching almost 100 million beneficiaries who include pregnant and nursing children in schools, and the Public Distribution System (PDS) reaching over 800 million people. The National Nutrition Strategy (NNS) has set very ambitious targets for 2022 and the *Poshan Abhiyaan* has also specified three-year targets to reduce stunting, undernutrition and low birth weight by 25 each year, and to reduce anaemia by 3 per cent each year. Besides, the government efforts, multiple sustained interventions like increased availability and accessibility of nutritious food, potable water, hygiene and sanitation, primary healthcare will help in reduce of malnourishment.

The charge officer Mr. Deepak Soni took care of nourishing the children. He visited regularly *Anganwadi* centres to make sure that nutritious food is provided to the children. Sudden visits were made to *Anganwadi* centres and he used to take lunch along with the children. This assured that each and every child should be fit mentally and physically. The undernourished children were given a special attention and provided the nutritious food until they grow as a normal child. Widows, old age people were assisted under the National Social Assistance Programme. The *pucca* (proper) houses were provided for the poor for decent living in better houses.

SDG-4: Quality Education: "Let us pick up our books and pencils. They are our most powerful weapons"—Malala Yousafzai.[27] "The children are the future of the country. Education enables them to acquire skills, knowledge, values and attitudes necessary to become responsible and active citizens of India."[28] Right to Education Act (RTE) was enacted on 4 August, 2009 by the Parliament of India. The Act makes education as a fundamental right. It emphasizes free and compulsory education for children between the ages of 6 to 14 years in India under the Article 21A of the Constitution of India. After passing the Act, India became one of 135 countries to make free and compulsory education to the children between the ages of 6 to 14 years. Compulsory education is an obligation of the Government and local authorities to provide and ensure admission, attendance and completion of elementary education by all children in the 6-14 age groups.

Education is very important tool for everyone to succeed in life. It helps in lessening the challenges of difficult life. Knowledge gained through the education enables every individual confident about their life.[29] *Education* is the key to success in personal and professional life. It provides us various types of knowledge and skills. Education is continuous process of entire life.[30] Education brings success and confidence in everyone's life.

The children's are the future of the globe. The children should be nurtured in mind and body. The education and school environment play a vital role in maturity of the mind and body of the children. The SDGs concept focuses on making the village as cent per cent literate. Initially, the literacy level of Joranda Jharia was very low. The initiatives of Deepak Soni and the people made success of cent per cent literate in the village. To initiate the process, education committees were formed. The teachers head the committees. The members are youth and students. The education committees visit different wards and take the special class in their houses. The SHG Members facilitated the process of evening classes and monitored the learning process. Students were instructed to make literate their parents.

The village is having high school and elementary school. The education committee assures 100 per cent attendance of children. The parent-teacher committee reviews the progress of the children. If any children, progress is slow, special classes will be arranged in the evening to improve their performances. Deepak Soni, Special Officer to the village visits the school often, at least twice in a week. He assures the children's as well as teacher's attendance. He takes special classes in English, Mathematics and equips them with the Current Affairs.

The researcher visited the school along with Mr. Deepak Soni and interacted with the students on current affairs. They are well versed with the geography of the states, capitals, countries. On political current affairs, they are up-to-date. On being asked the question, what you would like to be in the future, most of the students answered that they would like to be the teachers and quiet few of them has said that they would like to be police. The teacher is a role model, as everyday they interact with the teachers. As the village is a Naxal corridor, the police used to move in the village. They have said that they would like to become a police. It is surprised that no one would like to be Deepak Soni, who is an IAS Officer. The IAS is beyond their grasp. The dream of the students is not big, as they are surrounded with the environment of teachers and police. They feel that they should become either teacher or police.

SDG-5: Clean Water and Sanitation: "Let us built a clean India, Country can do it", the Prime Minister Shri Narendra Modi's clarion call is to make 'India as a clean country'. The Prime Minister has launched 'Clean India Mission' on 145th birth anniversary of Mahatma Gandhi on 2nd October in 2014. Clean India Mission is a major policy of Prime Minister Shri Narendra Modi. This is to make the country as a clean India by 2nd October, 2019, by 150th birth anniversary of Mahatma Gandhi. This is to fulfil the dream of Mahatma Gandhi towards clean India.

The mission is a massive mass movement to initiate the theme of cleanliness all through out India. The mission aims to cover all the rural and urban areas to make India as an ideal country before the world. The target of the mission is to eliminate open defecation, converting insanitary toilets into pour flush toilets, eradicating manual scavenging, complete disposal and reuse of solid and liquid wastes. The mission also aims to bring behavioural changes of people to practice health practices, spreading cleanliness among the people.

"Sanitation is more important than Independence", Mahatma Gandhi has said before declaring India's Independence. He emphasised cleanliness and sanitation in daily lives of the people. But the campaign has failed because of lack of people's participation. After 68 years of Independence, the most effective campaign was launched, requesting all sections of the people to participate in this mission and to make India as the clean India.[31]

Swachh Bharat Mission aims to achieve an Open-Defecation Free (ODF) India by 2 October, 2019, the 150th birth anniversary of Mahatma Gandhi by constructing 90 million toilets in rural India.[32] The mission also aims to establish an accountable mechanism of monitoring of toilet use.

Building a toilet at home and using it regularly is a healthy habit and should be practised by everyone irrespective of their age and gender.[33] To initiate the process, swachh committees were formed. Slogans were written as "Swachhta by the people and for the people." The swachhta rally was conducted; the street plays were enacted about harm of open defecation and the benefits of household toilets. The members of the swachh committees are students, teachers, SHG members, village elders and Panchayat Members. These committee members used to get up early in the morning and go to different directions where the villagers go for open defecation. Anyone is found; they will blow a vigil and instruct him to go back his/her house for defecation. This vigilance made them to construct the household toilets. The Gram Sabha has decided that all the villagers should voluntarily contribute *shramdan* (Voluntary labour) to construct the toilets.

The charge officer, Deepak Soni, has utilised the problems of village to opportunity to develop the village. In Gram Sabha, he has asked all the villagers, "Would you like to suffer with scorpion bite or die with the snake bite or trample by the elephant by going out for open defecation." So his slogan was "construct toilet and live long." Most of the villagers suffered scorpion bite and also snake bite. Few people died because of snake bite. This village is a passage for elephants, the elephants used to pass at any time. The villagers have to run to their houses, as soon as they see elephant and run for lives. As the village is a snake corridor, elephant corridor, they preferred the choice to live. All the villages agreed to construct the household toilets and community toilets at the *anganwadis* and at schools. The people contributed voluntary labour and the funds were taken from the MGNREGA and Swachh Bharat Mission. In the village all the households have toilets and they are utilising the toilets. Each household is supplied with the torchlight, to identify the snake/scorpion in the toilets. Jorandjharia achieved the status of ODF. But it has struggle a lot to achieve ODF status.

Joranda Jharia is a clean village. The streets are very clean and the houses are clean and hygiene. The schools, *anganwadis* are hygiene. The pictures on the walls expresses not only hygiene but expresses the objectivity of the schools and *anganwadi*. The Gram Panchayat assured that each street is clean and each house is clean. The tribals, may be poor economically, but rich in hygiene. The houses are very clean. Everyday the wet waste and dry waste is separated. The Panchayat staff will come and pick up the waste and put in dumping yard.

SDG-6: Decent Work and Economic Growth: The first priority of governance is to end poverty and zero hunger. The livelihoods promotion is a vital concept for decent work and economic growth. Decent work is provided to the people of the village by providing livelihood activities. Livelihood is a "means of economic activity to secure basic amenities such as—food, water, shelter, clothing, education and health of life." It provides the dignity of life and protects the culture of the community.

In Joranda Jharia village livelihood promotion was one of the objectives to develop the village. To initiate the decent work, the focus was to involve the women into economic activities and provide them with the entrepreneur skills. To initiate the process, the women have organised as Self-Help Groups (SHGs). Each group was allowed to select the economic activity depending upon the interest. Young girls choose tailoring and computer education. The women choose lac cultivation, which is suitable to that area. The Charge Officer Mr. Deepak Soni facilitated the marketing of goods. The second focus was on youth. The youth were given technical skills, depending upon their choice of interest. The young boys choose bike repairs and service and computer skills. The youth of village got employed in nearby towns, after acquiring skills. The Charge Officer, Deepak Soni took a special care of the youth not to join in Naxalite movement, which was very active in the region.

SDG-7: Gender Equality: Gender equality is a fundamental human right, and foundation for a peaceful, prosperous world. Gender equality refers equal access to resources and opportunities regardless of gender. This includes equal opportunity in education, livelihoods, and decision making. In India, the women were discriminated, politically deprived and it is a male dominated world. At local level (District Panchayats, Block Panchayats and Gram Panchayats), the 33 per cent of women was mandatory. In few provinces in local institutions, the representation of women has increased to 50 per cent. But, in decision making, male domination still persists.

In the parliament, the highest political body at federal government, state assemblies, although the number of women has increased, it is still in less number. The Women's Reservation Bill or the Constitution (108th Amendment) Bill, (2010) is still pending in the Parliament of India. It reserves 1/3rd of all seats in the Lower

House of Parliament of India, i.e., in the Lok Sabha, and in all state legislative assemblies for women. The Rajya Sabha passed the Bill on 9 March, 2010.[34] However, the Lok Sabha never voted on the Bill.[35] The Bill is still pending as it never went to the Lok Sabha.[36]

"India is the most dangerous nation for women", says Thomson Reuters Foundation[37] poll. The government have a greater focus on women's safety after the gang rape of Ms. Jyoti Singh Pandey, Physiotherapist on December 16, 2012 in a private bus. This did not deter the perpetrators. In 2016 nearly 40,000 rapes were reported.[38] India's capital New Delhi is dubbed as an "India's rape capital". The official data says nearly 40 crimes against women takes place every hour.[39] Women in India—from executives to women in middle-class homes, in factories or farms—face the dangers of sexual violence and harassment. According to World Bank data (2005) at least 20 million women have left the workforce due to their poor treatment and at present only 27 per cent work.

Thomson Reuters Foundation's poll of 548 experts on women's issues, found that "India was the most dangerous country for women in terms of human trafficking including sex slavery and domestic servitude." The Government passed "Nirbhaya Act" on April 3, 2013, i.e. new anti-rape law to deal with serious crimes against women. The Act prescribes life imprisonment as the maximum sentence for rape and death penalty for repeat offenders. Insulting modesty of women, by uttering any word or gesture shall be punished with jail up to three years.

The recent incident of Kathua rape case (abduction, rape and murder of an 8-year-old girl, Asifa Bano, in Rasana village near Kathua in the state of Jammu & Kashmir in January 2018) and Unnao rape case, i.e. rape of a 17 year old girl on 4 June, 2017 has brought a crime on women particularly, girl children are vulnerable to the rape and killings.[40] In India it was recorded that 106 rapes per day and four out of ten victims are minors.[41]

Recently, a six year girl was raped and killed on 2.9.2021 in Hyderabad city of Telangana province. According to police, the six-year-old girl was allegedly raped and murdered by 30-year-old neighbour in Hyderabad on Thursday (2.9.2021). The incident took place in the Saidabad Police Station area of Hyderabad. The Deputy Commissioner of Police, East Zone, Dr. Ramesh had informed that the girl went missing on Thursday morning (2.9.2021) and the police received a complaint. Immediately, they started the search operation but could not find her. Her body was found at the accused's residence on Friday morning (3.9.2021). The police has informed that the accused was currently absconding. To nab the culprit, Hyderabad City Police has announced a reward of Rs. 10 lakh for information leading to the arrest of Pallakonda Raju (30) who allegedly raped and murdered a 6-year-old girl in the Saidabad area of the city.

To the rape and murder of 6 year old girl, many prominent persons responded. The Tollywood (Telugu movies) Actor Mahesh Babu took to Twitter on Tuesday (14.9.2021) to condemn the sexual assault and murder of a six-year-old girl in Hyderabad, saying, "Will our daughters ever be safe?" is always a lingering question. "The heinous crime against the 6-year-old in Singareni Colony is a reminder of how far we have fallen as a society", he added.[42] The question of Tollywood actor Mahesh Babu "Will our daughters ever be safe?" is remaining unanswered. There are many Acts to stop the crimes against women, but not implemented properly.

The National Crime Records Bureau (NCRB)'s "Crime in India 2016" report reveals that in 94.6 per cent cases, the perpetrators were none other than the victim's relatives including brothers, fathers, grandfathers or acquaintances. The report showed that in the year 2016, a total of 38,947 cases of rape were registered in the country under Protection of Children from Sexual Offences Act (POCSO) as well as Section 376 and other related sections of the Indian Penal Code. Among these 38,947 cases, in 36,859 matters, accused are related to the victims, it said. The conviction rate is very low. The conviction rate is very low compared to all cognisable crimes. India's conviction rate for rape is at 25.5 per cent, remains low compared to all cognisable crimes—those that do not require a magistrate's permission to investigate—under the Indian Penal Code (46.9% in 2015). In 2016, only one in four rape cases in India ended in conviction—the lowest since 2012—according to national crime data.

In fact, crime against children has increased. Crime against children in 2019 is 4,212 and in 2020 are 4,200. Crime against women increased by 12 per cent. According to National Crime Record Bureau (NCRB), the crime in 2020 are 77 rape cases everyday, 80 murder incidents daily on an average, and 84,805 cases of kidnapping and abduction.[43] Overall, 3,71,503 cases of crime against women were reported across the country in 2020.

Table 3.1: Crime against women

Sl. No.	Year	Crimes recorded in 2020 by NCRB
1.	2018	3,78,236
2.	2019	4,05,326
3.	2020	3,71,503

Source: NCRB data-2020.

Table 3.2: Rape Cases against women

Sl. No.	Year	Rape cases recorded on women in 2020 by NCRB
1.	2016	38,947
2.	2017	32,559
3.	2018	33,356
4.	2019	32,033

Source: NCRB data-2020.[44]

According to NCRB (2020) data, among States and Union Territories, the maximum 5,310 rape cases were registered in Rajasthan in 2020 followed by 2,769 in Uttar Pradesh, 2,339 in Madhya Pradesh, 2061 in Maharashtra 1,657 in Assam. National Capital Delhi registered 997 rape cases in 2020.[45] Most of the crimes committed against the women were personally known to them. They are husband or relatives.

According to NCRB (2020) data, there were 62,300 cases of kidnapping and abduction. Besides rape, there were 85,392 cases of "assault to outrage modesty and 3,741 cases of attempt to commit rape." There were 105 cases of acid attack registered in the country. The country also recorded 6,966 cases of dowry deaths with 7,045 victims.[46]

The girls are insecure in the house and outside of the house. In Joranda Jharia to travel to the town/city, the companion is necessary. In order to protect themselves from the perpetrators, the girls and women were taught self-defence skills to combat in any untoward incident. The girls were given training in Karate and Kung fu to defend themselves. The self-defence skills gave self-confidence, courage to meet any challenge in the life. Now the girls can go to towns/cities on their own without accompanier. Interacting with the girls in the school, they explained that initially they had a fear to talk to men mainly strangers. Now they do not fear anyone as they know how to defend themselves in any untoward incident.

Conclusion

Joranda Jharia was a backward and underdeveloped village. But with the efforts of young civil servant, Mr. Deepak Soni, the village was transformed as a model for implementation of global goals (SDGs) with actions at local level. In fact, Mr. Deepak Soni has owned this village and put his creative efforts to make Joranda Jharia as one of the model villages.

There are many factors which helped the successful implementation of global goals in the village: (1) First and foremost was commitment of Mr. Deepank Soni, towards development; (2) Rapport building with the people and taking the confidence of the people by the administration; (3) Through People's Planning campaign, the people were nurtured and prepared for the preparation of village development plan and development of the village; (4) Before, planning, the problems of the villagers like, Naxalite corridor, elephant corridor and snake corridor, was identified. All these problems were transformed into opportunities to develop the village; and (5) Main weakness of the villagers, i.e. liquor consumption was identified. Mr. Deepak Soni understood that unless the liquor consumption is stopped, the development will not happen. So his goal was to wean the people from liquor consumption. This paved the way to prepare the people towards development.

Role of Women and SHGs in Implementing Global Goals

The success of Joranda Jharia is women's participation. To initiate the process, the women were formed as Self-Help Groups. SHGs were given a prominent role in development of the village. Women (SHGs) were active in preparation of situational analysis, resource mapping and in preparation of Village Development Action Plan. Self-Help Groups (SHGs) were in forefront of every development activity.

The unity among the women has strengthened them and they have become frontrunners in all the movements. The women are the most sufferers due to liquor consumption by the men. The women are in forefront in *Nasha bandi* (Liquor stopping) and united to stop the preparation and consumption of liquor and the consumption of the liquor was stopped in the village. They are in forefront in making the village as open defecation free (ODF). Open defecation is hazardous, as they go out for open defecation, particularly in the nights they face problems with the scorpions and snakes. The women participated in construction of toilets and made the men to participate in construction of toilets. The SHGs monitored the *Anganwadis*, to provide nutritious food to the malnutrition children. The SHGs ensured 100 per cent attendance of children and the teachers in the schools, providing special classes to improve the quality of education in the village. The SHGs monitored the developmental activities, mainly to reach the developmental schemes to the needy people, checking the quality of the works, in construction of toilets, houses and roads. The SHGs assured water supply in overhead tanks and checking the quality of water supplied in tanks. The SHGs assured technical skills to youth of the village and assured their placements in different places. This was done to wean the youth from the Naxalites. SHGs assured the best infrastructure in the village and moral values were incorporated among the villagers. To implement the global goals in Joranda Jharia, and making the village as a model village, the women and SHGs played a crucial role.

To summarise the active role of SHGs, the villagers painted the houses, buildings with pink colour and they call it as 'Pink Joranda'. According to their culture, the pink stands for unity, happiness, prosperity and development. In terms of community led social development, Pink Joranda has become a true Model Village for implementation of global goals (SDGs) in rural areas.

The main lacuna in development process was failure to develop the leadership among the villagers and institutionalisation of development process. The civil servants will be transferred after 3 years and elevated to higher positions. After Mr. Deepak Soni's withdrawal from the development process, the development may be weakened in the village and the village may go back to the underdeveloped stage. Dr. G. Narendra Kumar, Director General, National Institute of Rural Development and Panchayati Raj aptly puts it by saying "In any village, developing leadership and strengthening of local institutions is vital in sustainable development process."[47] To sum up, to implement global goals or to transform village, the leadership building and strengthening local institutions is a must for local action and is an essential element in sustainable development process.

Notes

1. T.M. Thomas Isaac, (2021). https://thekudumbashreestory.info/index.php/history-and-evolution/the-kudumbashree-idea/the-peoples-plan-movement, Date: 10-9-2021.
2. M. Thomas Isaac, https://www.newindianexpress.com/opinions/2020/jul/23/celebrating-24-years-of-peoples-plan-in-kerala-2173605.html, Date: 11-9-2021.
3. *Ibid.*
4. *Ibid.*

5. *Ibid.*
6. Stan Burkey (1993). *People First: A Guide to Self-Reliant Participatory Rural Development,* Zed Books, London and New York.
7. *Ibid.*
8. Mao Zedong also known as Chairman Mao. Mao was a Chinese communist revolutionary. Founding father of the People's Republic of China, Mao ruled China as the Chairman of the Communist Party of China from 1949 until his death in 1976.
9. Rural-Women-food-poverty (2018). http://www.unwomen.org/en/news/in-focus/rural-women-food-poverty, 8-08-2018.
10. In Local Government, Gram Panchayat is having 2-3 villages.
11. https://www.google.com/search?q=villages+in+india&rlz=1C1CHZL_enIN791IN791 & oq=Villages + in + India, Date: 18-9-2021
12. *Ibid.*
13. *Ibid.*
14. World Poverty (2018) https://world poverty.io/index.html, Date: 21-08-2018.
15. *Ibid.*
16. https://www.google.com/search?q=Poverty+-+definitions, Date: 13-9-2021.
17. *Ibid.*
18. https://www.worldvision.org/sponsorship-news-stories/global-poverty-facts#how-many, Date: 14-9-2021.
19. Thiruvalluvar was a celebrated Tamil poet and the philosopher.
20. https://www.worldvision.org/sponsorship-news-stories/global-poverty-facts#how-many, Date:14-9-2021.
21. *Ibid.*
22. Press Information Bureau (2010). "Prime Minister's Address to the Nation on the Fundamental Right of Children on Elementary Education", Pib.nic.in, 1-9-2010.
23. *Ibid.*
24. *Ibid.*
25. *Ibid.*
26. *Ibid.*
27. Malala Yousafzai is a Pakistani activist for female education and the youngest Nobel Peace Prize laureate in 2014.
28. *Ibid.*
29. *Ibid.*
30. *Ibid.*
31. *Swachh Bharat Abhiyan* (2018). https://www.indiacelebrating.com/essay/swachh-bharat-abhiyan-essay/13-08-2018.

32. Wikipedia (2018). https://en.wikipedia.org/wiki/swachh_bharat_Misssion#cite, note-bs-1
33. SBM (2018) #SBM pic.twitter.com/DbefYVM…13-08-2018
34. https://en.wikepedia.org/wiki/women's Reservation Bill#cite_Note-3, Date:14-9-2021.
35. *Ibid.*
36. *Ibid.*
37. *Ibid.*
38. Indian Express (2018). https://indianexpress.com/article/india/executives-to-maids-women- across-India-face- the-dangers-of-sexual-violence-and-harassment-5233583/27-09-2018
39. *Ibid.*
40. Wikipedia (2018). https://en.wikipedia.org/wiki/Kathua_rape_case and https://en.wikipedia.org/wiki/Unnao_rape_case: 27-08-2018
41. https://inshorts.com/en/news/will-our-daughters-be-safe-mahesh-on-6yrolds-rape-in-hyderabad-1631703693839, Date: 15-9-2021.
42. https://www.news18.com/news/india/77-rape-cases-daily-80-murders-a-day-in-2020-ncrb-report-shows-spike-in-crime-against-scst-4206896.html, Date: 16-9-2021.
43. https://www.news18.com/news/india/77-rape-cases-daily-80-murders-a-day-in- 2020-ncrb-report-shows-spike-in-crime-against-scst-4206896.html, Date: 16-9-2021.
44. https://www.news18.com/news/india/77-rape-cases-daily-80-murders-a-day-in-2020-ncrb-report-shows-spike-in-crime-against-scst-4206896.html, Date: 16-9-2021.
45. https://www.news18.com/news/india/77-rape-cases-daily-80-murders-a-day-in-2020-ncrb-report-shows-spike-in-crime-against-scst-4206896.html, 16-9-2021.
46. https://www.news18.com/news/india/77-rape-cases-daily-80-murders-a-day-in-2020-ncrb-report-shows-spike-in-crime-against-scst-4206896.html, 16-9-2021.
47. *Ibid.*

References

Stan Burkey (1993). *People First: A Guide to Self-Reliant Participatory Rural Development*, Zed Books, London and New York.

Beetham, D. (1994). "Key Principles and Indices for a Democratic Audit", in Beetham, D., (ed.). *Defining and Measuring Democracy*, Sage Publications, New Delhi, p. 1.

Buch, Nirmala (2003). *Panchayats in India—Forum for Citizens' Participation in Local Governance: Representation and Participation of Rural Women—Experience and Challenges*,http://www.ciff.on.ca/Reference/documents/MX-36_1_files/Papers/Buch.htm, 1/9/03, p. 1.

"United Nations Development Programme" (1993). *Human Development Report,* New York, p. 1.

Prachett, Lawrence. (1999). "New Fashions in Public Participation: Towards Greater Democracy", *Parliamentary Affairs*, Vol. 52, No. 4, October. New Delhi.

Vinita Bhali (2018). "No Child Left Behind", *The Hindu,* August 18, p. 10.

Malnourished Children (2018). https://www.livemint.com/Politics/16-08-2018 Thomson Reuters Foundation is the London-based charitable arm of Thomson Reuters, a Canadian global information and news network. The Foundation is a registered charity in the United States and United Kingdom and is headquartered in Canary Wharf.

Press Information Bureau (2010). "Prime Minister's Address to the Nation on the Fundamental Right of Children on Elementary Education", Pib.nic.in, 1-9-2010.

4

Strategies to Enroll Private Sector in Public Healthcare

An Indian Experience

Madhu Thawani

Introduction

Health is a state of complete physical, mental, and social well-being and not merely the absence of disease or infirmity. It is a precondition to the realization of human potential and for attainment of happiness. Thus, health is both a social and an economic good. The Constitution of India under healthcare allocates various services to the Central or State Governments based on 3 lists, viz. (a) Central List includes research, establishment of tertiary level institutes etc., (b) State List includes provision and regulation of basic preventive, promotion and curative services, establishment of public health and sanitation services, hospitals and dispensaries etc., and (c) Concurrent List includes programmes like population control, family planning, medical education, registration of births and deaths etc. The Central Government provides guidelines and the respective State government implement them. On the whole, provision of majority of health services is States' responsibility.

The healthcare service in the country is provided by (i) Public sector (Government hospitals, dispensaries primary health centres, community health centres, sub-centres and other healthcare facilities etc.), (ii) Non-Profit Medicare Centres (This sector managed by Charitable Institutions, NGOs, trusts, missions and churches etc.), (iii) Organized profit-making private sector (Corporate hospitals private hospitals, clinics and private practitioners etc.), and (iv)Private informal sector includes practitioners not having any formal qualifications (traditional healers, herbalists, *vaidyas* etc.).

The Central and State Governments over the years have expanded the healthcare delivery system. The country has 1,36,815 sub-centres, 22,962 primary health centres, 2,708 community health centres, 38,605 hospitals and over eight lakhs hospital beds. It has been taking proactive steps to control the spread of communicable and non-communicable diseases to promote health of the people through various healthcare programmmes and schemes. The 11th Plan had set six health outcome indicators as time-bound 'goals'. These included lowering maternal and infant mortality, malnutrition among children, anemia among women and girls, and fertility, and raising the child sex ratio. Though, there has been progress on all these fronts, except child sex ratio, the goals have not been fully met. Low public spending on health (1% of GDP), high out-of-pocket payments (71%) leading to impoverishment, high levels of anemia (56% among ever-married women aged 15-45 years) reflect in high levels of malnutrition among children (wasting 22.9%, stunting 44.9%, high infant mortality—47/1000 live births) and maternal mortality (212 per 1 lakh live births). Non-communicable diseases like cancers, diabetes, cardiovascular diseases, chronic obstructive pulmonary diseases etc. burden has grown to 53 per cent of total diseases burden by 2008 according to World Health Organization. Communicable diseases continue to be a major public health problem in India. Non-communicable diseases account for 42 per cent of all deaths and about one-quarter of all deaths in the country are due to diarrhoeal diseases, respiratory infections, tuberculosis and malaria. India's

Human Development Index score is also very poor 0.519 which put India at 119 rank out of 169 countries.

Total population of India according to 2011 is 121 crore of which 72.2 per cent of the population lives in some 6,38,000 villages and the rest 27.8 per cent in about 5,480 towns and urban agglomerations (Census, 2011). Availability of healthcare services is skewed towards urban centres, 28 per cent of the country's population, enjoying access to 66 per cent of India's available hospital beds, while the remaining 72 per cent, who live in rural areas, have access to just one-third of the beds. Approximately, 29 per cent of the Indian population (almost 300 million people) live below the poverty line and depend on free health services from the public sector. As India is one of the world's highest levels of private out-of-pocket financing (87% estimated in World Bank report 2011) it has adversely affected the poor leading to liquidation of assets or indebtedness. It is estimated that more than 40 per cent of hospitalised people borrow money or sell assets to cover expenses, and 35 per cent of hospitalised Indians fall below the poverty line because of hospital expenses.

Private Sector in Healthcare

Over the years, the private health sector in India has grown remarkably. At Independence, the private sector in India had only eight per cent of healthcare facilities but recent estimates indicate that 93 per cent of all hospitals, 64 per cent of beds, 85 per cent of doctors are in private sector (World Bank, 2001). 78 per cent of out-patients in rural areas (81% in urban areas) and 58 per cent in-patient services (hospitalisation) in rural areas (62% in urban areas) access healthcare services in private sector according to National Sample Survey Organisation (NSSO, 2006).

The private sector is also dominant in medical education as well as manufacturing of medical equipment, pharmaceuticals, and provision of diagnostic services as out of the 381 medical colleges in the country, 205 are in the private sector (Medical Council of India, 2013). To reap the benefits of private sector in healthcare industry private healthcare sector is recognized as an integral part of the Indian Healthcare by the National Health Policy 1983 and thereafter National Health Policy 2002, National Population Policy 2001 and National Rural Health Mission.

PPPs in health sector is promoted in the following four areas. These are: (a) Health infrastructure PPPs (for investing in creating or expanding health facilities); (b) Service delivery PPPs (for managing government-owned health facilities and/or delivering health services); (c) Financial protection PPPs (using demand-side financing instruments such as vouchers or service coupons for purchasing services from any empanelled private sector provider); and (d) other forms of private sector engagement (e.g. social marketing, research, advocacy etc.).

Various State Governments have tried to improve the quality of healthcare service making it affordable and accessible which are as follows:

1. Management of primary health centres (PHCs)/urban health centres (e.g. Karuna Trust) Karnataka, Odisha, Assam, Arunachal Pradesh and Andhra Pradesh.
2. Management of community health centres (CHCs) (e.g. Shamlaji) Gujarat and Uttarakhand.
3. Management of specialty care hospitals [e.g. Apollo Hospital, Raichur; Bombay Suburban Electric Supply Company (BSES), Mumbai], Karnataka, and municipal bodies of Mumbai and Pune.
4. Management contracts of mobile health services, emergency transport [e.g. Uttaranchal Mobile Hospital and Research Centre (UMHRC) , Health Management Research Institute (HMRI) and Government of AP Launched Mobile Health Units, Janani Express] Uttarakhand, Andhra Pradesh, Madhya Pradesh, Rajasthan, Tamil Nadu (Seva Nilayam NGO) and Bihar.
5. Contracting and co-location for laboratory, diagnostic services, and other clinical services (e.g. SMS Hospital, Jaipur) Rajasthan, Tamil Nadu, Andhra Pradesh and Bihar.

6. Land subsidy/joint ventures/BOT for hospitals, specialty units, diagnostic units, and medical colleges (e.g. Indraprastha Apollo; Coronation Hospital, Dehradun; Medall, Andhra Pradesh), Delhi, Uttarakhand, Punjab, Gujarat, Odisha, and Andhra Pradesh.
7. Demand-side financing options, including vouchers/health cards (e.g. Chiranjeevi, Sambhav Voucher, Janani Sahyogi) Gujarat, Uttarakhand and Madhya Pradesh.
8. Community-based health insurance and other forms of health (e.g. Yeshasvini, Rashtriya Swasthya Bima Yojana, Arogyashree etc.) Karnataka, Andhra, and almost all states.
9. Contracting non-clinical hospital support services (e.g. hospital waste, house-keeping, laundry, and diet) etc.
10. Social marketing—All of the private providers Hindustan Latex Ltd., Population Services, International (PSI), DKT International and Hindustan Latex Family Planning Promotion Trust (HLFPPT) have created standard sales distribution systems for supplying the contraceptives to their assigned areas through their field personnel, Uttar Pradesh.
11. The National Malaria Control Programme has involved the NGOs and private practitioners at the district level for the distribution of medicated mosquito nets (LOGISTICS).
12. Tele-medicine provides access to areas that are underserved or un-served. The Government of Karnataka, the Narayana Hrudalaya Hospital in Bangalore and the Indian Space Research Organization initiated an experimental tele-medicine project called 'Karnataka Integrated Tele-medicine and Tele-health Project' (KITTH), which is an on-line healthcare initiative in Karnataka.
13. The National AIDS Control Programme has involved both the voluntary and private sector to spread awareness about the HIV/AIDS, making free condoms available to the people for outreaching the target population through Targeted Interventions.

14. The Revised National Tuberculosis Control Programme has involved the private practitioners and the NGOs for the rapid expansion of the DOTS strategy.
15. Under the National Blindness Control Programme, District Blindness Control Societies have been formulated, which are represented by the Government, Non-Government and Private Sectors are given annual grants by government for their recurring expenditure. This is applicable to certain dispensaries run by NGOs in tribal areas also.
16. Training Programmes—Indian Society of Health Administrators (ISHA), has conducted over 100 training programmes for Central Government Health Scheme medical personnel; for NGOs, and for senior managerial personnel of Central and State public sector enterprises. Large number of NGOs is involved to provide training in various areas including TB, Leprosy, Malaria, Family Welfare, Immunization, HIV-AIDS, blindness prevention, and related areas.
17. Awareness Programmes: Central and State Governments and international agencies have partnered with NGOs to conduct awareness programmes in various fields, specifically for HIV/AIDS—family welfare, Maternal Child Health Care, Disasters Preparedness etc.

PPP Project in Healthcare

Majority of the Public Private Engagement is to provide healthcare service to the poor people who cannot afford or access the healthcare services have been addressed, it can be seen from the following case studies:

1. The Yeshasvini Co-operative Farmer's Healthcare Scheme is a health insurance scheme targeted to benefit the poor. It was initiated by Narayana Hrudayalaya, super-specialty heart hospital in Bangalore, and by the Department of Co-operatives of the Government of Karnataka. The Government provides a quarter (Rs. 2.50) of the monthly

premium paid by the members of the Cooperative Societies, which is Rs.10 per month. The incentive of getting treatment in a private hospital with the Government paying half of the premium attracts more members to the scheme. The card-holders could access free treatment in 160 hospitals located in all districts of the state for any medical procedure costing up to Rs. 2 lakh.

2. The Rajiv Gandhi Super-speciality Hospital in Raichur Karnataka is a joint venture of the Government of Karnataka and the Apollo Hospitals Group, with financial support from OPEC (Organization of Petroleum Exporting Countries). The basic reason for establishing the partnership was to give super-speciality healthcare at low cost to the people Below Poverty Line.
3. The Government of Andhra Pradesh has initiated the Arogya Raksha Scheme in collaboration with the New India Assurance Company and with private clinics. It is an insurance scheme fully funded by the government. It provides hospitalization benefits and personal accident benefits to citizens below the poverty line who undergo sterilization for family planning from government health institutions.
4. The Uttaranchal Mobile Hospital and Research Center (UMHRC) is three-way partnership among the Technology Information, Forecasting and Assessment Council (TIFAC), the Government of Uttarakhand and the Birla Institute of Scientific Research (BISR). The motive behind the partnership was to provide healthcare and diagnostic facilities to poor and rural people at their doorstep in the difficult hilly terrains. TIFAC and the State Government shares the funds sanctioned to BISR on an equal basis.
5. To make healthcare facilities more accessible to remote villages of Andhra Pradesh, the Government of Andhra Pradesh and Health Management Research Institute (HMRI) have joined hands. They have designed and

launched Mobile Health Units (MHUs) called '104 Mobile' which provide basic healthcare facilities. The technology-enabled van offers a range of health services to villagers located beyond three kilometres of the PHC.

6. The Bombay Suburban Electric Supply Company (BSES) municipal hospital (88-bed maternity hospital) was originally built on the municipal corporation land by Bombay Suburban Electric Supply Company or BSES, a private company, as part of their corporate social responsibility (CSR) initiative and handed over to Brihanmumbai Municipal Corporation (BMC) in 2000. Due to budgetary constraints, the BMC could not run the hospital. In 2002, it signed a contract with Global Hospital and Research Centre Trust (GHRC), (Bramhakumari Trust) to manage the hospital. The GHRC would hire staff, deploy additional equipment, and manage the hospital. The contract is for a period of 30 years. The contract specifies the GHRC to provide 40 per cent of out-patient department (OPD) services and 33 per cent admissions to the poor as per the user fees charged in the BMC hospitals.
7. SMS Government Hospital, Jaipur in 2004 signed a contract with a private company to operate and maintain CT and MRI machines within the hospital premises, for a period of 7 years. The negotiated tariffs were almost 60 per cent cheaper than private operators in the vicinity. Services would be free for BPL patients (estimated at 20% of all patients).
8. Fortis Escort Hospital, Dehradun—Pandit Deen Dayal Upadhyay Hospital (DDU), Dehradun, is one of the largest government hospitals in the state. But due to shortage of specialist doctors, the hospital was unable to offer any super-specialty services. In 2011, the government decided to engage Fortis Hospitals to build and operate a 50-bed cardiac care unit (CCU) within the premises of DDU. The initial contract would be for 10 years. Under the contract, 25 in-patient beds (out of 50) would be reserved for BPL

patients at government stipulated rates. Services provided to the Below Poverty Line (BPL) patients are reimbursed by the government. The government also agreed to pay Rs. 99,200 per month per occupied bed as a grant. Each day, OPD consultation is free of charge for all patients and at a specified time of the day.

9. Gujarat Government Chiranjeevi Yojana—A PPP model has helped in increasing the number of institutional deliveries and reduced the maternal mortality rate by utilizing the private ob/gyn services and attracting the pregnant women belonging to BPL category to avail of the facilities with practically no expenditure to be incurred by them. 868 gynaecologists have volunteered to work under this Yojana, 14,832 complicated cases and 14,535 c-section cases were dealt out of total deliveries (2,35,289) under Yojana.

In spite of the political support being provided by the Government to private sector in providing healthcare and encouraging it to complement and supplement its efforts, there are number of reasons due to which the Private Sector is still hesitant to enroll itself in Public Health Care Schemes.

Issues in PPP Healthcare

1. It will affect their OPD and their Commission at pharmacy, pathology and radiology;
2. Private sector feels that the schemes are complicated and not flexible and keep changing;
3. Red Tapism/Corruption to get contracts from the Government;
4. Political Interference;
5. Too much emphasis for achieving quantitative targets;
6. Too much of Paper Work and Reporting;
7. Frequent transfer of personnels in the Government affect the implementation of programme;
8. Slow process of PPP projects;

9. Autonomy to private sector is not given to carry other healthcare service if they enroll under government programmes;
10. Resources (finance, staff, medicines, equipment purchases and repairs) are not provided on time , it constrain the service delivery;
11. Payment of remunerations/incentives to physicians participating in PPM is very less and (under RNTCP per patient initially private practitioner use to get Rs. 250 per patient now it has been increased to Rs. 1000 and compensation paid under Chiranjeevi Yojana of Gujarat for Cesarean delivery was also very low);
12. Remuneration is not paid on time;
13. General practitioners are not ready to enroll under RNTCP programme as it will affect their normal OPD due to social stigma of the disease;
14. Private practitioners are not ready to Sign MOU with Public health sector due to legal complications;
15. Private Sector Involvement is not encouraged at planning stage, this leads to mismatch between real needs and government agenda;
16. Supervision and monitoring mechanism is not mutually acceptable. For example Senior Tuberculosis Supervisor supervising the doctor is not acceptable under RNTCP programme; and
17. Government lacks—Technical and managerial skills to run successful PPPs.

Conclusion

Public Private Partnership engagement to provide healthcare has helped the Government of India to provide affordable, accessible and quality healthcare at the doorstep of the people. It has worked out well but still at some stage private sector is not ready to enroll themselves in Government healthcare schemes due to low incentives, red-tapism, political interference, delay in getting resources and incentives problems are to be addressed to ensure public private partnership in healthcare on sustainable basis.

References

Arya Suhasini, B. (2012). Synopsis of Ph.D. thesis "A Comparative Study of Public and Private Health Services in Mumbai Region—Availability and Utilisation Pattern", SNDT Women's University, Mumbai.

Government of India, Planning Commission, Twelfth Five Year Plan (2012-2017) Social Sectors, Volume III, Sage Publications India Pvt. Ltd.

Gudwani Ayushi *et al.* (2012). "Indian Health Care: Inspiring Possibilities, Challenging Journey", Prepared for Confederation of Indian Industry by Mckinsey & Company.

Health Division, Planning Commission (2012). Report of Steering Committee on Health for the 12th Five Year Plan.

Kapilashrami, M.C. *et al. Involvement of Private Sector in Health: Suggested Policy Guidelines and Mechanisms.*

Rao, P.H. (2012). "The Private Health Sector in India: A Framework for Improving the Quality of Care", *ASCI Journal of Management, 41*(2): 14-39.

Raman A. Venkat. *Private Sector and Public-Private Partnership in Health Service Delivery in India.*

Reddy Sunita & Marry Immaculate (2013). "Aarogyasri Scheme in Andhra Pradesh, India: Some Critical Reflections", *Social Change, 43*(2), 245-261. Sage Publications.

Thadani Khusbhu, B. (2014). "Public Private Partnership in the Health Sector: Boon or Bane", *Social and Behavioral Sciences, 157*, 307-316.

5

Snakebite Envenoming in India

Public Health Issue and Beyond

Nafeesath Sabida, S.M. and *A. Shahin Sultana*

Snakebite envenoming is a potentially life-threatening disease that results from injecting a mixture of toxins (venom) following the bite of a venomous snake. Envenoming can also be caused by having venom sprayed into the eyes by certain snake species that can spit venom as a defence measure (WHO, 2017). Envenoming by snakebite creates medical emergencies involving different organs and tissues, depending on the species responsible for the bite. Most severe cases result from Viperidae family members' bites (pit vipers and true vipers) and Elapidae (cobras, kraits, mambas, coral snakes, Australasian species, and sea snakes). All these very poisonous snakes are found in the Indian subcontinent (WHO, 2007).

Snakebite is one of the most neglected public health issues in poor rural communities living in the tropics. Because of serious misreporting, the actual worldwide burden of snakebite is not known. South Asia is the world's most heavily affected region due to its high population density, widespread agricultural activities, numerous venomous snake species, and lack of functional snake bite control programmes (Alirol, 2010).

Objective

This chapter attempts to narrate the issue of snakebite in India from a holistic perspective by reviewing research articles and information available in the public domain of academia.

Methodology

An extensive electronic search on *PubMed*, *Elsevier*, *British Medical Journal*, and Google Scholar is carried out using keywords like snakebite in India, snakebite envenoming, neglected tropical diseases, and anti-snake venom. The literature is further scrutinised based on the objective and analytically reviewed.

Snakebite in India

WHO officially listed snakebite envenoming as a highest priority neglected tropical disease in June 2017. Snakebite is a neglected public health issue of many tropical and subtropical countries. Nearly 5.4 million snakebites take place each year, resulting in 1.8 to 2.7 million cases of envenoming, between 81,410 to 1,37,880 deaths and a large number of amputations and other permanent disabilities each year. Extensive community-level research on snakebite deaths in India estimated at 45,900 deaths in 2005, which is over 30 times more than the Government of India's authorised figure. Revised estimates based on verbal dissections and other data now put forward that as many as 1.2 million Indians lost lives from snakebite envenoming between 2000-2019 (average of 58,000/year). Annual snakebite deaths were most significant in the state of Uttar Pradesh (8,700), Andhra Pradesh (5,200), and Bihar (4,500). The number is 30 fold higher than the number declared from official hospital records (Mohapatra, B. *et al.*, 2011). Assessing the actual consequences of snakebite is difficult because the cases reported to health ministries by clinics and hospitals are often only a trivial proportion of the substantial burden. After all, many victims never reach primary health centres and are so unreported. This is coloured by socio-economic and cultural factors that influence treatment-seeking behaviour, with many victims choosing traditional practices rather than hospital care (WHO, 2021).

A Disease of Poverty

As a disease of poverty, snakebite envenoming has failed to draw requisite attention for public health policy inclusion and investment for dynamic, sustainable efforts to reduce the medical and societal burden. This is primarily due to the socio-demographics of the affected populations and their lack of political voice (Williams, D.J. *et al.*, 2019). The literature on snake envenoming is rich with references associating rural agriculture with a high incidence of morbidity and mortality.The survival of the economically deprived rural population depends on their non-mechanised, low-cost farming techniques, and ironically these practices place them at high risk of snakebite. Their feet, legs, and hands are most frequently affected by snakebite (Whitaker *et al.*, 2009 & Sharma, S.K. *et al.*, 2004). Globally the tremendous burden is experienced in underdeveloped countries or nations that suffer from poor governance, political and social conflict, resource scarcity or food insecurity. The negative association between snakebite mortality and government disbursement on health confirms that the burden of mortality is highest in countries with difficulty meeting the considerable financial cost of snakebite. India, a nation with a medium human development index and human poverty index, has the highest snakebite mortality in the world. It suggests that there are other factors like vast variation of income within the country, complex considerations of population, venomous snake densities, antivenom effectiveness and clinical practices and guidelines leading to the alarming situation (Harrison *et al.*, 2009).

Snakebite is an occupational, environmental and domestic health hazard with a significant economic fallout on the individual and the family. In India, 70 per cent of bites are in males between 20 and 50 years of age (Alirol *et al.*, 2010). It shows that bites are most common in the active, productive members of the family. The economic repercussion is remarkable as in most villages; males are the sole earning members the family depends on. Insufficient infrastructure in villages, including lighting, sewage systems, roads and in-house water supply, co-contributes to snakebites,especially at night. Poor transport facilities in the rural areas lead to a massive delay in the transfer of patients to a secondary or tertiary centre (Menon, J.C. *et al.*, 2017).

A Public Health Crisis

Hence, the number of snakebites is misrepresented; it directly affects the country's estimation of needed Anti-Snake Venom (ASV). Primary healthcare centres often do not have the stock of ASV and trained professionals to treat snakebite. Unwillingness on the part of the medical and paramedical professionals at the village centre to admit and treat snakebites is because of the complications and reactions to ASV. Many centres are not equipped with respiratory support to deal with these situations. ASVs made in the developing world tend to generate a higher rate of adverse reactions than those produced in the developed world. The cost difference explains the relationship between cost and quality (Simpson, I.D. *et al.*, 2009). The low quality of ASV is influenced by factors like lacunas in the standardisation of the ASV and the absence of centralised quality control on the process of ASV manufacturing as its absence of regional or zonal pools of snake venom. The venom used to manufacture ASV for the entire country is from one or two sources limited to a small geographical area. Presently, the Irula Co-operative Society, near Chennai, is the only authorised supplier of venom for the manufacture of Anti-Snake Venom (ASV). Venom researchers have proved regional variation in venom constituents and chemical properties, intra-species, which calls for regional/zonal venom centres to develop the facilities to manufacture ASV for a particular region (Menon, J.C. *et al.*, 2017).

Medical education in the developing world, including snakebite treatment, is often based on textbooks from developed nations. These typically contain guidelines and recommendations that are inept in a developing world scenario because of the general focus on well-equipped tertiary hospital treatment rather than on treatment in primary care centres, which are closer to the victim but less well equipped.While infrastructure plays a vital role in transport, the delay is often because professionals in closer health centres are not sufficiently trained to manage snakebites and lack confidence. Therefore, they tend to send patients to more distant, better-equipped centres. Research in India has exposed that 94 per cent of doctors knowhow to treat snakebite from key US textbooks or inappropriate local textbooks by forensic medicine specialists who do not treat snakebite. Nearly 40 per cent of doctors expressed no confidence in their ability to treat snakebite (Simpson, I.D., 2008). In 2016, India responded to these concerns by producing and implementing protocols developed regarding the local conditions and involving local expertise, supported by bedside material and training. The development of protocols targeted at each segment of the health service has had a significant response in encouraging primary care institutions to treat snakebite effectively.

Traditional treatments are often considered an obstacle in the delivery of scientifically proven medicines for snakebites. In rural India, the population opts for traditional and alternative medicines for snakebite treatment due to socio-cultural reasons. Snake is widely worshipped in India, and snakebite is often connected to the population's belief system. There are many ways the traditional healers treat snakebite envenoming, such as incision, suction, application of herbal plants, and administering natural and synthetic substances (G.K. Raman, 2013). Common traditional methods are cutting the bite site, using a tourniquet, freezing, burning, and shocking; ingestion of plant extracts; and the local application of poultices and ingestion of alcohol. People bitten by snakes often prefer to see *ojhas*, or traditional faith healers, rather than attend hospitals because of their poor educational and economic backgrounds. Cultural beliefs play a big part in such customs; the bodies of people who have died from snakebite are often disposed of on rafts made from banana trees on the rivers in eastern India, particularly in the Sundarbans (Bhaumik, S., 2013).

Human-Wildlife Conflict

In many ways, snakebite has more in common with traditional human-wildlife conflicts that involve physical harm inflicted on humans (Pandey *et al.*, 2016). However, while not caused by a pathogen, snakebite envenoming is more analogous to a disease than a physical injury because it involves complicated and prolonged physiological and immunological effects and treatments. Snakebite risk can also be viewed as the result of overlaps in snake and human distributions, modified by patterns in their abundance, activity, and population dynamics, similar to vector-borne diseases (Pintor *et al.*, 2021). Despite the global burden, conflicts between humans and snakes usually expressed through snakebites still have not received sufficient attention. Considering that climate change might shift the geographic distribution of venomous snakes, it is crucial to develop strategies to identify and manage hotspots of potential contacts between people and dangerous snakes (Zacarias *et al.*, 2019).

Discussion

As a neglected public health issue, dealing with snakebite envenomation is crucial for health professionals, administrators, politicians, and policymakers. The World Health Organization admits that the shortage in antivenom availability is the biggest hurdle in reducing snakebite envenomation's mortality and morbidity. From the review, it is comprehended that snakebite is more than a medical and public health issue. Its implication spread through a wide range for a country like India. It is a socio-economic, cultural and ecological issue that needs to be thoroughly studied and analysed from all these perspectives. Mitigating the issue of snakebite thus be done through a holistic approach. Like many other unexpected illnesses, beliefs around snakebites are associated with deity penance, witchcraft, or other powerfully persuasive phenomena that are often very locally specific. Effective engagement with health decision-makers at regional and national levels has strong evidence in the success of disease interventions and stimulates trust in outcomes and hence productive participation in mitigation (Williams, D.J. *et al.*, 2019).

Conclusion

India has a vital role in working towards WHO's goal of achieving the global target to halve the number of deaths and disabilities due to snakebite envenoming by 2030. Snakebite Healing and Educational Society of India (SHE-India) is a nationwide multipronged organisation that campaigns for and delivers effective healthcare and education and works to reduce human-snake conflict. This society delivers proper education and awareness about snakebite, its first aid and encourages hospital-based treatment by collaborating with the forest department, educational institutions, community groups and local government (Kadam *et al.*, 2021). They are setting up a practical example for achieving the WHO's identified objective of empowering and engaging local communities in reducing snakebite mortality and morbidity by 50 per cent. A governmental and non-governmental organisation's collective effort in executing workable models like this could bring about substantial change in the snakebite crisis faced by the nation.

Recommendations

1. Encouraging community-based research to acquire actual data of snakebite envenoming and the need for ASV.
2. Improvement of ASV production protocol as per WHO standards and check the supply of low-quality ASV in the market.
3. Production and milking of venom from different regions in India to deal with the issue of regional variations in treatment outcomes.
4. Appropriate training for medical and paramedical professionals to manage snakebite according to regional needs.
5. Awareness and educational campaign at the grassroots level to promote healthy behaviour to reduce the incidence of snakebite.

6. Development and distribution of first-aid manual in regional languages across the country.
7. Strategic and sustainable work to mitigate human-snake conflict.

References

Alirol, E., Sharma, S.K., Bawaskar, H.S., Kuch, U. & Chappuis, F. (2010). "Snakebite in South Asia: a review." *PLoS neglected tropical diseases, 4*(1), e603.

Bawaskar, H.S., Bawaskar, P.H., Punde, D.P., Inamdar, M.K., Dongare, R.B. & Bhoite, R.R. (2008). "Profile of snakebite envenoming in rural Maharashtra, India." *JAPI, 56*, 88-95.

Bhaumik, S. (2013). "Snakebite: a forgotten problem." *BMJ*, 346.

G.K. Raman, (2013, November,11). "A vanishing breed of snakebite healers in Kerala." *The Hindu*. Retrieved from: https://www.thehindu.com/news/national/kerala/a-vanishing-breed-of-snakebite-healers-in

Harrison, R.A., Hargreaves, A., Wagstaff, S.C., Faragher, B. & Lalloo, D.G. (2009)." Snake envenoming: a disease of poverty." *PLoS neglected tropical diseases, 3*(12), e569.

Indian Red Cross Society (2016). *Indian First Aid Manual*. Retrieved fromhttps://www.indianredcross.org/publications/FA-manual.pdf

Kadam, P., Ainsworth, S., Sirur, F.M., Patel, D.C., Kuruvilla, J.J. & Majumdar, D.B. (2021). "Approaches for implementing society-led community interventions to mitigate snakebite envenoming burden: The SHE-India experience." *PLoS Neglected Tropical Diseases, 15*(2), e0009078.

Menon, J.C., Joseph, J.K., Jose, M.P., Dhananjaya, B.L. & Oommen, O.V. (2016). "Clinical profile and laboratory parameters in 1051 victims of snakebite from a single centre in Kerala, South India." *J. Assoc Physicians India, 64*(8), 22-29.

Mohapatra, B., Warrell, D.A., Suraweera, W., Bhatia, P., Dhingra, N., Jotkar, R.M. & Million Death Study Collaborators (2011). "Snakebite mortality in India: a nationally representative mortality survey." *PLoSNegl Trop Dis, 5*(4), e1018.

Pintor, A.F., Ray, N., Longbottom, J., Bravo-Vega, C.A., Yousefi, M., Murray, K.A. & Diggle, P.J. (2021). "Addressing the global snakebite crisis with geo-spatial analyses–Recent advances and future direction." *Toxicon: X, 11*, 100076.

Sharma, S.K., Koirala, S., Dahal, G. & Sah, C. (2004). "Clinico-epidemiological features of snakebite: a study from Eastern Nepal." *Tropical doctor, 34*(1), 20-22.

Simpson, I.D. & Norris, R. L. (2009). "The global snakebite crisis—a public health issue misunderstood, not neglected." *Wilderness & Environmental Medicine, 20*(1), 43-56.

Simpson, I.D. (2008). "A study of the current knowledge base in treating snake bite amongst doctors in the high-risk countries of India and Pakistan: does snake bite treatment training reflect local requirements?" *Transactions of the Royal Society of Tropical Medicine and Hygiene, 102*(11), 1108-1114.

Snakebite envenoming, 08.04.2019, WHO Retrieved from: https://www.who.int/news-room/fact-sheets/detail/snakebite-envenoming

What is snakebite envenoming? 01.03.2021 World Health Organization, Retrieved from https://www.who.int/snakebites/disease/en

Whitaker, R. (2015). "Snakebite in India Today." *Neurology India, 63*(3), 300.

Williams, D.J., Faiz, M.A., Abela-Ridder, B., Ainsworth, S., Bulfone, T.C., Nickerson, A.D. & Warrell, D.A. (2019). "Strategy for a globally coordinated response to a priority neglected tropical disease: Snakebite envenoming." *PLoS neglected tropical diseases, 13*(2), e0007059.

World Health Organization (2007). *Rabies and envenomings: a neglected public health issue: report of a consultative meeting, World Health Organization, Geneva,* 10 January, 2007. World Health Organization.

Zacarias, D. & Loyola, R. (2019). "Climate change impacts on the distribution of venomous snakes and snakebite risk in Mozambique." *Climatic Change, 152*(1), 195-207.

6

Politics of Childcare

'Access to Childcare' as a Public Policy in Odisha

Swapna S. Prabhu

Introduction

Quality childcare is a birth right of the new born and should not be compromised on any grounds. In India, the government's intent to optimistically enhance various indicators of child rights has been consistently evident in many of its policy formulations as well as in its commitment to international ratifications, the most prominent being the UN Convention on the Rights of the Child adopted in 1989. However, the matters pertaining to day care related public policy in the state of Odisha requires addressing issues of both social and political choice, such as, the amount of public support and encouragement to be given to working mothers; the extent of redistribution to families with young children; the modes of childcare which need to be given social sanction and the extent of intervention by the public sector in childcare (Krashinsky, 1977: 137). The chapter investigates the primary childcare needs of low-income families and the challenges they face in supporting childcare for their children in the absence of governmental support. There needs to be a realisation that although parents are generally seen to be free to choose the facilities they deem most appropriate for their child, access to good quality care is very often highly limited and unequal. Hence, it must be the responsibility of the state to generously subsidise and support parents to access childcare.

Further, mothers are faced by time and energy constraints in providing adequate care to the young one especially when they work outside. A general assumption is that childcare for children under the age group of two years must be provided at home by their mothers given the requirements of breast feeding and intense care required by the children during the initial years of their lives. It needs to be noted here that the first time women in India were granted maternity benefits was in a law passed in Bombay in 1929. Although maternity entitlements aim at protecting women against income loss and job discrimination, while ensuring that they have adequate time 'to give birth, to recover and to nurse their children' as was specified by the International Labour Organisation (of which India was a founding member), most of the productive legislations for working women have been like a double-edged sword (Chhachhi, 1998: L21-L29). The laws providing women with better working conditions in response to their specific needs have very often been used against them and at times become an obstacle to their work opportunities.

The Rationale for Day Care and Early Childhood Care

The rationale for childcare and its relevance as a public policy emerges on the following grounds:

(a) Custodial and protective day care has traditionally been advocated by child welfare authorities for children from 'troubled' homes (i.e. motherless or fatherless families, where mothers work outside or are emotionally unable to provide full-time care). However, more recently, child development specialists have supported day care to children from educationally and economically backward sections of the society by providing a setting which stimulates and develops the child's cognitive and sensory abilities. Further, such an arrangement would free the children from a patriarchal nuclear household (in rural households) by providing a society of peers with greater stimulation and freedom. The study seeks to support developmental/liberation ethics, as mentioned above, as a requisite for any legislation on 'access to childcare.

(b) The study also signifies the demands of the women's rights groups who argue that women have a right to pursue employment and careers for reasons of self-fulfilment and quality day care facilitates female career advancement without sacrificing child welfare.

(c) Access to childcare and other day care services promote social change by infusing the values of group cooperation in the young and facilitating contact among different socio-economic groups. This would help the state in advocating community values among the people over individualism.

Objectives of the Study

The present study was undertaken:

(i) To draw a possible link between access to childcare and social security for women workers in unorganised sectors *via* state and societal recognition of childcare as an integral part of the care ethics.

(ii) To examine the subject of "childcare" as a public policy in Odisha.

(iii) To highlight the primary childcare needs of low-income families and the challenges they face in supporting childcare for their children in the absence of governmental support.

(iv) To understand how socio-economic inequalities and wider structural factors contribute to care disparities.

(v) To investigate into how care and vulnerability figure into the social construction of childhood.

Hypotheses

On the basis of the above mentioned objectives, the following hypotheses were formulated for empirical research:

(i) Segmental and fragmented approach towards childcare as a public policy in Odisha has resulted in childcare being viewed, in the state, not as an end in itself but rather as a tool for the achievement of other social, economic and political goals.

(ii) Availability of childcare is intimately linked to parental labour market participation and their income, in particular that of mothers.

Methods of Study

The main thesis of the study focuses on the pertinent questions associated with gender inequalities and the concept of 'care deficit' in very young children belonging to the marginalised sections of the society. The study is placed both conceptually and empirically within the larger framework of childcare.

Area of Study: The study was conducted in 5 locations in the city of Bhubaneswar in Odisha which are the daily meeting points for the construction workers for work distributions by the contractors. The locations identified were Kalpana Square, Salia Sahi, Jaydev Vihar, Lingaraj Temple area and Niladri Vihar and the reference period was 2019-20.

Sampling Method: A purposive stratified random sampling methodology was adopted for selecting labour gathering locations in the city of Bhubaneswar, women workers and Anganwadi Centres (AWCs). Focused Group Discussions (FGDs) and wherever required personal interviews were done with the target groups.

Sources of Data: Data from the Women and Child Development Department of Government of Odisha and Odisha State Council for Child Welfare were collected for primary inputs. Personal Interviews and Focused Group Discussions with the target group consisting of women workers from the selected areas of workplace and data from four AWCs in the city of Bhubaneswar nearer to the selected areas of study were used for primary data analysis. Besides this, various books, journals, published reports/ government records; published reports from research studies/

Case studies, and interviews with the target group; newspaper articles, other media coverage, information through the Internet, official records of the National Food Security Act, 2013, Building and Construction Workers Act of 1966, and Contract Labour (Regulation and Abolition) Act of 1970 were also referred.

Sample Size: A total sample of 149 women labourers engaged in construction work having children below the age group of 3 years were chosen on the basis of stratified random sampling from 5 locations across the city of Bhubaneswar and four AWCs from the city nearer to the selected areas were studied separately.

Selection of Focus Group Discussions (FGDs): More than twenty women labourers from each of the 5 selected areas (accounting to a total of 149) in the city of Bhubaneswar were considered for FGDs. Further, each of these women workers from each area were again divided into a group of five to six depending upon the convenience of the workers. Each group was involved in FGDs on a daily basis spanning across 15-16 days each. Similarly, FGDs were conducted with women workers in other areas of work as well. The entire process of FGDs was completed within a period of 6 months (September 2019-February 2020). The FGDs were conducted in the morning times between 7.00 am to 8.30 am during which the labourers from all across the city gather for labour work distribution.

Maternal Work and Child Care in Odisha: Policies and Schemes

Odisha ranks 25th among the Indian states in human development index given the fact that the birth rate, infant mortality and maternal mortality rates are very high in the state compared to other states. Besides this, the state has also been in news recently for a declining child population. Against this backdrop when we look at the legislations passed with regard to Infant Foods, Breast Milk Substitutes and Feeding Bottles Act, 1992 regulating the sale and marketing of infant foods and feeding bottles, we realise that these legislations have been conceptualised ignoring the role of mothers as working women. Since women with full time jobs, especially those engaged in the unorganised sectors including women working in the construction industry face difficulties while breastfeeding due to lack of flexible working hours, no childcare facility at workplace, long distances between the place of work and the residence of the women where the child resides, strict working schedule mostly in polluted environment leaving no scope for women to take personal care of themselves at the first place thereby resulting in most of these women complaining lack of breast milk to feed their child. This denies the child of her fundamental right to grow in a healthy manner and also the child's 'right to care'.

Maternity benefits and childcare services are an important part of social protection systems. They allow workers to earn an income when their children are young and give them time, to care for them, at home. This is particularly important for women workers from marginalised sections.

The Government of Odisha launched a state specific scheme called *MAMATA* in 2011 for pregnant women and lactating mothers to address the issue of maternal and infant under nutrition. It is a conditional cash transfer maternity benefit scheme which provides monetary support to pregnant and lactating women to improve their nutritional status. The limitations of this scheme reflect in fact that it focuses exclusively on feeding practices of children and women's health thereby neglecting the fact that in order to be able to ensure sound health for the child, the presence of the mother is a prerequisite which tends to be missing in case of women working in the unorganised sectors like the construction industry where there is hardly any scope for work time flexibility. Secondly, in order to be a beneficiary of the scheme, the woman should be registered with the nearest Anganwadi Centre (AWC) that would sponsor her name to the government for availing cash transfer. Here, again the possibility of registration with AWC by a woman whose workplace is highly uncertain due to changing construction sites is very limited.

Further, for the overall well-being of children, the *Odisha State Council for Child Welfare* was established in the State in the year

1959 which is affiliated to the Indian Council for Child Welfare, New Delhi. The Council is functioning under the aegis of Women and Child Development Department, Government of Odisha and is supported by the District Councils for Child Welfare in implementing various programmes and projects of both the Central Government and the Government of Odisha. Besides, the welfare of children, adolescents and expected and nourishing mothers, the scheme aims at undertaking various schemes and projects for the overall welfare of children.

The world's largest integrated early childhood programme, the *Integrated Child Development Services* (ICDS) established in 1975 has more than 70,000 sanctioned centres in Odisha which provides services throughout the state. The beneficiaries under the Scheme are children in the age group of 0-6 years, pregnant women and lactating mothers.

ICDS was launched with the following objectives in different parts of the country:

- to improve the nutritional and health status of children in the age-group 0-6 years;
- to strengthen and encourage the psychological, physical and social development of the child;
- to address and reduce the incidence of women and child mortality, morbidity, malnutrition, undernutrition and also cases of school drop-out;
- policy coordination between various departments to promote overall child development; and
- to make the mother capable of looking after the basic health and nutritional requirements of the child by generating proper awareness.

Women belonging to the poorer sections of the society and economically deprived families across the country are the most vulnerable when it comes to work and maternal health. In the Eleventh Five Year Plan document, the Planning Commission rightly observed that given the plight of poor women wage labourers, who neither can stay at home during late pregnancy nor can afford to stay at home to fully recover after delivery, what is required is a modest maternity benefit so as to partly compensate for their wage loss.

Again, most of the women and childcare centric schemes do not holistically address the issues regarding the woman's compulsions to work right up to the last stage of pregnancy and resumption of work soon after child birth. Therefore, effective measures in the form of Conditional Cash Transfer was deemed necessary by the Women and Child Development Department of Government of India to provide partial compensation of wage loss as maternity benefit to working women. Thus, Indira Gandhi Matritva Sahayog Yojana (IGMSY) was initiated in 2010 to improve nutritional and health status of pregnant and lactating women across the country by partly compensating for their wage loss and encouraging increased access to supplementary nutrition under ICDS Scheme.

The Orissa State Commission for Protection of Child Rights (OSCPCR), which was constituted in September 2010 plays an important role in safeguarding the rights and privileges of children besides examining factors inhibiting child rights. Although the Commission is committed to safeguarding child rights what remains missing is a realization by the Commission that if its objectives are to be accomplished, it should also think of developing a framework for providing training and financial incentives to groups willing to provide childcare services in the form of crèches or day care centres. Besides this, since the Commission is also involved in research studies and data analysis on issues pertaining to child rights, the Commission should work out ways to understand how laws and policies relating to maternity and childcare can be strengthened and how the productive and the reproductive roles of the working mothers can be reconciled thereby protecting them from the painful experience of choosing between work and childcare.

Further, malnutrition in Odisha continues to be a major and deadliest challenge despite the claim by the State Government that it is well under control. The recently released report by the

Registrar General of India (RGI) titled 'Medically Certified Cause of Death (MCCD)' maintained that as many as 26,184 children suffered from malnutrition and fell in the severely underweight category in 2018. Unfortunately, the causes of only 11.7 per cent deaths annually were being certified in the state. Further, the India Health of Nation and States-2017 (IHNS-17) report had rated malnutrition, especially child and maternal, as the prime risk factor in driving most of the deaths and disabilities in the state. Under five year children lost nearly 1.8 per cent of life-years owing to nutritional disorders. In fact, the report further stated Odisha recorded a whopping 69 per cent of deaths happen prematurely among all the age groups (Sahoo, 2019).

Odisha has high levels of poverty. It has faced several development challenges over the years, including insurgent movements, large pockets of extreme deprivation, social disparities, and natural disasters in comparison to other states. Despite these challenges, Odisha has demonstrated significant commitment to reducing undernutrition, has expanded nationally sponsored nutrition-specific programmes, and has launched state-led initiatives relevant to improving nutrition. This commitment in the face of adverse circumstances has paid off, to some extent. The state has made significant progress in reducing child undernutrition and this progress has been more rapid than many other richer states. Despite these improvements in child survival there do not appear to have been significant reductions in the proportion of children who are stunted and wasted. Malnutrition is not just a food or a health issue, but a broader development issue requiring a long-term and coordinated response across multiple sectors.

The existing feeding practices in the country to promote child growth as cited by the National Family Health Survey-3 (2005-06) is rather dismal. As per the study, Odisha, the state where the study was carried out is one of the lowest performing states of India with an Infant Mortality Rate of 51 per 1000 live births against the national average of 40 (Sample Registration System, 2013). Although the state in the recent past has shown sincere commitment in bringing about a positive change in the health sector, the existing health indicators prove that a much more favourable political and programmatic environment is required to achieve this end. To achieve this goal, the Odisha Voluntary Health Association (OVHA) implemented a project SURAKHYA- Promotion of Infant & Young Child Feeding Practice in Odisha covering all 30 Districts with 314 Blocks and 1,570 Gram Panchayats and 9,420 villages in March 2011 with active support of UNICEF, Bhubaneswar branch and has been quite successful in understanding the urgent needs, challenges and policy concerns pertaining to health and family welfare in the State (Kar Bhattacharjee & Samantaray Biswal, 2016: 40-41).

Under the Constitution of India, Article 41-43 of Directive Principles of State Policy (Part IV) stand for the right of livelihood where the Constitution directs the State to secure right to work, education, decent living, and assistance towards unemployment, old age, sickness, disability and maternity. Despite this provision, the situation of social security policy and its execution remains highly ambiguous both at the Centre and State level. A look at the wide range of policies/schemes framed by different departments under various ministries of Union Government at different points of time in the past reveal the directionless and half-hearted efforts towards a comprehensive policy on social security. The prominent ministries which have so far pronounced some of such social security schemes for young children and working mothers are Department of Food & Public Distribution, Health & Family Welfare, Housing & Urban Poverty Alleviation, Social Justice & Empowerment and most importantly the Ministry of Labour & Employment which has the prime responsibility of framing and implementing the labour laws. Every scheme is thus designed with specific purpose of targeting a selective group of beneficiaries ignoring the rest and in the present case the 'rest' includes the women working in the unorganised sectors. As per the report of the Eleventh Five Year Plan, the big challenge and contradiction lie in the fact that the same group of beneficiaries get covered in multiple schemes and those with dire need of support end up being excluded from the planning process either due to practical or political reasons.

In other words, the life of the workers in the *unorganised sectors,* mainly the construction workers is marked by work with no job security, no workplace safety, no minimum wage, no maternity leave and more importantly no childcare arrangements for working mothers. Construction workers often leave their very young babies unattended for long hours while they work. Under such circumstance, even breast-feeding becomes difficult.

Analysis of the Data

Some of the basic characteristics of the sample selected for the study indicate that the mothers (women workers) are fairly young, with an average of 72 per cent of women in their early twenties. Further, a sizeable proportion of these women live in extended families/ joint families, with nearly 80 per cent and above living with their mothers-in-law and a relatively small proportion with their own mothers/parents. Surprisingly, about 52 per cent of women in this sample are literate with an ability to read and write in their local language (Table 6.1).

Table 6.1: Personal profile of women workers

Area of field study (with No. of respondents from each area)	Age Group (20-30 yrs.) (in numbers and percentage)	(Number & percentage of literate workers	Number & percentage of workers having more than one child	Respondents with husbands as daily wagers (in Nos. & percentage)	Family composition Joint Family* Nuclear Family** (in Nos. & percentage)	
Kalpana Square (23)	18 (78)	15 (65)	14 (60)	23 (100)	21 (91)	02 (8)
Salia Sahi (28)	19 (68)	13 (46)	23 (82)	28 (100)	27 (96)	01 (3)
Jayadev Vihar (29)	25 (86)	18 (62)	21 (72)	29 (100)	24 (82)	05 (17)

(*Contd.*)

Area of field study (with No. of respondents from each area)	Age Group (20-30 yrs.) (in numbers and percentage)	(Number & percentage of literate workers	Number & percentage of workers having more than one child	Respondents with husbands as daily wagers (in Nos. & percentage)	Family composition Joint Family* Nuclear Family** (in Nos. & percentage)	
Lingaraj Temple area (21)	20 (95)	16 (76)	20 (95)	21 (100)	21 (100)	00 (0)
Niladri Bihar (48)	26 (54)	16 (33)	44 (91)	48 (100)	46 (95)	02 (4)

Source: Field Study (2019-2020).

* For the purpose of the present study, Joint family would mean those households having more than four members.

** For the purpose of the present study, Nuclear family would mean households having four or less than four members.

Further, the demographic as well as the personal profile of the women workers (target group) explains that the family dynamics and the cultural factors associated with these dynamics such as having more number of children in a family, age factor, family structure and so on play a vital role in children being neglected at all levels of childcare and accepting inequality within existing social and economic institutions as given. Being solely focused on the existing conflict between children's care needs and mothers' economic needs, we very often tend to ignore other domestic responsibilities that women usually engage in. Besides the data clearly shows as to how an average of 60 per cent and above number of women workers had extra familial concerns on account of having more than one child, with nearly 80 per cent and above having joint family structures putting more pressure on them to work extra time at home at the expense of childcare (See Table 6.1). The next level of analysis in this study also reveals that family support towards childcare was not so easily available for most of the women in spite of having joint families compelling them to take their children along with them to their hazardous workplaces with no support from their employers either (Table 6.2).

Table 6.2: Childcare (CC) arrangements during working hours

Area of field study (with numbers of respondents from each area)	CC by self during working hours (In numbers & percentage)	Family support for CC (In numbers & percentage)	Number & percentage of women receiving CC support from governmental institutions/ agencies (crèche/day care)
Kalpana Square (23)	15 (65)	07 (30)	Nil
Salia Sahi (28)	11 (39)	17 (60)	Nil
Jayadev Vihar (29)	23 (79)	06 (20)	Nil
Lingaraj Temple area (21)	14 (66)	07 (33)	Nil
Niladri Bihar (48)	13 (27)	35 (72)	Nil

Source: Field Study (2019-20).

Gender inequality plays a pivotal role within the political economy in shaping the intra-family dynamics associated with women's employment. Very often our concern is confined to the notion that maternal employment means that the mother is the 'natural' caretaker for her young children. As a result, when the mother is employed outside, especially when she works at a distance from home, children are left in the care of other siblings or grandparents and in some cases without any care support. Under such circumstances, these children may not be appropriately fed or may be more vulnerable to other health hazards including accidents. Childcare in the present study does not only imply feeding, giving bath to children and other related activities rather it also includes the quality time spent by the mother in watching children play and being with them when they need them the most during the day.

The study shows that an average of around 60 per cent of women interviewed revealed that they themselves are responsible for childcare even during working hours that questions the feasibility and relevance of the governmental childcare programmes and practices existing in the state of Odisha and its access and availability to women working in the unorganised sectors such as construction labour. Women who were themselves taking care of their children at workplaces maintained that they leave children in the open spaces sometimes left alone and sometimes with children of other labourers. Implicit in this statement is the vulnerability and insecurity that both mother and child have to go through during working hours (Table 6.2).

The percentage of family support that most women have an access to needs to be understood in a more realistic manner. In other words, regardless of the time spent towards economic participation outside, women end up spending great deal of time in the domestic activities ranging from cooking, cleaning, washing clothes, fetching water for the family and so on there are certainly incompatible with caring for their young children. As such, even though an average of 48 per cent of women admitted to having access to family support towards childcare during working hours, it needs to be understood that apart from paid labour outside, unpaid domestic labour takes away much of the time a mother can spend with her child and as such almost all women rely substantially on elders in the family or older siblings at home and sometimes even neighbours to look after their younger children (Table 6.2).

Certain common childcare challenges before the low income families as revealed through the present study are:

1. Low wages,
2. Non-standard or changing working hours,
3. Inflexible work schedule,
4. Job insecurity,
5. Absence of paid/sick leave, and
6. Lack of time and information regarding childcare arrangements.

In addition to the cost towards childcare, low income families also face challenges which are otherwise unreported and ignored while making childcare legislations/schemes. Firstly, childcare centres (such as Anganwadi Centres) do not offer care during evenings or on weekends, when many poor families may need them more. Secondly, families with lack of any private transport facilities find childcare options even more limited. Thirdly, location of most of these care centres in poor neighbourhoods make it insecure for the children. Fourthly, for single mothers, availability of care by relatives can also be limited because of distance from one's immediate household. Finally, receiving quality care for children in formal childcare settings need not be good enough to stimulate their development.

As rightly pointed out by many scholars writing on childcare, three factors generally complicate our understanding of childcare: (i) conceptualisation and measurement of childcare; (ii) conceptualisation and measurement of women's work; (iii) causal link between maternal work and childcare (Short, Chen, Entwisle and Fengying, 2002: 32-33). Besides, the role incompatibility that arises from activities relating to mothering and work lead to negative consequences of role strain among the working mothers especially among the wage workers engaged in unorganised sectors.

As pointed out by the 'new home economics' model of decision making, decision regarding allocation of time towards childcare arises from a process of utility maximisation that is affected by the decisions and characteristics of individual household members. In such cases women generally forego their work opportunities for the sake of childcare which also includes other household activities. This leaves the burden of 'opportunity costs' on women workers especially in wage labour in the absence of any childcare support from the state.

In the absence of necessary wage structures, established rules and social security measures, conducive working environments, social protection to care for their own children, women working in the unorganised sectors are very often left to fend for themselves when it comes to providing care to their young children. The state very often fails to understand that maternity benefits and childcare services are an important part of social protection systems.

One of the examples of challenges arising out of lack of flexible working hours among working mothers is limited access to exclusive breast-feeding to very young children. As per one of the studies conducted by Kalinga Institute of Medical Sciences (KIMS), Bhubaneswar, Odisha, in 2015, Exclusive Breast Feeding (EBF) was calculated as 48 per cent and early initiation of breast-feeding was nearly 46 per cent. What was alarming was that the feeding indicators calculated for children between 6-23 months age group showed dietary diversity of 27.4 per cent and minimum meal frequency of 29 per cent. Despite the provision of iron syrup and folic acid tablets under the National Rural Health Mission (NRHM), for 6-59 months old children, the consumption of iron rich foods in the state of Odisha was reported to only 6.8 per cent. This indicated high levels of morbidity among children under the age of five in the state (Kar, Bhattacharjee, Samantaray & Biswal, 2016: 39). The above mentioned study also facilitates our understanding of how absence of flexible working hours to women workers directly results in health hazards for children, especially for those who require exclusive breast-feeding.

Table 6.3: Health and childcare (cc) practices

Area of field study (with number of respondents from each area)	**Whether provided with flexible working hours during late pregnancy? (in numbers & in percentage)**		**Whether flexible working hours provided for CC? (in numbers & in percentage)**	
	Yes	**No**	**Yes**	**No**
Kalpana Square (23)	09 (39)	14 (61)	14 (61)	09 (39)
Salia Sahi (28)	03 (10)	25 (89)	10 (36)	18 (64)
Jayadev Vihar (29)	02 (6)	27 (93)	22 (76)	07 (24)
Lingaraj Temple area (21)	11 (52)	10 (47)	15 (71)	06 (6)
Niladri Bihar (48)	11 (23)	37 (77)	41 (85)	07 (14)

Source: Field Study (2019-20).

The present study indicated that whereas about 91 per cent of women workers admitted to absence of any facilities regarding flexible working hours during late pregnancy, nearly 38 per cent maintained that there were no facilities at the workplace as well no flexible working hours provided for care of very young children, most of whom used to accompany their mothers to the workplaces (Table 6.3).

The study also revealed that although nutrition and food security remains the prime concern of the women workers with nearly 90 per cent of the women respondents ascertaining the point, it is quite disheartening to learn that only one per cent of the respondents showed any interest towards addressing to the mental and psychological needs of the young children and only four per cent of them were concerned about giving prime importance to the safety and security of their children. These findings reveal the fact that the risk factor pertaining to the safety and health conditions of children of these construction labourers is very high

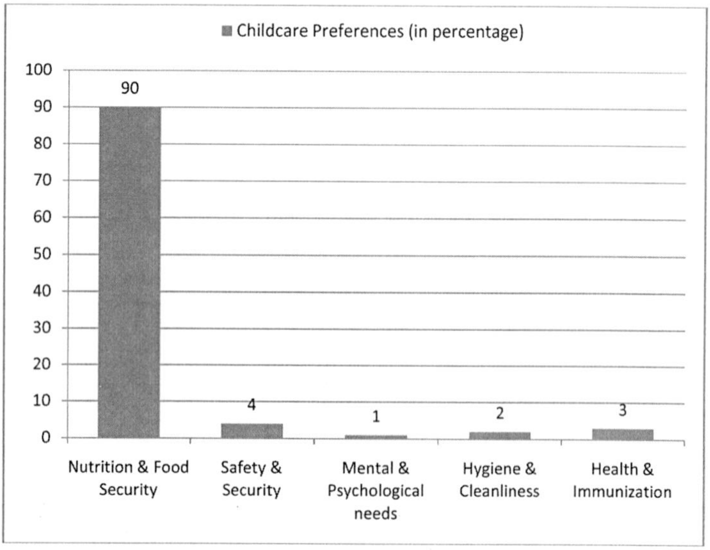

Fig. 6.1: Childcare priorities of women workers

Source: Field Study (2019-20).

and is often neglected not only by the state but also by the society at large which seldom gives it any attention while claiming their socio-economic demands from the state. Women workers, being the most vulnerable, socially and economically, on the other hand, find no time and energy to talk about or raise these issues before the government for any social security measures (Fig. 6.1).

As the state of Odisha makes an attempt to reform and redesign its childcare policies, it has to seriously take into account three important aspects, viz. affordability, access to it by poor working mothers and quality and reliability.

Conclusion

The findings of the study reveal that the best way to understand the extent of access, women workers have towards childcare is by considering the following aspects:

(i) Time and energy constraints that women workers experience due to their daily household chores coupled with workplace commitments and time slots for each activity.

(ii) Structural deprivations that women experience due to lack of social support towards maternal and childcare and also on account of the patriarchal family structures.

(iii) Availability of reliable local solutions for childcare.

(iv) Conducting anthropometry of children below the age group of 3 years and their mothers. (Anthropometry has not been conducted for the present study.)

The extent to which a woman gets access to childcare in India, depends to a great extent on her economic and social strata in the society. The lower your economic strata in the society, the lesser the time you get to attend to your young child. Here, 'access' is to be considered as a luxury not available to all. Physical compulsions related to economic efficiency, which is very often measured by the number of hours you put in towards your profession with extra labour, prevents women labourers from paying expected attention to their children. 'Access' here also has to be taken as a birth right coming naturally to the child that is yet to be granted a constitutional status so as to enable it to be recognised as significant.

Further, a society and the state as a whole get affected when economic efficiency is compromised. Similarly, a child's moral, physiological and psychological rights are compromised with in the absence of a right to 'access to care'. The young child of today will represent our present generation in the future. Thereby, the health, morality, efficiency and prosperity of a nation necessitates a state policy that gives primacy to 'access to childcare' as one of the foremost goals of its public policy.

Besides, woman labour force forms an integral part of our human resource. They form an important segment of our social capital. Hence, when we talk of human resource development, this section of the population demands serious consideration. Women labourers having children below the age group of five years have to be guaranteed protection by the state *via* a combination of policies supporting and enhancing the access to childcare. In this regard, the state must consider the following factors determining the success/ failure of its policies towards early childcare:

(a) Socio-economic status of the family,
(b) Cultural predispositions as far as their (women labourers) family structures as concerned,
(c) Kind of work they are engaged in (to assess time and energy constraints),
(d) Number of children in the family below the age of five years,
(e) The working hours per day in proportion to their daily wage,
(f) The existing childcare arrangements at home,
(g) Structural deprivations experienced by women in some communities, and
(h) Understanding the scope to adopt and implement local solutions (mainly through community participation).

Keeping the above-mentioned factors in mind, the state must enable the policy-makers to understand the link between health and timely access to nutritious food, time and space constraints, structural deprivations experienced by certain specific communities, public and private spheres of a woman's life, economic efficiency and socio-psychological requirements of the women and most importantly, the link between the present circumstances and the future prospects.

Some of the indicators that can enable policy-makers to measure access to childcare among women labourers in unorganised sectors include:

(i) Total time spent per day towards care giving of young children.
(ii) Prevalence of malnutrition and undernutrition among children below the age of three.
(iii) Dietary practices of both the child and mother.
(iv) Rules regarding recess at workplace.
(v) Childcare practices adopted during working hours.
(vi) Any community support towards childcare.
(vii) Childcare priorities of parents with regard to nutrition, health, personal hygiene, quality of childcare and so on.
(viii) Conducting anthropometry of children below the age of three years and their mothers.
(ix) Family support towards childcare at home.

When these factors and requirements are taken into consideration, significant strides can be made towards policy making in favour of early childhood development. Especially, in states like Odisha, Bihar, and Rajasthan where a large number of children suffer from malnutrition, lack of early healthcare assistance, where maternal mortality rates are comparatively high, maternal healthcare facilities in most of the rural areas is negligible and where daily wage of the labour class working in the unorganised sectors is either very low or remains undefined/unregulated, the need to have state regulated mechanisms for 'access to early childcare' becomes a basic necessity on humanitarian grounds.

Some of the policy initiatives at the state level may include:

(a) Generating awareness about childcare, nutritional and health requirements among women labourers at their workplace. This may be done through community contact programmes inciting discussions and interactions among the members of the labour class once in every month. This will also facilitate gender sensitisation among the workers.

(b) Community supported crèche facilities within 2 km of the work premises for children between the age group of one year to three years. In this case, *anganwadi* workers (women and men) who are professionally trained by the state agencies and subsequently monitored at frequent intervals by the state authorities concerned can be employed.

(c) Legislations enabling flexible working hours for women workers till the child attains the age of three years. For this purpose, a survey may be conducted to find out the time and space expectations of the women workers in order to attend to their child's physical and psychological needs.

(d) 'Work from home' policy alternatives to be identified so as to enable women workers to judiciously channelise and manage their time for work and childcare.

(e) Childcare to be treated as a subject of 'Corporate Social Responsibility' (CSR). The officials associated with this task may be referred to as childcare entrepreneurs to be trained and supported by a public-private partnership (PPP) mode. The PPP mode can be utilised for:
   (i) Infrastructure building;
   (ii) Training to the supporting staff to equip them well with childcare management skills;
   (iii) To run counselling centres for parents of the young children;
   (iv) Research support on childcare to the trainees; and
   (v) Financial assistance for training and salary payments can be borne by the state.

(f) Collaboration with local and national level NGOs can be encouraged primarily in three areas:

 (i) Training for childcare workers/staff and *anganwadi* workers.

 (ii) Providing logistic support to community based crèche facilities.

 (iii) Counselling to women workers to educate them about childcare.

Apart from the policy initiatives, certain potential pathways that can ensure quality childcare for women workers may include the following:

- Women's collectives and workplace crèches.
- Maternity benefits and policies not to be seen as paternalistic benevolence to women but as a psycho-emotional aspect essential to strengthen the bond between the mother and the child.
- Concerns of Social Security Costs need to addressed (loss of job, leave benefits, promotion avenues etc.).
- Sexual division of labour in childcare emphasising on provisions for paternity leave that would eventually lead to much awaited transformations in gender relations.
- Maternity Benefits to be made a Fundamental Right instead of Directive Principles of State Policy (DPSP) under the Constitution of India.
- Need to categorically differentiate between the number of crèches in the country in general and in the states, in specific, which are statutory in nature and those which are voluntary or run by community initiatives. The structural, financial, administrative aspects and professional ethics of the above mentioned crèches need to be clearly validated.

The irony of the policies/schemes and legislations enunciated and established by the governments both at the Centre and in the States is that while on the one hand these policies and laws promote breast-feeding, child nutrition and mother's health, on the other hand it remains totally silent on how to address all stages of childcare, right from pregnancy, child-birth, lactation, and more significantly infant care and day care, as one thereby necessitating a single law meant for early childhood development that includes women's access to childcare at least till the child attains the age of six. Therefore, to genuinely promote the health and welfare of mothers and children, the need of the hour is to promulgate a strong legislation that considers maternity and childcare services jointly and also by subsequently providing positive social support measures for the working women especially those engaged in the unorganised sectors.

7

Impact of Child-Parents Relations on Child Development

A Comparative Study of Students of Lucknow City of Uttar Pradesh

Deepa Awasthi

Introduction

'Child is a Father of Man' and he is ought to become a citizen of his country and contribute for its development. Development of a child largely depends upon its surrounding. Family, friends, school, peer group and the society in which he is residing affects the personality of an individual to a great extent. Out of these factors affecting the child family is foremost and within family parents are the most important from child's development point of view. For all-round development of child, it is mandatory that child and parent have healthy relations among them but now-a-days a shift is being observed. Educators and psychologists are coming across a number of children who are not able to perform in their studies, games and other fields during adolescence while they were performing much better before. The main cause of the problem was found to be rooted in unhealthy child-parent relations and these unhealthy relations are continuously affecting their physical and mental development, leading to anxiety among them hindering their educational growth also.

Growing age leads to physical and mental changes in children, this is not only challenging for children but also for parents. Parents have to adapt to new situation accordingly. Parenting is not only growing the children, it is much more than that. Parents have to change their parenting with growth of their children. If more than one child is there in family, parents have to shift their style of parenting every minute and every second. For parents if one thing does not work well, they cannot stop for a while. They have to look out for new ways, new solution and possibilities. Parent has to change their style of parenting according to gender of child as well.

Children learn about the world around them through a positive parent-child relationship. As they are growing and changing children look upon their parent to determine whether or not they are secure and loved. It is also the foundation from which they will build their future relationships (Dorn, 2020).

According to Thakur (2009), the informal relations between child and parents should be healthy and close. Parents should keep on changing their behaviour according to the situation. Along with parent they have to play the role of teacher, mentor and friend as well from time to time. Recently, degradation in child-parent relation is seen in society making the environment of family unhealthy. For maintaining healthy relation among child and parent, the responsibility lies on parents, they should understand the needs and emotions of children.

With growing age due to physical and mental development child expresses emotional instability, making them tense. If parents fail to understand the change in child's behaviour then relation between child and parent becomes pathetic, especially during age of adolescence (Arora, 2009).

Finally, communication is the last parent-child relationship component that either makes or breaks the bond between parents and their kids. This being so, adolescents become particularly sensitive to certain 'you' statements directed at them by their parents (Pagani *et al.*, 2009).

Reasons for Depreciating Child-Parent Relations

There could be number of reasons for depreciation in parent-child relations, the real reason depend upon situation. Here are the few reasons been discussed which are responsible for weakening the parent-child relations:

(a) **Excess Control of Parents:** Some parents still follow the centuries old pattern of parenting where children are kept under excessive control. Children in these families have to take permission of their parents for each and every activity they do. Ultimately later on it affects the relation between child and parents.

(b) **Working Parents:** Usually, families where mother father both are employed, parents are daily out of home for work, and parents hardly have time for their children. Even when parents are at home after work they are unable to spend quality time with children due to office tension or tiredness. Similar condition exists with the parents where both of them run a family business together. In such situation children find themselves alone within the four walls of home. Questions arising in their little mind remain unsolved, caretakers fails to answer their curiosities.

(c) **Size of Family:** Size of the family also affects the child-parent relationship. Big families having more number of children, parents find it difficult to focus on every child equally. Child, who remains unattended by parents feel ignored, leads to weaken their relations not only with parents but also with their siblings.

(d) **Socio-economic Status of Family:** In families with low socio-economic background, child usually held parents responsible for their situation while children belonging to upper socio-economic background where their needs and luxuries are fulfilled they feel pride in being member of the family. In such families, members have better relations with each other.

(e) **Relation between Parents and other Family Members:** Relation between parents and other family member also affects child-parents' relationship. Families where mother and father keep on quarrelling with each other, children face loneliness and are confused, with whom they are close with. Similarly, when siblings don't have healthy relations among themselves, all-round growth of children are badly affected.

(f) **High Expectations from Parents:** Blind race of standing first also have adverse impact on child-parents relations. Due to growing competition parents expect that their child should remain ahead of everyone. Although parents know that this competition has no end, it is ought to grow continuously. It is not possible for children to fulfil the expectation of parents always.

(g) **Occupation of Parents**: It is seen that children sometimes compares the occupation of parents in their peer group and they hesitate in telling the occupation of their parents when they find that their parents' occupation is less respectable in society. So the occupation of parents affects child-parent's relationship.

Need and Justification

This can be derived from above discussion that child-parent relationship plays a vital role in physical and mental development of child. We find that number of studies has been carried out on this issue but no comparative study has been conducted on the child-parent relationship between secondary level students of government and private schools of Lucknow city. Any child will only be able to become a good citizen of country contributing to development of nation when he/she gets the full chance to flourish and develop to its full potential. Any obstacles in their development will ultimately going to affect the society in whole. So there is great need of study.

Statement of the Problem

'Impact of Child-Parents Relations on Child Development:

A Comparative Study of Students of Lucknow City of Uttar Pradesh'.

Objectives

- To compare parent-child relationship of male and female students of government schools.
- To compare parent-child relationship of male and female students of private schools.
- To compare parent-child relationship of students of government and private schools.

Hypothesis

- There will be no significant difference in parent-child relationship of male and female students of government schools.
- There will be no significant difference in parent-child relationship of male and female students of private schools.
- There will be no significant difference in parent-child relationship of students of government schools and private schools.

Research Methodology

This study is descriptive in nature. Survey method has been used to collect data.

Population and Sample

All the students of class IX of government and private schools of Lucknow City were the population of the study. Sampling has been done in two stages. At first stage, total 6 secondary level government and private schools have been selected through random sampling out of which 3 were government schools and other 3 were private schools. At second stage, total 120 students were selected through incidental sampling. 20 students (10 male and 10 female students) from each school have been selected as sample.

Tools

Parent-Child Relationship Scale (PCRS): Parent-Child Relationship Scale, constructed by Dr. Nalini Rao has been used to collect data. This scale includes 100 items related with 10 dimensions, i.e. protecting, symbolic, punishment, rejecting, object punishment, demanding, indifferent, symbolic reward, loving, object reward, and neglecting of parent-child relationship. Respondents rated their mother and father separately for the same item on five point rating scale.

Personal Data Schedule

Along with parent-child relationship scale, a self developed Personal Data Schedule has been used to collect detailed information about the respondents such as name, age, sex, educational qualification etc.

Procedure

After sampling, students were requested to fill Parent-Child Relationship Scale (PCRS) along with Personal Data Schedule.

Statistics Used

Mean and t-test were used to analyse the data.

Results

Results can be presented as below:

Table 7.1: Difference in Parent-Child Relationship of Male and Female students of Government Schools

Groups	N	M	t-value	Significance
Male Students of Government Schools	30	586.2	0.21	Not significant at 0.05 level
Female Students of Government Schools	30	589.9		

Table 7.1 indicates the mean scores of male and female students of government schools on parent-child relationship scale. Mean

scores of male students has been found 586.2 and for female students mean scores was 589.9. t-value has been calculated for the above data distribution which has been found 0.21. It is not significant at 0.05 level of significance. Thus hypothesis-1, that there will be no significant difference in parent-child relationship of male and female students of government schools has been accepted. These findings can be presented through Fig. 7.1.

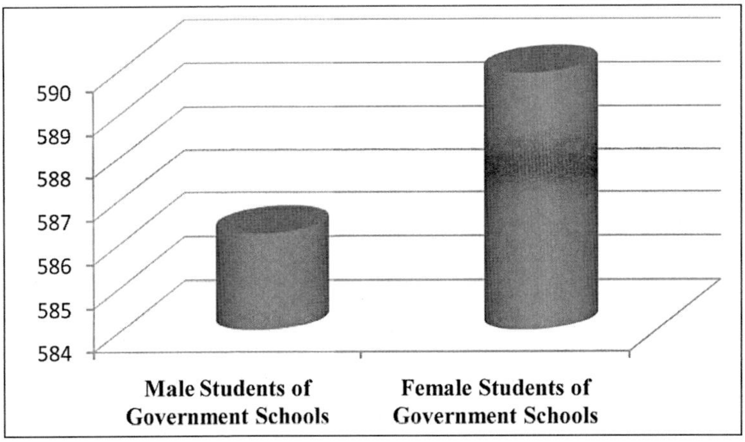

Fig. 7.1: Difference in Parent-Child Relationship of Male and Female students of Government Schools.

Figure 7.1 has very well presented the difference between mean scores of male and female students on Parent-Child Relationship Scale in favour of female students of government schools. However, this difference is found not significant but mean in favour of female students has shown their better parent-child relationship.

Table 7.2: Difference in Parent-Child Relationship of Male and Female students of Private Schools

Groups	N	M	t-value	Significance
Male Students of Private Schools	30	569.3	2.58	Significant at 0.05 level
Female Students of Private Schools	30	580.2		

Table 7.2 indicates the mean scores of male and female students of private schools on parent-child relationship scale. Mean scores of male students has been found 569.3 and for female students mean scores was 580.2. t-value has been calculated for the above data distribution which has been found 2.58. It is significant at 0.05 level of significance. Thus hypothesis-2, that there will be no significant difference in parent-child relationship of male and female students of private schools has been rejected and alternative hypothesis has been accepted in favour of female students of private schools. These findings can be presented through Fig. 7.2.

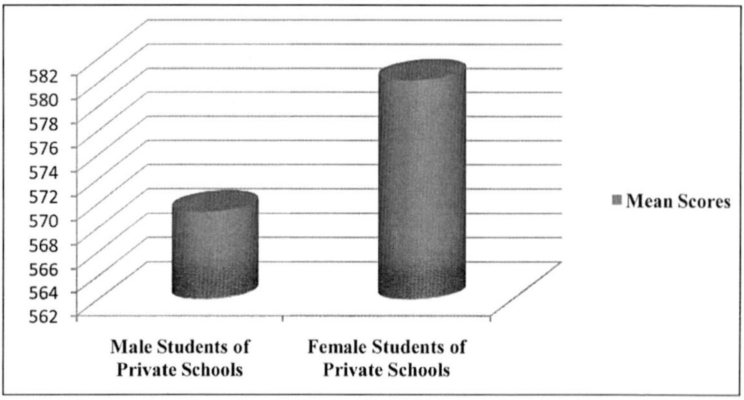

Fig. 7.2 Difference in Parent-Child Relationship of Male and Female Students of Private Schools.

Fig. 7.2 clearly depicts the difference between mean scores of male and female students of private students on Parent-Child Relationship Scale in favour of female students of government schools.

Table 7.3: Difference in Parent-Child Relationship of Students of Government and Private Schools

Groups	N	M	t-value	Significance
Students of Government Schools	60	588.05	2.63	Significant at 0.05 level
Students of Private Schools	60	574.75		

Table 7.3 indicates the mean scores of students of government and private schools on parent-child relationship scale. Mean score of students of government schools has been found 588.05 and for students of private schools, mean scores has been calculated 574.75. t-value has been calculated for the above data distribution which has been found 2.63. It is significant at 0.05 level of significance. Thus, hypothesis-3, that there will be no significant difference in parent-child relationship of students of government and private schools has been rejected and alternative hypothesis has been accepted in favour of students of government schools. These findings can be presented through Fig. 7.3.

Fig. 7.3 indicates the difference between mean scores of students of government and private schools on Parent-Child Relationship Scale in favour of students of government schools.

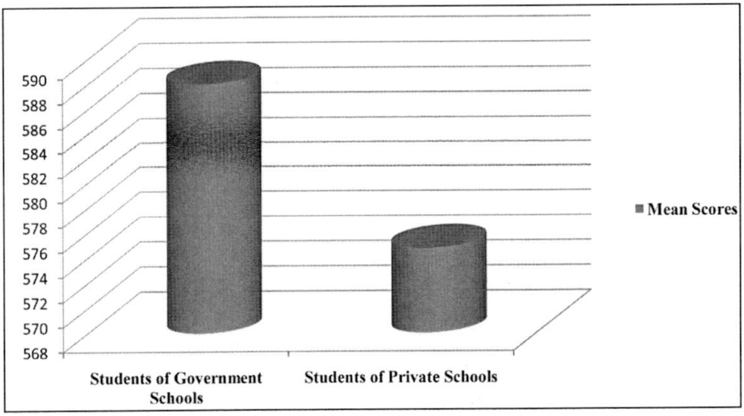

Fig. 7.3: Difference in Parent-Child Relationship of Students of Government and Private Schools

Findings

Respondents have shown strong parent-child relationship. On the basis of analysis of data it has been concluded that:

1. No significant difference in parent-child relationship has been found between male and female students of government schools. Mean scores have shown that female

students of government schools have better parent-child relationship with their parents than male students.

2. Significant difference in parent-child relationship has been noticed between male and female students of private schools in favour of female students.
3. Significant difference in parent-child relationship has been found between students of government and private schools in favour of students of government schools.

Discussion

Parents are the source of energy and motivation for well-being of their children as well as their success. Positive relations play a vital role in overall personality development of children. In case of youth, role of parents become more important and influence their personal and professional life. Both male and female need the same affection, confidence, trust and positivity from their parents but studies have shown differences in these relationships. Shaban & Mattoo (2012) and Agarwal (2020) have found significant differences in parent-child relationship of male and female students. These findings support the findings of present study as there is significant difference in parent-child relationship between male and female students have been noticed in case of private school students in favour of female. In case of government schools, mean score of female students have supported their better relation with their parents. Shakila (2017) has found in her study that female students have better cordial relationship with their parents. This study also has coherent status with findings of present study. Shakila (2017) have also concluded that type of schools (municipal or government or private) have significant impact on parent-child relationship. Students from municipal and government schools have shown better relation with parents than students from private schools. This also support the conclusions of present study as students from government schools have shown better relationship with parents than students from private schools. However, Sarita *et al.* (2016) in their study of secondary students have found contrary results in favour of better parent-child relationship of male students than female students. Reason behind this finding may be attributed to the strong patriarchal set-up where the study was conducted by Sarita *et al.* Their study was conducted in Haryana, which remains victim of low sex ratio from long time. Favourable perception of people towards boys and negative towards girls may be the reason behind that.

Suggestions

(a) Parents should administer the level of control over children. They should play a role of guide or mentor rather than interfering in their each and every decision. Let them learn by doing mistakes. Mistakes will act as a lesson for them, guiding them towards success. A trust among them will pave the way for healthy relations.

(b) Parents should motivate their children by setting an example because knowingly unknowingly children copy their parents. We find that moral values followed by family are easily acquired by children in their day-to-day life.

(c) Parents should use the concept of reward and punishment very carefully. It is responsibility of parents to let their children know about right and wrong, they should be criticised for their wrong acts in the manner that they should aware of what is right.

(d) Parents should try to make their children self-dependent, it will develop a notion of confidence and self-respect among them. This confidence will sail them through all the struggles of their life.

(e) Parents should develop a democratic environment in family discussion so that children may also get the chance to express their views. Their serious views must be accepted by family members. According to Strohschein and Mathew (2015), adolescents who receive parental support and encouragement are less likely to rebel against parents.

(f) Parents should know that every child cannot be first or best. Getting first position in class or living a successful life are two different things and the second one is more important than other one. Parents should motivate their children for studies in the way different from comparing them from other children of similar age group. Parents should accept that every child is unique and different from others.
(g) In case where both parents are working should try to spend good time with their children especially on weekends and holidays. They should utilize summer and winter vacation of children for developing friendly relation with them. Parents should be available at least when they need their parent's support, care and help.
(h) Parents should try to answer the curiosities of their children. A meaningful answer to their questions will add up in their confidence while avoiding their questions will have an adverse impact on their relationship affecting child development.
(i) Parents should limit the size of their family so that the various needs of children could be fulfilled at least to limit where they may not feel inferior to others in their peer group.

Conclusion

Child-Parent relations are the backbone of child development. Unhealthy relation with parents and other family members will restrict the development of child. Every child in this world is unique; the concept of one key for all locks is not applicable in case of human beings. Parents must understand the psychology of their children and nourish them accordingly. We can understand that students studying in same school with similar socio-economic background perform differently in their life, the one the only one reason behind this difference is the input of their parenting and their surroundings.

References

Agarwal, R. (2020). "A Comparative Analysis of Parent-Child Relationships between School & College Students." *IOSR Journal of Humanities & Social Sciences, 25*(1), 17-21. Retrieved from http://www.iosrjournals.org/iosr-jhss/papers/Vol.%2025%20Issue1/Series-9/C2501091121.pdf

Arora, S. (2009). *Abibhavak Shiksha*, Agra: Agrawal Publication, p. 47.

Dorn, P. (2020). 8 Ways to Strengthen a Parent-Child Relationship, www.familyservicesnew.org published on July 28, 2020 and accessed on June 26, 2021.

Lamb, M.E. & Lewis, C. (2005). "The Role of Child-parents Relationship in Child Development", *Developmental Science: An Advanced Textbook*, pp. 429-468, Lawrence Erlbaum Associates Publishers. www.psycnet.apa.org

Pagani, L., Tremblay, R.E. *et al.* (2009). "Risk Factors Models for Adolescents Verbal and Physical Aggression towards Father", *Journal of Family Violence,* 24, 173-182.

Positive Relationship between Parents and Children: How to Build Them, www.raisingchildren.net.au

Ramirez, N.E. Diana (NA). Parent-Child Relationships and its effect on Adolscence, submitted to Mckendree University, www.mckendree.edu.net accessed on June 25, 2021.

Rao, N. (1989). *Manual for Parent-Child Relationship Scale (PCRS).* Agra: National Psychological Corporation.

Saraswat, M. (2010). *Shiksha Manovigyan ki Rooprekha*, Lucknowe: Alok Prakashan, pp. 166, 640.

Sarita, Sonia & Pooja (2016). "A Comparative Study of Parent & Child Relationship of Male & Female Secondary School Students in Private & Government Schools." *International Journal of Applied Research. 2*(6), 1000-1002. Retrieved from https://www.allresearchjournal.com/archives/2016/vol2issue6/PartP/2-6-75-236.pdf on July 7, 2021.

Shaban, S. & Matto, N.H. (2012). "A Comparative Study on Adolescent-Parent Relationship among Boys and Girls in a Rural Setting." *Studies on Home & Community Sciences. 6*(2), 121-125. Retrieved from https://www.tandfonline.com/doi/abs/10.1080/09737189.2012.11885377

Shakila, J. (2017). "Parent-Child Relationship of Secondary School Girl Children in the Context of Locality and Different School Background." *Scholarly Research Journal for Interdiscipilnary Studies*, *4*(37), 8452-8459.

Strohschein, L. & Mathew, A. (2015). "Adolescent Problem Behaviour in Toronto, Canada: Association with Family, School and Neighbourhood Social Capital." *Sociological Inquiry*, *85*(1), 129-147.

Thakur, Y. (2009). *Samaveshi Shiksha*, Agra: Agrawal Publication, 113.

8
Mapping the Vulnerabilities and Deprivations of the Child Bride
Critical Pathways and Policy Imperatives

Moushumi Pattnaik

Moral and spiritual precepts often qualify, rationalise and even sanctify the institution of marriage. Precepts like—'Marriages are made in heaven', 'Marriage as a union of souls', 'Marriage as a sacrament', strongly attach a sense of divinity to this age-old socio-cultural practice. Marriage is often lauded as a 'Holy ordinance' and an important 'Sanskara'. However, the spike in feminist research and literatures have exposed the surreality of such epithets citing the gender-based discriminations, exploitations and vulnerabilities women face more distinctly after marriage. More so, when it comes to marriage among children, feminist research is outrightly vocal and poses a paradigmatic challenge to this practice because it opens up the Pandora's box of vulnerabilities, insecurities and indignation for the young bride. The study aims to explore the critical pathways and nuances relating to child marriage and its inter-sectionality with other manifestations of gender inequality and oppression. The chapter intends to scan through policy imperatives to curb this practice. It is a work not only of diagnosing the problem but envisaging measures on how to respond.

Ubiquity of Child Marriage

"Child Marriage is truly a global problem that cuts across countries, cultures, religions and ethnicities. Child brides can be found in every region in the world, from the Middle East to Latin America, South Asia to Europe" (Girls Not Brides, 2016). According to Pew Research Centre, around 117 countries around the world allow child marriage to happen and it impacts negatively on a nation's economies (Gray, 2016). National and international communities are increasingly recognising child or early marriage as a serious problem, both as a violation of girls' human rights and as a hindrance to key development outcomes. International studies bear testimony to the devastating effects of child marriage on the life of the young girl. Child marriage virtually puts an end to a girl's education. A child bride's lack of education and peers limit her support systems, and without skills, mobility, and connections, she is constrained in her ability to overcome poverty for herself, her children, or her family. The International Centre for Research on Women has also pointed out that child brides are at heightened risk of violence in their homes.

The frequency and veracity of child marriage is regularly computed by national and international institutions. The latest international estimates indicate that worldwide, more than 60 million women aged 20-24 were married before they reached the age of 18. India is estimated to have over 24 million child brides. 40 per cent of the world's 60 million child marriages take place in India according to the National Family Health Survey. The State of the World Report states that in India 51 per cent of young women with no education and 47 per cent with only primary education had married by the time they had reached 18 years (24). Looking at the gravity of the problem, the Government of India has come up with the 'Prohibition of Child Marriage Amendment Bill' 2021 to fight malnutrition, MMR, IMR and other morbidities so as to usher gender equity, empowerment, female participation in labour market, autonomy and better health outcomes for women.

The prevalence of child marriages among girls in India is reported to be 23.3 per cent. Though it is decreasing as compared to the previous National Family Health Surveys but in absolute terms the numbers are quite high. India has the 14th highest rate of child marriage in the world, according to the International Centre for Research on Women. Marriage systems and practices vary by region, caste and tribe. Rates of child marriage are higher in the North-West and lower in the South-East of the country. The states with the highest rates of child marriage (50% and above) are Bihar, Rajasthan, Jharkhand, Uttar Pradesh, West Bengal, Madhya Pradesh, Andhra Pradesh and Karnataka. But even in low prevalence states there may be pockets with high rates of child marriage.

Perusing Literatures

Kimball and Dwivedi (2021) observed that for too long the conventional focus on increasing the age of girls at marriage has driven incomplete or misdirected interventions in their research article "Recollections of How Child Marriage Field Has Evolved." Their frame of analysis seeks an urgent shift from the age factor to a multiplicity of factors that underpin a centuries old cultural norm. They suggest the following: (a) Marriage needs interrogation not just it takes place at the age of 16 rather than 18 but because of its potentially negative life consequences for girls. We need focus on girls' lack of agency, the social conditions of marriage, and the experiences of married girls with regard to divorce, inheritance and other structural factors, (b) Consider adolescents' own aspiration and ambition and not view them simply as children lacking agency and aspiration. If young people are not empowered to make decisions about education, livelihoods, employment, or marriage, then a decision not to marry, in itself, will never be an empowering experience. Girls and boys often marry because it is their only pathway to adulthood. It is a genuine aspiration because there is no other. Therefore, the fundamental question is how do we understand and empower young people from a broader social and economic perspective, and (c) To promote critical education and perspective building, enabling girls to think about their future lives in terms other than marriage. If young girls do not have support for their decisions—through an enabling education, the skills to negotiate with their parents, then those decisions will backfire on them.

Quite a radical stance is taken by Jha, Kathurima, Uribe and Nthamburi (2021) who in their chapter "Building a Global Movement to Respond to Child Marriage" state that contemporary laws relating to marriage and sexuality complicate matters, example conflating age of consent with age of marriage may perversely incentivise early marriage. Besides weak or non-existent registration systems and the fact that many people lack birth certificates undermine the efforts to regulate age at marriage. In a society where marriage is the only socially sanctioned way to express sexuality, the movement against child marriage needs to be nuanced in the light of promoting sexual rights and well-being of girls and women. Invoking only legal measures against child marriage would unseat efforts to fight for sexual/LGBTQ rights. Therefore, strategies to fight child marriage need to respond to the complexities of the context and go beyond laws to community-level dialogue and interventions that promote gender equality and sexual rights. Going forward there is need for governments to go beyond enacting legislation defining or revising the age of marriage to able the roots of the practice. Millions of girls continue to marry early because of the lack of secondary schools and employability beyond school. Making options other than early marriage available to them should be a policy imperative. Unpacking sexuality, transforming gender roles and making contraception accessible to both married and unmarried individuals would play a significant role in making sure that choices are possible to make and they are supported. "Delinking age of consent and age of marriage would go a long way towards respecting adolescent sexuality and recognizing their evolving capacities in line with the Convention on the Rights of the Child."

Roost, Horn, Koski (2021) in their research article, "Child Marriage or Statutory Rape? A Comparison of Law and Practice Across the United States" have made a unique observation that in many US states children can legally marry at an earlier age than they can legally consent to sex, leading to situations in which sex between spouses may be a criminal act. They assume that as some states exempt sex between married persons from their definition of statutory rape, which may create perverse incentives for child marriage. Their results highlight the blurred legal and conceptual boundaries between child marriage and sexual violence. The simultaneous legality of child marriage and marital exemptions to statutory rape law provide legal loopholes for sexual acts with children that would otherwise be considered crimes. Marital exemptions to statutory rape laws may also incentivize a substantial portion of child marriages. These exemptions suggest that, in the eyes of the state, marriages cannot be exploitative in the same manner as non-marital relationship and therefore, married children do not require the same protections.

Muthengi *et al.* (2022) find that the two most common reasons given by girls for marrying or cohabiting were poverty and pregnancy and sometimes both. Premarital pregnancy tends to lead to cohabitation more that to marry and with cohabitation often unsupported and unrecognised by parents, families and communities, cohabitating girls are at greater risk of isolation and couple dissolution. Incidents of abuse in cohabitating union are likewise high and cohabitating girls often lose spousal benefit when their relationship dissolves or their partner dies.

The chapter by Edmeades (2021) and colleagues find that early marriage among boys is determined by their entry into economic activity. Given the centrality of bread winner role for men, child marriage for boys increases with employment and dropping out of school. The earlier a boy leaves school and begins earning a leaving, the sooner he marries. It is the opposite for transition of girls, where leaving school means leaving behind opportunity to support herself and her family economically and her marriage is driven in part through norms regulating their sexual and reproductive behaviour.

Jejeebhoy, Raushan (2021) in their research article titled "Marriage Without Meaningful Consent and Compromised Agency in Married Life: Evidence from Married Girls in Jharkhand, India" have mentioned that marriage without meaningful consent persists in India, yet early marriage programmes have rarely addressed consent, and research on the practice and its consequences for married life are limited. This study explores how consent in marriage decisions affect married life, specifically, agency, gender attitudes, spousal communication, contraception and marital violence outcomes.

Jejeebhoy and Raushan describe earlier research from India, Nepal, and Pakistan showing that girls in self-arranged marriages were more likely than those in fully family-arranged marriages to display agency, hold positive attitudes, communicate with their husbands, and practice contraception. However, they have found that marital violence was unrelated to marriage arrangements. Girls in self-arranged marriages report freedom of movement, self-efficacy, equitable gender role attitudes, and attitudes espousing girls' right.

Nanda, Das, Datta (2021), in their study "Education, Sexuality, and Marriage ability: Overlapping Tropes in the Lives of Adolescent Girl in Haryana, India" strongly argue about nuanced insights on the value of girls' education and overlapping domains of marriage. Girls' capabilities and opportunities through education are curtailed by pervasive gendered restrictions. Without challenging norms around girls' sexuality and essentiality of marriage, we are likely to see fewer gains from schooling for girls' empowerment. Education is considered key to enhance girls' prospect for marriage. The intrinsic benefits of education may enable some girls to chart better life trajectories, though its value is largely understood within a bounded space of girls' marriage ability. The persistent focus on marriage structures, girls' daily school routines bounded by strict restrictions and scrutiny around their mobility, sexuality, and conduct. They conclude that achieving gender parity in education alone is insufficient to achieve broader gender equality goals.

Without contextually grounded approaches to change the cultural narratives around girls' education, its transformative potential is appropriated within the prevailing norms that privilege marriage as a key destiny for girls. Further interventions need to address the quality of education, associated work trajectories and restrictive social norms for girls to truly take advantage of their increased educational attainment.

Montoya, Graham, Lopez, Cohen (2021), in their research study "Gender Norms, Control Over Girls' Sexuality, and Child Marriage: A Honduran Case Study" establish strong links between 'Marianismo' (a powerful gender norm) and girls' mobility, sexuality and child marriage in rural areas of Honduras. Marianismo is a cultural arch type which views girls and women as modest, innocent, sexually abstinent, nurturing, passive abnegated and family centred, i.e. a good mother or a good wife. Beliefs around the expectations of girls having impeccable behaviour leads to excessive protectiveness of girls. The belief that intimate and sexual relationships should occur only within the context of marriage encourages girls to see marriage as only way to be involved in a romantic relationship. Girls are expected to live up to these exceptions and live in restrictive environment that control their mobility, socialisation opportunities and sexuality. However, at the same time, the girl is also undergoing through normal psycho-social development processes. They are developing a greater sense of autonomy and experiencing interest in intimacy and sexual relationship which comes in conflict with the strict gender conceptualisation pertaining to marianismo. Thereby to come out of this doldrum, the young girls decide to enter child marriage because they see it as best option given the limited choices. The authors make a submission that educational institutions that explain and normalize the changes that occur during adolescence (particularly around the attraction and intimacy) and challenge social norms and constructs that promote gender inequality should be a central component of child marriage programming for adolescent parents and community members. They have developed a unique intervention programme known as HEY or Holistic

Education for Youth to challenge sexist gender norms and prevent the harmful practice of child marriage.

Baird, Murphy, Seager, Jones, Malhotra, Alheiwidi, Emirie, Rashid, Sultan (2021) in their research article titled "Intersecting Disadvantages for Married Adolescents: Life After Marriage Pre- and Post-COVID-19 in Contexts of Displacement" have focused upon the experiences of married girls in refugee settings and how their development trajectories diverge from those of their non-married peers, particularly in the context of the COVID-19 pandemic. Drawing on cross-national panel data from Bangladesh and Jordan, this article explores diversity in child marriage experiences in contexts affected by forced displacement. Their findings show that refugee girls are at significantly greater risk of child marriage than their host community counterparts, and face heightened vulnerabilities overall. Capability deprivations are experienced by married girls across all settings, i.e. both in Bangladesh and Jordan. However, for Jordanians child marriage is associated with better physical and mental health outcomes, lower levels of hunger, and lower likelihood of psychosocial stress. This may in part reflect the economic insecurities of the natal families for which they arrange marriages of girls in families with better financial prospects than their own. Further married Syrian girls fared even better than Jordanian girls.

Elnakib, Khoury, Salameh, Sacre, Abirafeh, Robinson, Metzler (2022) in their research article "Investigating Incidence, Correlates, and Consequences of Child Marriage Among Syrian Refugees Residing in the South of Lebanon: A Cross-Sectional Study" say that research on child marriage has increased in volume but remains scarce in humanitarian settings. This study aimed to investigate rates, correlates, and consequences of child marriage among Syrian refugees in South Lebanon. Several factors, which mirror drivers of child marriage in stable settings are associated with hazard of child marriage in this context. They additionally found important sexual and reproductive health gaps among child brides, such as low levels of knowledge of the dangers of early childbearing and closely spaced births as well as high rates of early and multiple births. Their study confirms and builds upon existing literature that highlights the association between household characteristics and child marriage. Like other studies they find that higher levels of parental education are associated with lower hazard of child marriage. They also find that girls who were orphaned were very likely to be married off compared to their counterparts.

Parsons *et al.* (2015) in their article "Economic Impacts of Child Marriage: A Review of Literature" suggest that social and cultural norms including those related to faith, influence the age at which a girl is expected to marry. Child marriage is most common among the poor who have fewer resources and opportunities to invest in alternative options for girls. Assigned gender roles of girls restrict them to household only and do not prioritise them in labour force participation or education. Further, the financial transitions around marriage also contribute to the practice of child marriage. Interventions are most powerful when they empower girls with information, skills and support networks; enhance the accessibility and quality of formal schooling for girls and offer economic support and incentives for girls and their families to keep girls in school, so that they marry later. The article is structured in five sections. Each section documents the economic impact of child marriage in a specific area: participation and decision making, educational attainment, labour force participation, violence and health. Apart from negative consequences at the individual level child marriage may also have far reaching consequences at the national and global level in the form of lost earnings and inter-generational transmission of poverty.

Naved, Kalra, Talukder, Laterra, Nunna, Parvin and Mamun (2021) in their research study titled "An Exploration of Social Norms that Restrict Girls' Sexuality and Facilitate Child Marriage in Bangladesh to Inform Policies and Programs" provides insight into how to accelerate reductions in child marriage in Bangladesh exploring the norms that drive the practice. These norms place significant expectations and pressure in families to preserve girls' chastity and maintain family honour through their daughters' virginity and reputable marriage in this patriarchal and predominantly Muslim society. While declines in child marriage are correlated with increased rates of education and while interventions that promote retention in and completion of school, build empowerment and life-skills of girls, facilitate economic participation, and provide positive incentives, have been shown to decrease child marriage in the short term, without understanding and addressing the norms driving the practice of child marriage, any progress made in changing attitudes and behaviour risks being low-impact and short-lived.

Shaheen, Othman, Hamdan, Albqoor, Atoom, Langer, and Gausman (2021) in their research article titled "Child Marriage in Relation to the Syrian Conflict: Jordanian and Syrian Adolescents' Perspectives" have explained child marriage under the backdrop of Syrian civil war and considering the perspectives and Jordanian adolescents as refugee and vast population.

The Syrian conflict has changed practices relating to child marriage, fostering a renewed reliance on child marriage in light of increasing instability, leaving both Jordanian and Syrian adolescents increasingly vulnerable. Many adolescents reject the practice, thus offering an opportunity for social change. Although some of the underlying drivers related to financial insecurity, safety, and education are thought to interact to make girls and young women more vulnerable to child marriage, other factors appear to be protective, such as changing social norms through new contacts with host communities. They conclude that more efforts are needed to empower girls and increase their agency to take over control over their lives, which is one of the core elements of the ecological framework that often is overlooked in an effort to foster change at higher contextual levels.

Why Child Marriage?

Multiple reasons can be cited for the occurrences of child marriage. People's traditional mind-set and the deep-rooted cultural beliefs consider a girl as a liability and a burden to be married off and sent to her in-laws' place as soon as possible. Social pressure that is pressure from neighbours and relatives is also an important cause for the parents to get their children married young.

Other reasons underlying the practice consist of the importance attached to virginity. Rural families consider the virginity of the girl as important and a matter of family honour. There is a high degree of insecurity and anxiety related to safeguarding a girl's virginity. Marriage is considered 'safe' to protect the girl from unwanted sexual advances. Without such security, a girl who is unmarried and no longer a virgin is considered to ruin the family reputation. If a girl loses her 'virgin status'—whether through consensual sex or forced sexual assault—she is no longer considered suitable for marriage. In a society which puts a high premium on the patriarchal values of virginity and chastity of girls, girls are married off as soon as possible.

The Planning Commission of India identified the complex causes of child marriage to include, "the growing insecurity of girls and increasing violence against them, adolescent pregnancy resulting from sexual ignorance and neglect, increasing drop-outs from post-primary schooling due to various reasons, and deep neglect of the physical and cultural development of girls, with no provisions for games/sports, healthy entertainment and reading facilities."

Dowry is yet another key reason for the existence of this practice. Many a times greater dowry is demanded from parents of older girls. Hence, poverty-stricken parents are forced to marry their daughters to avoid such dowries. Further, in families where there are many daughters, parents solemnise their marriages on the same day to save money.

Some of the other causes of child marriage are economic hardship and poverty of the parents, low level of education of the parents as well as of the girls and gender disparity. Besides the lack of political will and poor implementation of the existing laws results in the practice to continue unabated.

Consequences of Child Marriage

Child Marriage deprives the girl of both physical and mental well-being. As her education is put to an end she loses her employability. Heavily engrossed in gender roles she lacks agency and peer group memberships. She becomes exposed to greater health risks, the greatest being early pregnancy and childbirth which leads to reproductive health problems and contribute to high Maternal Mortality Rates (MMR) and Infant Mortality Rates (IMR).

Maternal Mortality Rate (MMR): Reports reveal that MMR in India is still high with more than 1,00,000 women in India dying every year from causes related to pregnancy and childbirth. A woman dies every seven minutes in the country due to complications related to pregnancy. The Maternal Mortality Ratio for India (2014-16) is 130 per 1,00,000 live births. However, it has declined to 113 per lakh live births in 2016-18.

Complications during Childbirth: As young girls are physically immature to bear a child, childbirth causes a major threat to their health and life expectancy. Two million women worldwide suffer from obstetric fistula, a debilitating complication of childbirth especially common among physically immature girls. According to The State of the World's Report, The older the girl, the higher is the dowry the parents have to pay. In India, one out of every three adult women is underweight and therefore, at risk of delivering babies with low birthweight.

Infant Mortality Rate (IMR): Child marriage not only affects the girl child but also the child born due to early pregnancy. The mother's young age and lack of proper nutrition lead to the improper growth of the baby. Sources indicate that the overall, infant mortality rate declines sharply with the mothers' increasing education. It ranges from a high of 87 deaths per 1,000 live births for illiterate mothers to a low of 33 deaths per 1,000 live births for mothers who have at least completed high school (NFHS-02). It ranges from a high of 22.9 per cent (NFHS-04- 2015-16) per 1000 to a low of 12.9 per cent (NFHS-05-2019-21).

Trafficking and Sale of Girls: Child marriage also results in the trafficking of children for various purposes, including prostitution, labour and exploitation. Young girls are lured/forced into marriage for the purpose of selling them to other states. Trafficking of married girls is rampant in Rajasthan, Uttar Pradesh, Chhattisgarh and even Kerala. A survey of victims of trafficking revealed that 71.8 per cent of the respondents were married when they were children (i.e. when they were below 18 years). This suggests that child marriage is among the key factors that make women and children vulnerable to trafficking.

Vulnerable to Domestic Violence: A UNICEF study points out that India has one of the highest levels of domestic violence, whereby 67 per cent of women who were married at below 18 years faced domestic violence. It has the highest levels of domestic violence cases among women compared to other countries like Zambia, South Africa, Cambodia etc. Domestic violence is a major problem among adolescent girls who marry early. Women who marry younger are more likely to be beaten, threatened or sexually abused. They are sometimes likely to believe that a husband is justified in beating his wife. Owing to the age difference between the partners, young girls are more vulnerable and susceptible to domestic violence, as well.

Illiteracy among Girls: Child marriage denies girls' access to schooling and their right to education, which is necessary for their personal development and effective contribution to the future well-being of society. Sometimes, girls who prefer to go to school before or after marriage may not be allowed to pursue higher studies. Usually they are removed from school, thus ending their education and individual development, and making them vulnerable. Many parents believe that investment in a girl's education is a waste of money because ultimately, she would have to get married and move to her husband's house where she will take care of the household. Withdrawal from school in order to get her married limits her opportunities to become an informed and self-reliant individual. In many cases, these girls are also not allowed to socialize and make friends outside their family.

Lack of Decision-Making Powers: Girls are not able to discuss issues related to pregnancy, childbirth and contraceptive use when they are married at a young age, thus denying their basic reproductive rights. Child marriage takes children out of school and thereby the end of their education. This serves to perpetuate cycle of low literacy and limited employment opportunity.

Legislative Interventions and Policy Imperatives

Government of India enacted the PCMA 2006 to enforce legal action against child marriage in the country. Child marriage is established as a cognizable and non-bailable offense under the PCMA, which aims to prohibit the solemnization of child marriages. "Child marriage" is defined as a marriage where either of the contracting parties is a "child", defined as 21 years of age for a male and 18 years for a female. The PCMA establishes the power of courts to issue injunctions to prohibit solemnization of a child marriage either *suo motu* (on its own motion) or in response to complaints filed by any person or non-governmental organization having reasonable information relating to a child marriage.

Despite the well-intentioned legislation and elaborate structures and mechanisms in place, the implementation of PCMA is observed to be sub-optimal. Deep rooted traditional beliefs and social norms among people often over-ride the legislation. Lack of knowledge of communities on both legal provisions and negative impact of child marriage has been one of the major reasons against the community taking legal recourse.

The key strategies for ending child marriage require heavy administrative engagements based on the situational analysis, regional consultations with various stakeholders such as adolescents, community, civil society, and functionaries at different levels. Moreover, ongoing government programmes that empower adolescents and prevent child marriages should be reviewed and inputs must be drawn from different departments. End term evaluation as well as mid-term evaluation of programmes become very important in this regard. To address the problem of child marriage an all-encompassing and holistic approach is required. Political will and direction coupled with administrative commitment is the need of the hour. The administration must pay attention to and ensure the following:

1. Efforts must be made to retain all girls in school. The girls should complete secondary school. The schools must have separate functional toilets and availability of sanitary pad for girls in schools to reduce absenteeism.
2. There should be availability of adequate higher secondary schools to cater to the demand of transition from secondary to higher secondary school.
3. Prepare older adolescent girls for livelihoods and school-to-work transitions. Ensure transition of students of vocational education from high school to ITI and Polytechnic.
4. Encourage sports as a career option for girls and boys, including increasing sports hostels for girls. Initiate career counselling in all high schools so that both boys and girls are aware of career options and opportunities and take advantage of them.
5. Introduce market oriented and livelihood based vocational training for out of school and drop-out adolescents.
6. Build girls' agency and empower them to exercise life choices. Creation of girls' clubs would be an important step in this regard.

    - Encourage access to positive role models.
    - Leverage social protection programmes, notably Conditional Cash Transfer (CCTs) and other entitlements.
    - Sensitise influential community members so that they can bring awareness in the village community.
    - Enhance boys' understanding and support for gender equality through counselling programmes in schools.
    - Address the vulnerability and social isolation of married adolescent girls.

- Enhance implementation and knowledge of laws concerning gender equality, and notably child marriage.
- Enhance the reach and quality of facilities, services and entitlements.
- Harness the potential of the media to promote gender equality.

References

Baird Sarah, M.M. (2021, December 01). "Intersecting Disadvantages for Married Adoloscents: Life After Marriage Pre- and Post-COVID-19 in Contexts of Displacement." *Journal of Adolescent Health*. Retrieved from https://doi.org/10.1016/j.jadohealth.2021.12.001

Child Marriage Prohibition Act, 2006 (2006). *The law defines"hild" as a person who, if a male, has not completed twenty-one years of age, and if a female not Completed eighteen years of age.*

Dwivedi Archana, K.D. (2021). "Recollection of How the Child marriage Field Has Evolved." *Journal of Adolescent Health*, S7- S8. Retrieved from https://doi.org/10.1016/j.jadohealth.2021.12.010

Edmeades Jeffrey D., M.K. (2021). "Child Grooms: Understanding the Drivers of Child Marriage." *Journal of Adoloscent Health*. Retrieved from https://doi.org/10.1016/j.jadohealth.2021.08.016

G.B.P. (2015). Child Marriage in India: A Study of Situation, Causes & Enforcement of Prohibition of Child Marriage Act. *Supra note*. Retrieved from https://ideas.repec.org/p/ess/wpaper/id6900.html

HRLN (2017). *Child Marriage: The Worst Form of Slavery.* Human Rights Law Network.

ICRW (2006). *Too Young to Wed: Education and Action Towards Ending Child Marriage.* International Center for Research on Women (ICRW). Retrieved from https://www.icrw.org/wp-content/uploads/2016/10/Too-Young-to-Wed-Education-and-Action-Towards-Ending-Child-Marriage.pdf

India, G.O. (2006). *Prohibition of Child Marriage Act 2006.*

India, L.C. (2006). *11 Proposal to amend the prohibition of Child Marriage Act 2006 and other Allied Laws.* Retrieved from https://indiankanoon.org/doc/116780787/

Jejeebhoy Shireen J., R.M. (2021, July 5). "Marriage Without Meaningful Consent and Compromised Agency in Marriaed Life : Evidence From Girls in Jharkhand, India." *Journal of Adoloescent Health*. Retrieved from https://doi.org/10.1016/j.jadohealth.2021.07.005

Burckhardt, Jacob. (2014). *The Civilization of the Renaissance in Italy*. Auckland, New Zealand: The Floating Press.

MDW&S . "Archival ." August 2015. www.mdws.gov.in. <www.mdws.gov.in/guidelines-swachh-bharat-mission-gramin-11102017>

Peace Corps. *Water Purification, Distribution and Sewage Disposal: Appropraite technologies for development*. Washington DC, The USA: Information Collection and Exchange, 1984.

Strachman, D.P. (1989). "Hay Fever, Hygiene and Household Size." *British Medical Journal*, 1259-1260.

WHO and UNICEF. (2014). *Progress on Drinking Water and Sanitation*. Geneva: WHO Press.

WHO, Sanitation (2015). <http://www.who.int/topics/sanitation/en/>

World Commission on Environment and Development (1987). "Our Common Future."

9

Gender and Development

A Study of Maternal and Child Healthcare Policies in Odisha

Padmalaya Mahapatra

Introduction

Gender discourse within the field of development has come a long way from building a case of 'inclusive' growth which prevents the marginalization of women to questioning of the predominant notions of development itself. The body of feminist critique continues to traverse new terrains and posit new challenges. The neo-liberal vision of society with a strong undercurrent of economic determinism often celebrates the atomistic, unconnected, self-maximizing individual—a conception which largely inhibits the space of both culture and development. Women's limited access to and control of material resources and limited decision-making power within the household can produce high fertility rates, under-investment in aspects of family welfare such as child nutrition and education, and sub-optimal allocations of human capital in the economy. Maternal morbidity and mortality along with infant mortality rate is universally considered as human development indicators in a country and determines the health status of the people. In spite of very good plans and programmes, the reduction in MMR & IMR is much below the target set in Odisha. The present study is based on both primary and secondary sources of data. The chapter attempts to analyse the impact of maternal healthcare policies on women's health status in Odisha. It mainly focuses on maternal mortality relating to socio-economic characteristics of deceased, status of ante natal care, major causes that led to maternal death, major steps taken through various policies and programmes initiated by Government of India/Government of Odisha and their achievement.

Gender and Development

The **Gender** Related **Development Index** (GDI) is an index designed to measure gender equality. GDI together with the Gender Empowerment Measure (GEM) were introduced in 1995 in the Human Development Report written by the United Nations Development Programme. The GDI measures differences between male and female achievements in three basic dimensions of human development: health, education and command over economic resources. GDI is the ratio of female HDI to male HDI. To calculate it, the HDI is first calculated separately for females and for males. India ranks 130 in Gender Inequality Index: UN. According to the United Nations' Human Development Report, India is ranked 130 out of 155 countries on the Gender Inequality Index (GII). The gender index takes into account reproductive health, empowerment, and economic activity.

Maternal Health—Concept, Definition and Components

Maternal health refers to the health of women during pregnancy, childbirth and the *post-partum* period. While motherhood is often a positive and fulfilling experience, for too many women it is associated with suffering, ill-health and even death. Maternal healthcare is a concept that encompasses family planning, preconception, prenatal, and postnatal care. Goals of preconception care can include providing education, health promotion, screening and interventions for women of reproductive age to reduce risk factors that might affect future pregnancies. Prenatal care is the comprehensive care that women receive and provide for themselves throughout their pregnancy. Women who begin prenatal care early in their pregnancies have better birth outcomes than women who receive little or no care during their pregnancies. Postnatal care issues include recovery from childbirth, concerns about newborn care, nutrition, breastfeeding, and family planning.

Women constitute nearly half (49.5%) of the State's total population as per Census 2011. As such their socio-economic development is a *sine qua non* for sustainable growth of the economy. Generally, women experience considerable disadvantage and discrimination in the society owing to gender differentiation. The gender bias propels disparities in terms of literacy, access to public health services and social development indicators. The female literacy of Odisha as per 2011 Census was 64 per cent which was at par with national averages. But gender gap in literacy as per 2011 Census was the highest in Nuapada district and lowest in Khordha district.

Infant Mortality in Odisha has made quantum leap with 56 points decline by reducing IMR from 96 (SRS 2000) to 40 in 2015-16 (NFHS-4) which is the highest point decline in the country far ahead of national average decline of 27 points and better than major States like Gujarat (28 points), Rajasthan (38 points), Chhattisgarh (25 points), Jharkhand (26 points), MP (36 points), UP (19 points). This translates into 51,000 more children being saved annually compared to the year 2000. IMR in rural Odisha was 43 as compared to 21 in urban areas in 2015-16. At the national level, IMR stood at 41 and varied from 46 in rural areas to 29 in urban areas in 2015-16.

Infant Mortality Rate Point decrease: Odisha-56, India-27

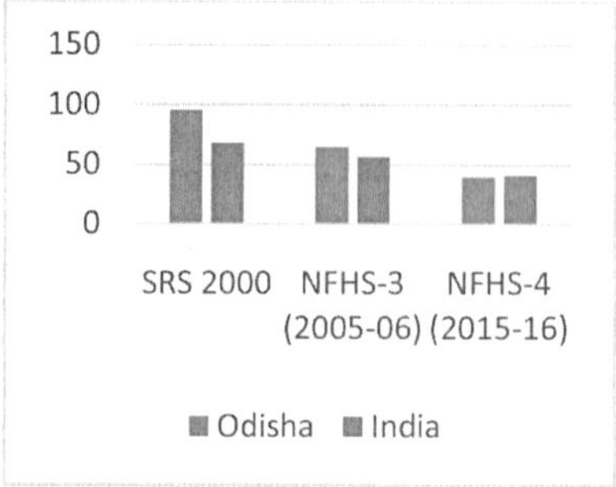

Source: National Family Health Survey.

Gender inequality, human rights and its effects on maternal health

Despite the country's growing economy and an ambitious rural health initiative, over 1,00,000 women die from pregnancy-related causes each year, more than anywhere else in the world. Many more suffer debilitating complications that they endure in silence due to impunity and lack of accountability in the health system. The medical causes of maternal mortality are well known and largely preventable, yet government policies have failed to have an impact.

Promotion of maternal and child health has been one of the most important objectives of the Family Welfare Programme in India. The current Reproductive and Child Health Programme (RCH) was launched in October 1997. In order to improve maternal health at the community level, a cadre of community level skilled birth attendant who will attend to the pregnant women in the community is being considered.

Review of Literature

Miller (1989), Murthi, Anne and Dreze (1995), Gupta and Bhat (1997), George (1998), Bhat and Zavier (2003), Mishra, Roy and Rutherford (2004), Dyson and Moore (1983), Krishnaji (1987), Siddhanta, Nandy and Agnihotri (2003), Pandey (2003), Hill and

Upchurch (1995) and Acharaya & Kumar (2004) explained the extent of gender differences in infant and child mortality in terms of gender differences in health status, disease incidence, preventive and curative treatment and social status.

> "In many parts of the world, women receive less attention and healthcare than man do and particularly girls often receive very less support than boys. As a result of this gender bias, the mortality rates of females often exceed those of males in these countries. This is an important issue because gender discrimination that contributes to poorer health status for girls than for boys is likely to be the main pathway for excess female child mortality. Such discrimination occurs in (a girl) receives less attention than would be bestowed upon a son. She is less warmly clad, she is probably not so well fed as a boy would be and when ill, her parents are not likely to make the same strenuous efforts to ensure her recovery."

Sugathan, Mishra and Rutherford (2001), Kishor and Parasuraman (1998), Stephenson and Tusi (2002), Bourne & Walker (1991), McNay, Arokiasamy and Cassen (2003), Dyson and Moore (1983) and Rustagi (2004) evaluated the status of women in India with different indicators such as of women's work, education, health, survival, safety and participation in public/ private decision-making.

Sudha, Rajan, (1999) George (2002), Rutherford and Roy (2003), Bose (2007), Visaria (2007) examined the causes for eliminating the girl child. It indicates that they are rooted in rituals and perceptions that go back centuries: the fear of having to pay for a girl's dowry, the belief that for true salvation a son should perform the last rites, the conviction that lineage and inheritance run through the male line and that a son will look after his parents in their old age, whereas the daughters will belong to another family. Tied up to all this is the old perception of seeing only men as the bread earners.

Whatever our stance is on feminist economics, however, we need to be aware of these issues when analysing the effect of gender related issues on development at the macro level. Indeed, some of the newer fields in economics, such as behavioural economics, take some of these challenges more seriously. Another example of rising awareness of the need to consider changing social norms and culture is a recent book on economic growth by David Weil (2005), which gives considerable emphasis on culture and values.

During the 50 years from 1950 to 2000, mortality in all age groups greatly improved. The infant mortality rate (IMR) was 90 per cent lower in 2000 than in 1950, making infants the age group that saw the greatest changes over time. Men experienced a decline of at least one-third across all age groups. Women's death rates at ages zero to 80 fell by at least 50 per cent, while improvements above age 80 constituted at least 30 per cent of the decline over the 50-year period. These sex specific differences in mortality declines were also reflected in life expectancy. Women's life expectancy increase was almost linear over time. Men, on the other hand, initially experienced a slower life expectancy increase. From the late 1970s onward, male mortality declined faster in relative terms than female mortality (Luy, 2004).

While at the beginning of the period, infant mortality contributed significantly to East-West differences, old age became much more important over time. Until the mid-1970s, the lower IMR and more rapid improvements in this rate in the GDR were responsible for part of the initial advantage of GDR in male life expectancy (Nolte *et al.,* 2000a). The first few years after reunification, the IMR fell in both the East and the West, and the rates converged in 1997 (Nolte *et al.,* 2000b, 2001).

In a cross-sectional study, under-5 mortality was found to be strongly associated with maternal and infant health programmes. It was also strongly associated with the proportion of births attended by trained person. To raise the public health spending remains the main challenge in developing countries for improving the quality of maternal and child healthcare (McGuire, J.W., 2006).

A study was conducted to describe the association between under-5 mortality and socio-economic, political, and healthcare factors between rich and poor children. In this study, higher incomes were associated with lower under-5 mortality rates (Houweling *et al.*, 2005).

Global under-5 mortality has dropped from 11.9 million in 1990 to 7.7 million deaths in 2010. 33 per cent of these deaths occurred in South Asia and 49.6 per cent in Sub-Saharan Africa. Less than 1 per cent death occurred in developed countries. Compared to 1990 to 2000, there is accelerated decline in child mortality from 2000 to 2010 (Rajaratnam *et al.*, 2010).

In a study from India, under-5 mortality rate declined at a mean rate of 3.7 per cent per year between 2001 and 2012. According to this study, 222 districts were lagging in the process of achieving Millennium Development Goals. Female mortality rate was higher by 25 per cent in 303 districts (Ram *et al.*, 2013).

Objectives

The main objective of the study is to ascertain the level and pattern of maternal mortality among the selected rural groups in Odisha. More specifically the study tries to:

- Determine the level of maternal mortality among the selected population groups in Rural Odisha.
- Identify the Risk Factors of Maternal mortality, know their operational mechanism and find out their related risks.
- Recommend appropriate intervention modes to prevent and control risk factors in order to reduce maternal and infant mortality.

Research Questions

To what extent maternal and child healthcare policies influence to improve the health status of women in Odisha?

Method of Study

This study is based on both Primary and Secondary data. Data collected from empirical study in 2 Gram Panchayats of Cuttack district of Odisha. This study also involves personal interviews and discussions with several Women Leaders, Social Welfare Boards, and prominent members of NGOs etc.

- Field investigations, empirical surveys, direct interviews with villagers specially women, young mothers, traditional *dais*, *Anganwadi* workers, the Auxiliary nurse midwives, doctors and Self Help groups, *Panchayat sarpanchas* and members.
- Extensive scanning of published material on the subject.
- Scanning of a few previous and current Five Year Plan Provisions to reduce IMR & MMR. A special attention was given to the Midterm reviews not only of the Planning Commission but also of Reports of some Ministries, viz. Ministry of Health and Family Welfare, Ministry of Women and Child Development of the Centre and the States; National Rural Health Mission, selected local feedback from Panchayat Raj reviews and a few members of the Panchayats of the concerned States.

In any case, the problem of IMR & MMR is part of the Indian, "Social Complexity." To totally bring it down we need to take vigorous direct and indirect systemic reform steps. It is high time, we took not one but several, "first steps" some of them have been recommended here as we have to walk a thousand miles to bring down IMR/MMR in India.

Reduction of maternal and child deaths is one of the major challenges of the health system in Odisha. With several efforts from the State under the RMNCH+A campaign, it has been observed from the SRS reports, that there has been a decline in the State Maternal Mortality Ratio (MMR) and Infant Mortality Rate (IMR) over the years.

(Odisha State strategy for accelerated reduction of Maternal and Infant Mortality-Odisha 2020)

The maternal mortality has been defined by WHO as death of a woman while pregnant or within 42 days of termination of pregnancy, irrespective of the cause of death (and) is intended for countries that wish to identify deaths occurring in pregnancy, child birth up to 6 weeks after the end of pregnancy but where the cause of death cannot be identified precisely (WHO cited in Royston, Mauldin, 1994).

For women and adolescent girls of reproductive age, the biological functions of pregnancy and childbirth intersect with gender inequalities and poverty to expose women to maternal health risks. A lack of autonomy to make decisions about one's own healthcare, low levels of education circumscribing the ability to make informed healthcare decisions, limited control over financial resources, restricted mobility to access healthcare services and power differentials between healthcare providers and recipients are all factors which may preclude women from receiving the quality of care essential for ensuring healthy pregnancies and deliveries.

Though the maternal mortality ratio declined by 37 per cent between 2000-2015, there were an estimated 3,03,000 maternal deaths worldwide in 2015 due to complications in pregnancy and childbirth. Almost all (99%) occurred in developing regions, with the highest level (546 per 1,00,000 live births) in sub-Saharan Africa, followed by South Asia (182 per 1,00,000 live births).

Maternal and New Born Health

Sl. No.	Component	Rate
1	Proportion of women aged 15-49 who received post natal care within 2 days after giving birth (%)	62
2	Antenatal care coverage for at least four visits (%)	51
3	Proportion of births attended by skilled health personnel (%)	81
4	Caesarean section (%)	17
5	Proportion of women 20-24 years old who gave birth before age of 18	22
6	Number of women age 15-49 years with a live birth delivered in a health facility	79
7	Births who had their postnatal check-up within the first two days after birth (%)	24

Source: Other NS 2016.

Infant mortality is an indicator of the health status not only of infants, but also of the whole population and of their poverty ridden social and economic status in the country. They face excessive vulnerability, as underprivileged, to a hostile environment and suffer malnutrition and serious health problems; all this leads to high rates of infant mortality and morbidity. Infant mortality, i.e. deaths under one year of age in a year per 1000 live births, is an important indicator of child health and development.

(*Source:* The Socio-economic determinants behind Infant Mortality & Maternal Mortality, sponsored by the Planning Commission of India, 2006).

Child Health

Sl. No.	Component	% Rate
1	Children under age 5 whose births are registered (%)	72
2	Women aged 20-24 years who were first married on in union by age (%)	27
3	Children aged 5-17 years engaged in Child Labour (%)	12
4	Children aged 1 to 14 years who experienced any violent discipline (psychological aggression and/ or physical punishment) in the past month (%)	Not Available
5	Justification of Wife beating (female) (%)	47
6	Justification of Wife beating (male) (%)	42
7	Women aged 15-49 who have undergone female genital mutilation (%)	Not Available

Source: UNICEF/WHO, 2017.

In 2015, the world began working towards a new global development agenda, seeking to achieve, by 2030, new targets set out in the Sustainable Development Goals (SDGs). The proposed SDG target for child mortality aims to end, by 2030, preventable deaths of newborn and children under 5 years of age, with all countries aiming to reduce neonatal mortality to at least as low as 12 deaths per 1,000 live births and under-5 mortality to at least as low as 25 deaths per 1,000 live births.

Child Survival

Sl. No.	Component	Rate
1	Under-five mortality rate (U5MR), deaths per 1000 births	39
2	Number of Under-five deaths	989,167
3	Infant Mortality Rate (IMR), deaths per 1000 live births	32
4	Neonatal Mortality rate (NMR), deaths per 1000 live births	24
5	Under-five mortality rate (U5MR), deaths per 1000 live births (male)	39
6	Under-five mortality rate (U5MR), deaths per 1000 live births (female)	40

Source: IGME, 2018.

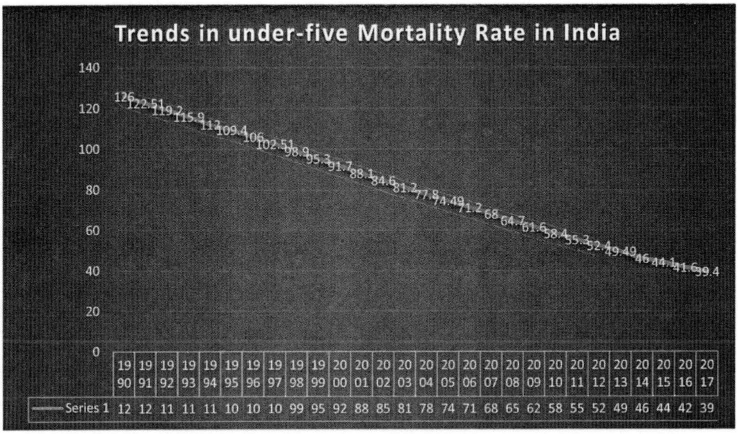

Existing Interventions for Reducing IMR & MMR in the State.

The world made remarkable progress in child survival in the past few decades, and millions of children have better survival chances than in 1990-95. 1 in 26 children died before reaching age five in 2018, compared to 1 in 11 in 1990. Moreover, progress in reducing child mortality has been accelerated in the 2000-2018 period compared with the 1990s, with the annual rate of reduction in the global under-five mortality rate increasing from 2.0 per cent in 1990-2000 to 3.8 per cent in 2000-2018. Despite the global progress in reducing child mortality over the past few decades, an estimated 5.3 million children under age five died in 2018—roughly half of those deaths occurred in Sub-Saharan Africa.

State is continuing its consistent efforts for reducing MMR and IMR through different strategies at community as well as facility level. The major interventions which are implemented currently are as follows:

Village Health and Nutrition Day (VHND)

These days are organized once in a month in every AWC on a fixed day basis (Tuesdays and Fridays) with joint effort of ANM, AWW and ASHA. The VHND provides quality ANC & PNC services for expecting and lactating mothers, counselling on family planning needs, Adolescent Health Day for adolescents, monitoring growth of child development where services like general health check-ups (Weight for age, BMI, Anaemia detection etc.), provision of essential drugs and micronutrients like IFA, albendazole, calcium are along with counselling and referral of identified high risk cases to appropriate institutions. Line listing and follow-up of anaemia cases is also done in this platform.

Comprehensive Abortion Care (CAC)

To provide safe and accessible abortion care services, doctors and paramedics are trained in different methods of MTP up to CHC DP level.

Review of Maternal Deaths

To reduce the incidence of maternal deaths, each and every cause of maternal death is analysed and corrective action is taken accordingly at appropriate level. These reviews are undertaken at various levels so that steps can be taken for avoiding similar deaths in future.

Screening of Syphilis and HIV in Pregnant Women

For early management of syphilis and HIV among pregnant

women, at all pregnant women are mobilized for screening test which is presently available up to delivery points. ANMs and ASHAs are mobilizing pregnant women for screening at the facility level and initiation of treatment, if found positive.

ANM Mentoring

This activity aims at improving knowledge and building defined skill sets of HW(F) for providing quality services in VHNDs and Sub-centre.

MAMATA Yojana

This scheme was launched in the year 2011 and is operational in the state to provide monetary support to the pregnant and lactating women of 19 years of age which enables them to seek improved nutrition and promote health seeking behaviour. The beneficiary will receive a total incentive of Rs. 5,000 in four instalments, subject to the fulfilment of specific conditions. Payment is made by e-transfer from the CDPO to the beneficiary account.

Janani Surksha Yojana (JSY)

JSY is a safe motherhood intervention scheme implemented with the objective of reducing maternal and neonatal mortality by promoting institutional delivery among all pregnant women with provision of cash incentive of Rs. 1400 and Rs.1000 for rural and urban area and Rs. 500 for home delivery cases belonging to BPL category respectively. The payment is made to the beneficiaries through Direct Bank Transfer (DBT) method only.

Janani Sishu Suraksha Karykram (JSSK)

JSSK assures cashless services to pregnant women, post-natal women up to 6 weeks after delivery and sick infants up to one year in government health institutions in both rural and urban areas.

New Born Care Corners (NBCC)

A special corner is established in the labour room of all delivery points with a set of equipment for immediate care of the newborn and Healthcare providers conducting deliveries have been trained in Navjat Sishu Suraksha Karyakram (NSSK) for essential newborn care and resuscitation.

Kangaroo Mother Care (KMC) Units

KMC units have been established in all health facilities with SNCUs for ensuring warmth and early initiation of breastfeeding in low birth weight, preterm hypothermia and other sick newborns.

Findings

It is estimated that about 15 per cent of all pregnancies can develop complications of which five per cent can be life threatening. These complications cannot be predicted but if detected and timely care is provided then maternal deaths and disability can be averted. Further, there are no evidences that antenatal care alone will have considerable impact on reduction of maternal deaths. However, antenatal care is a crucial aspect of birth preparedness and complication readiness where pregnant women can be screened, danger signs can be detected, treated or referred and to ensure that the pregnant woman and her spouse or family members are educated and counselled.

(*Source:* Odisha State Strategy for Accelerated reduction of Maternal and Infant Mortality, 2020).

The Maternal & Infant Mortality rate has been decreased significantly in India due to the innovative schemes adopted by the Government of India through the implementation of family welfare programmes. To improve the accessibility and affordability of quality healthcare especially for those residing in rural areas particularly the poor and vulnerable women and children, the government has launched National Rural Health Mission in 2005.

(*Source:* Maternal Mortality in Orissa: An Epidemiological Study, by MY HEART).

Under the study, attempt was made to collect qualitative information pertaining to maternal mortality, infant mortality and challenges faced by the pregnant women, service providers, ASHAs, ANMs, Anganwadi Workers, and other medical staffs or government staffs etc. Members in the focus group discussions in all the Sub-centre villages were Housewives who actively participated in the process of discussion. In all cases, SHG leaders as well as AWW/ANM moderated the focus group discussion. The findings from each focus group discussion on the present theme have been enumerated below.

Year	Preg-nant	Regist-ered	Child Birth	%	Reason			
					Miscarriage	%	Child Death	%
2017-18	49	48	46	94	2	4	1	2
2018-19	65	65	62	95	1	2	2	3

Data: In the year 2017-18, 49 women were pregnant, 48 were covered under MAMATA Yojana (Government Policy) but 1 could not come under the policy due to under age (below 18). There were only 46 child births and rest 3 were child death. 2 child deaths were due to miscarriage and 1 child death was due to disease.

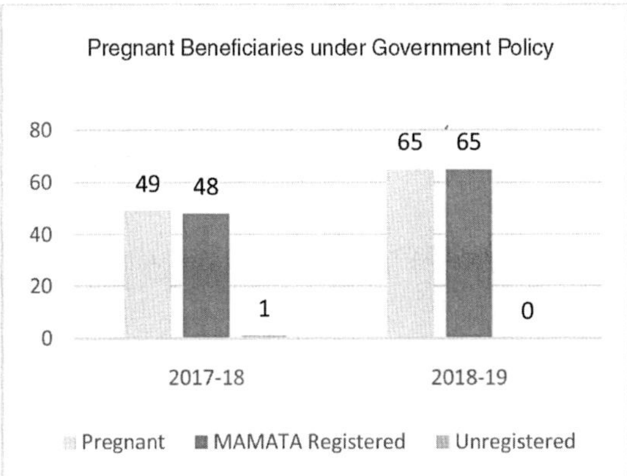

RIN

The State existing Interventions

In the year 2018-19, 65 women were pregnant, all were covered under MAMATA Yojana, but there were only 62 child births and rest 3 were child deaths. 1 was miscarriage and 2 were child deaths due to deficiency of vitamins.

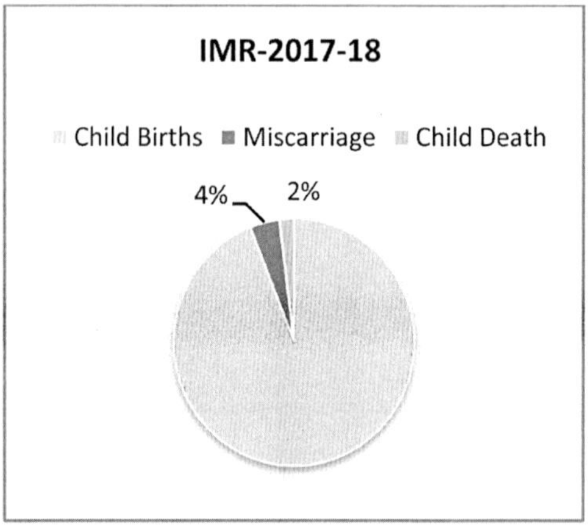

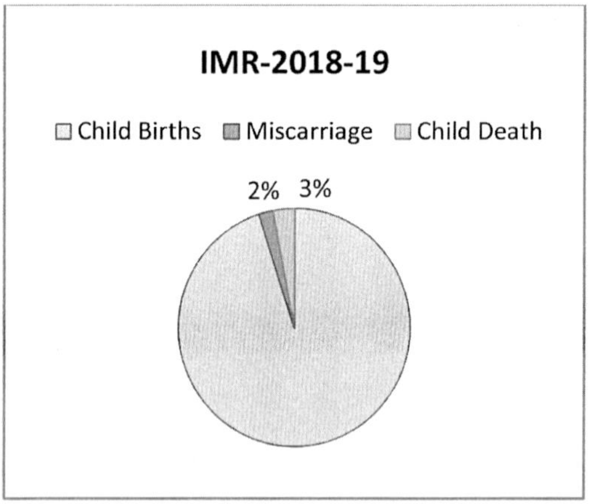

Antenatal Status of Women

Antenatal care generally implies that either a doctor, ANM or any other trained health personnel provides pregnancy related healthcare so as to avoid complication during pregnancy and child birth. Proper and effective counselling is also an integral part of

ANC such as preventive care, diet during pregnancy, delivery and postnatal care. According to guideline envisaged in Reproductive and Child Health Programme, ANC should include at least 3 health check-ups, measurement of weight, height and blood pressure, administration of 2 TT, consumption of IFA tablets and preventive measures for malaria.

Survival Status of Neo Natal

About 58 per cent of newborn were reported to be alive in the post-delivery period whereas only 29 per cent of newborn babies could not survive. It is to mention that many of the health institutions are not properly equipped to provide neo-natal care. On the other hand, there was lack of health education programme on the aspect of effective neo-natal care and a role of service providers towards community.

Concluding Observations

The present empirical study has reflected the gap between policy formulation and policy implementation. The author concludes the chapter with an optimistic viewpoint suggesting measures to remove the loopholes in Maternal and Child Health Care Policies in Odisha.

Suggestions

- There should be increased awareness programme on maternal health and safe motherhood.
- Treatment at right time during pregnancy and sufficient nutritional food intake by PWs should be major responsibility of elderly members in every family including the husband.
- Services and system in sub-divisional medical centres should improve to ensure quality maternal healthcare.

References

Mohan, R., Krishna, D.R., Shiva Kumar, A.K., Chatterjee, M., Sundararaman, T. (2011). *Human Resources for Health in India.* Lancet, 377 (9765), 587e598.

http://dx.doi.org/10.1016/S0140-6736(10)61888-0.

International Institute for Population Sciences (IIPS) and Macro International, 2008. National Family Health Survey (NFHS-3), India, 2005e06: Orissa. IIPS, Mumbai.

International Institute for Population Sciences (IIPS) (2010). District Level Household and Facility Survey (DLHS-3) 2007e08, Orissa, India. IIPS, Mumbai.

Ministry of Health and Family Welfare Government of India—Annual Report 2005-06.

Compendium of Research Projects in RCH (Ministry of Health & Family Welfare, Government of India).

Odisha Economic Survey, 2017-18, Planning and Convergence Department, Government of Odisha.

National Rural Health Mission (2005-2012) Mission Document.

Mapping India's Children—UNICEF in action 2004-2005.

Five year plans—Three volumes (2002-2007) Vol. I, Vol. II and Vol. III.

Mid-term Appraisal of the Tenth Five Year Plan.

10th Plan Strategies for Children.

Journal of Women's Health (An Analysis of the Determinants of Maternal Mortality in Sub-Saharan Africa) October 2004.

Determinants of Maternal Care in a Region of South India, Jagdish C. Bhatia and John Cleland (Institute of Management, Bangalore, Prof. of Medical Demography, Centre for Population Studies London School of Hygiene and Tropical Medicine, London, U.K.

Ministry of Health and Family Welfare Government of India—Annual Report 2005-2006.

National Rural Health Mission—Mission Document, Ministry of Health & Family Welfare, Government of India.

Compendium of Research Projects in RCH (Ministry of Health & Family Welfare, Government of India).

10

Food Security among the Socially Excluded Communities in India

Policy Options

Arun Kumar Nayak and *Padmalaya Mahapatra*

Introduction

Food is mankind's most essential need. Therefore, adequate production and even distribution of food have become a high priority global concern. More so, food plays a very vital role in maintaining proper health and also helps in the prevention and cure of diseases. A well-balanced, nutritive and correct diet is consequently most important for the maintenance of good health and the healing of diseases. Food meets physical, emotional, social, and physiological needs as well. The physiological need is the first and foremost important need emphasized by Maslow's Theory of Hierarchy of Needs (1943). A human cannot focus on other issues until the physical need has been addressed, for which food is the most essential and fundamental requirement for human existence. Hunger is the physical need for food and it is usually understood to refer to the distress associated with lack of food (IFPRI, 2014). Different types and forms of foods are needed for physical, mental, and social wellness. Therefore, food helps in maintaining the wellness of different forms and kinds. Experts believed that the food habits and food choices of individuals are mostly influenced by many factors such as social, cultural, religious, family, friends, and mass media. But at the macro level, the factors that affect the food supply are agriculture, environment, government policy, economics, technology etc. The global food scenario shows that there has been a continuous increase in food production, yet many people in developing countries are living with hunger, malnutrition, and poverty, which are the ultimate results of food insecurity. These arguments throw light on "chronic food insecurity" (continuously inadequate diet caused by the inability to acquire food) and "transitory food insecurity" (a temporary decline in a household's access to enough food). The former is caused by poverty and the latter is due to a sudden shortfall of food as in the case of drought, floods, or other natural or man-made calamities. Food insecurity is not primarily the result of a global shortage of food. Instead, the poor lack the income to purchase available food supplies. Reducing food insecurity and enabling food security is a primary duty of the global governments not only for the sake of present generations but also for future generations too.

Social exclusion and inclusion have been the most challenging issue of the contemporary world. In India, certain communities such as Scheduled Castes, Scheduled Tribes, and religious minorities experience systematic exclusion in the matter of taking advantage of development. Social Exclusion is a multidimensional concept. Marginalization of certain groups is a major problem in developing countries like India, where their counterparts enjoy considerable economic and social opportunities. Some social groups are struggling to fulfil their basic necessity of life, particularly, food. Despite significant consideration, investment, and participation to cope with these challenges, the results are not still at a satisfactory level. As per the reports, the gap between richer and poorer is continued to be widened. The societies of the developing countries are still heavily engaged in disparity and discrimination based on religion, race, caste, class, and ethnicity.

At the same time, every country in this world essentially has to be food to feed its population. India is one of the fastest-growing countries in the world, in terms of GDP and purchasing power. At the same time, India, with the second-largest population in the world, has been struggling to secure food for all irrespective of their socio-economic status. The country has many differences in almost every respect. Social diversity, economic differences, regional differences, rural-urban divide are different forms of differences that one could notice in India. Of all differences, the social and economic differences are found to have influenced each other in the same direction. Those who are socially backward are found to be economically backward too. As such, socially backward families undergo more economic stress in almost all walks of economic life. Food insecurity is not an exception to this.

Despite achieving self-sufficiency in food production, the problem of chronic hunger and malnourishment remains at a very high level. National Family Health Survey-5 (2019-20), indicates a decline in the nutritional status of children less than five years between 2015-16 and 2019-20. The Government of India has been implementing the largest food intervention programme called Public Distribution System (PDS) through which primarily food grains are distributed at a subsidized rate to all eligible households. The eligible households are given ration cards to buy fixed rations of food grains. Before 1997, a universal system of PDS was implemented and food grains were made available to all registered households in the rural and urban areas. But, the introduction of TPDS under the National Food Security Act, 2013 with dual pricing since then has run into serious problems with the exclusion of eligible/deserving households and inclusion of non-eligible households (Kannan, 2012).

Food Security as a Human Right

Food insecurity is one of the major problems faced by mankind in the world. This issue has been widely discussed at the international, national, regional, and local levels. Thus, food security is considered as one of the human rights, and, it is incorporated in the national and international laws that ensure the right to food. It is a well-known fact that food plays a crucial for the growth of human development and it is reiterated by the UN's one of the Millennium Development Goals (MDGs), viz. "Eradicate poverty and hunger", by 2015 and subsequently it is focused on the Sustainable Development Goals (SDGs) to be achieved by 2030. The right to adequate food is realized when each and every man, woman, and child have physical and economic access at all times to adequate food or means for its procurement. The term "Right to Adequate Food" is derived from the International Covenant on Economic, Social, and Cultural Rights (ICESCR, 1948). The right to adequate food may be defined as: "to have regular, permanent and unrestricted access, either directly or using financial purchases, to quantitatively and qualitatively adequate and sufficient food corresponding to the cultural traditions of people to which the consumer belongs, and which ensures a physical and mental, individual and collective fulfilling and dignified life free of fear."

The human right to adequate food recognizes for each human being a human rights standard, containing the following elements: (i) food is adequate in terms of nutritional quantity and quality, safe from adverse alien substances, and culturally acceptable in the context of the prevailing food patterns; (ii) food procurement is possible for all without conflicting with the satisfaction of other material and non-material basic needs; (iii) Access to food is sustainable overtime, and (iv) access to food is possible in human dignity. The States' obligations under the right to adequate food coincide largely with those under the right to an adequate standard of living.

The right to freedom from hunger is termed by Article 11.2 of the International Covenant on Economic, Social and Cultural Rights "a fundamental right." Governments are requested to take "appropriate steps" to ensure this right. According to the covenant, States have to improve methods of production, conservation, and distribution of food including specific programmes like developing or reforming agrarian systems (Kunnemann, 1999). The right to enough and assured food to live an active and healthy life with dignity is in principle also an essential component of the fundamental right to life, because life itself is impossible without food (Mander, 2012).

The right to food is about freedom from hunger. The right to food can be understood, as the right to have two square meals a day throughout the year. The right to food (i.e. to be free from under-nutrition) then links with a wide range of entitlements, not only to food itself but also to other requirements of good nutrition such as clean water, healthcare, and even elementary education. For this reason, on 28 November, 2001, the Supreme Court of India passed a significant "interim order" about eight nutrition-related programmes. These are Targeted Public Distribution System (TPDS), Antyodaya Anna Yojana (AAY), Mid Day Meal Scheme (MDMS), NOAPS, Annapurna Scheme (AS), Integrated Child Development Scheme (ICDS), National Maternity Benefit Scheme (NMBS), and National Family Benefit Scheme (NFBS). In brief, the interim order has three significant components: (i) it converts the benefits of these nutrition-related programmes into legal entitlements; (ii) it directs the State and Central Governments to adopt specific measures to ensure public awareness and transparency of the programmes, and (iii) it directs all State Governments to introduce cooked mid-day meals in primary schools within six months (Dreze, 2003).

Background of Food Security

The historical World Food Summit was held in Rome in 1996, in which 185 countries participated and signed the 'Rome Declaration on World Food Security.' The Rome Declaration reaffirmed the right of everyone to have access to safe and nutritious food. Consequently, the right to adequate food is recognized as a fundamental human right.

The world communities further pledged in 2000 to cut the number of the world's hungry people to half between 1990 and

2015, as one of the MDGs (UNDP, 2008). The Nobel Laureate Amartya Sen (1981) has suggested a framework of food entitlement to understand the genesis of hunger and the access to food. According to him, own production, stored wealth, employment, kinship, and government transfers are all possible sources of food entitlement. The concept of food security has been evolving in many ways and diversified since the first world conference in 1974. There are close to 200 different definitions for the concept of food security. The World Development Report (1986) defined food security as "access all people at all times to enough food for an active, healthy life." Hindle (1990) says that food security is an outcome, but it is more importantly an approach to development thinking. It is an organizing principle. Effective food security analysis should direct the government to put in place those policies, investments, and institutions dividing efforts that are consistent with the long-term reduction of food insecurity. Inter American Network for Agriculture and Democracy explains that food security is a fundamental human right; nutritional security is an internal part of food security (access to food is not enough if the nutritional quality is poor; food security must be compatible with resource sustainability and must be based on agriculture which preserves biodiversity and natural resources and the responsibility for food security must be shared by government and society as a whole. According to the FAO, food security refers to the availability of food at all times; the accessibility of food to everyone. The availability of the adequate nutritional quality of food, in terms of quantity, quality and variety, and cultural acceptability of the food to the population. Thus, the basic objectives of food security are: (i) ensuring production of adequate food supplies; (ii) maximum stability in the flow of supplies; and (iii) security access to available supplies on the part of those who need them or in other words production, availability, and access.

John Bongaarts in his article on "population pressure and food supply system in the developing world" has brought out the factors that determine the food security of any nation and they are: (i) proportion of potentially arable land used for growing crops; (ii) cropping frequency; (iii) proportion of the harvested area used for production of food crops; (iv) average crop yield; (v) trade multiplier; the proportion of domestic use for direct human consumption; and (vi) animal product multiplier. Therefore, it is concluded that food security is exactly kind of multi-spectral and multilayered topic, which needs global governmental intervention to tackle food insecurity. The most common and useful definition was given by the United Nations of the Food and Agriculture Organization, Rome in 2005. Food security as defined "exists when all people, at all times, have physical, social and economic access to sufficient, safe and nutritious food that meets their dietary needs and food preference for an active and healthy life." Household food security is the application of this concept to the family level, with individuals within households as the focus of concern (FAO, 2005). From the mentioned definitions, food security can be understood that availability, accessibility, and affordability of food to all people at all times in the country.

Concept and Dynamics of Social Exclusion

Social exclusion is a multidimensional concept. It relates to the alienation or disenfranchisement of certain people within a society. It may be an exclusion based on caste, religion, region, race, geographic location, class structure, personal habits, appearance etc. The concept of social exclusion is seen as covering a remarkably wide range of social and economic problems. Even in the practical context of identifying "the excluded" in France, Rene Lenoir, as secretaire d'Etatal's Action Social of the French government, spoke of the following as constituting the "excluded"—a tenth- of the French population: Mentally and physically handicapped, suicidal people, aged invalids, abused children, substance abusers delinquents, single parents, multi-problem households, marginal, asocial persons, and other social "misfits" (Sen, 2000). Indicators of social exclusion on the level of the nation-state or demos will measure the inaccessibility of rights and services to those who by definition of citizenship should have access to them.

Social exclusion means the inaccessibility, ignorance, or inability to receive those services which are available as a right as defined by the State. It also includes being discriminated which prevents access to those services (Yitzhak *et al.,* 2000). There are groups of people in all societies who are disadvantaged because they are discriminated against. Discrimination occurs in public institutions, such as the legal system or the education and health services, as well as in the household and the community.

The concept of Social Exclusion has multidimensional connotation."Social exclusion describes a process by which certain groups are systematically disadvantaged because they are discriminated against based on their ethnicity, race, religion, sexual orientation, caste, descent, gender, age, disability, HIV status, migrant status or where they live. Discrimination occurs in public institutions, such as the legal system or education and health services, as well as social institutions like the household" DFID (2005).

The Constitution of India and legal framework recognize the principle of non-discrimination and equal opportunity to all, irrespective of caste, race, religion, colour, sex, ethnicity etc. Despite several promises put forth by the Constitution, various forms of discrimination continue to persist in Indian society because the constitutional remedy is often inaccessible to the SCs, STs, and religious minorities, literally taking away the equal quotient eligible to them. Sachar Committee (2006), report of Indian government shows the intensity of exclusion towards Muslims in India in the fields of education, health, employment, and banking credit (Ziyauddin *et al.,* 2009).

The term social exclusion is multidimensional although its Western use is selective and confines to markets promoting equality separate it from the Indian emphasis on social justice as linked to ending discrimination of *Dalit* groups. The concept of social exclusion is inherently problematic as it faces three major challenges in India: (i) relates to the historical discrimination of certain groups and their exclusion; (ii) political economy of the excluded, and (iii) questions how equality responses are restricted within the framework of social exclusion.

Socially Excluded Groups in India

Anthropological Survey of India (ASI), has identified 2800 castes including 450 SCs, 461 STs, and 766 OBCs. All major assets of production are owned by the upper caste and the lower strata of the society, particularly the depressed classes (SCs/STs) are the section of people without assets. The unequal distribution of wealth compels the depressed classes to depend on the upper classes for their survival. This is the main reason for socio-economic exploitation and exclusion. In the socially excluded sections of the society are SCs/STs, called *Dalit*. Generally, SCs/STs are working in the unorganized sector and their socio-economic conditions are miserable as pointed out in various commissions' reports appointed by the Government of India. It has been found that though India is on the path of high economic growth, several people live below the poverty line. It is a matter of disappointment that still 79.0 per cent of unorganized workers, 88.0 per cent of SCs/STs population, 80.0 per cent of OBCs, and 84.0 per cent of Muslims belong to the poor and vulnerable group.

They are living in social insecurity, unsanitary environment, and excruciating conditions (Adhikary *et al.*, 2013).

India Exclusion Report (2013-14) says "education, urban housing, decent work in the labour market and legal justice about anti-terror legislations are very diverse, the dominant and striking finding from the report is that for these public goods the groups being most severely and consistently excluded are almost always the same: women, *Dalits*, *Adivasis*, Muslims and persons with disabilities. Members of these groups tend to be either excluded completely from access to these public goods or excluded on unequal and discriminatory terms compared to other sections of society."

Social Exclusion and Economic Development Process

The differing nature of social exclusion needs a different framework of analysis to inquire into the situation of excluded groups, their causes and forces, thereby addressing the issues of "exclusion from what", as well as "exclusion by what" and "by whom." Exclusion carries different patterns, for some it may be excluded from land, for others exclusion from secured jobs, and for some exclusion from opportunities to develop skills, all these patterns are linked to the process of development like as: (i) exclusion from goods and services, (ii) lab or market exclusions, (iii) exclusion from land; (iv) exclusion from security; and (v) exclusion from human rights. The central aspect of any analysis of exclusion is the idea that it is embedded in the ways societies function. Differences in the development paths and macro-economic and structural adjustment strategies imply some kind of social exclusion. Similar aggregate economic development may lead to quite different patterns of income inequality, quite different patterns of distribution of the benefits of the growth. In this, the institutional arrangements which mediate between economic and social development are crucial. They may include or exclude, limit gains to a few sectors or groups or spread advantage widely.

Landlessness and Social Exclusion

The land is one of the factors for the production and livelihood of poor people. According to Amartya Sen (2000) in his working paper "landlessness is similarly an instrumental deprivation. A family without land in a peasant society may be deeply handicapped. Of course, given the age-old value system in peasant societies, landlessness can also have to constitute importance in a world that values a family's special relationship with its land: to be without land may be seem like being without a limb of one's own. But whether or not a family attaches direct value to its relationship with its "own land", landlessness can also help to generate economic and social deprivation. India has had a long history of social discrimination, closely linked with denial of access to land. Specific land tenure systems prevailing at the time of independence also created their own set of problems. The deteriorating quality of land records administration over the last four decades has compounded the hardships of the poor. And in the recent past, the drive to acquire land for development has posed fresh challenges, most especially for the STs. The last few years have witnessed several new government initiatives, including the Hindu Succession (Amendment) Act, 2005 and the STs and Other Traditional Forest Dwellers (Recognition of Forest Rights) Act, 2006, which are a response to both historical injustices and recent challenges (GoI, 2012).

Marginalized people who are not given access to land, pastures, or fishing grounds lack access to food because they cannot produce enough on their marginal resource base. Hunger and malnutrition today are not a question of food availability, but of poverty: lacking access to food or food-producing resources (Kunnemann, 1999).

Linkages between Food Deprivation, Poverty and Social Exclusion

There is an interlinkages between food deprivation, poverty and social exclusion. High-income families can be spending more money on their daily life activities. They can spend more money on food, health, and education. But low-income families mostly depend on causal work. Especially, during the unemployment period, access to food is more challenging for the poor. Biradar (2012) pointed out why do SCs/STs experience a greater incidence of poverty due to: (i) lack of productive assets; (ii) lack of human capital; (iii) casualization of employment; (iv) limited occupational mobility; and (v) high degree of underemployment.

Poverty and Food Insecurity

There is a close link between poverty and food security. Poverty can involve not only the lack of the necessities of material well-being but the denial of opportunities for living a tolerable life. Life can be prematurely shortened. It can be made difficult, painful, or hazardous. It can be deprived of knowledge and communication. It can be robbed of dignity, confidence, and self-respect—as well as the respect of others. One of the educators from Colombia said "Poverty is criminal because it does not allow people to be people. It is the cruelest denial of all of us as human beings" (HDR, 1997). Income is the main desiring factor for purchasing power. Low-income families cannot purchase nutritious food in the open market. In this situation, landless households, unorganized sector labourers, SCs, STs, Women headed households were systematically excluded from the market economy.

Food Security and Sustainable Development

Physically and mentally healthy people are the real wealth of a nation. The basic objective of development is to create an enabling environment for people to enjoy long, healthy and creative lives. Here, purchasing power is one of the important factors for food security, because, it is related to jobs or livelihood opportunities. It is evident that even if the availability and access are satisfactory, the absorption of food in the body seems to be poor and littler elated to the consumption of clean drinking water as well as environmental hygiene, primary healthcare, and primary education, because of poverty.

Even if physical and economic access to food is assured, ecological factors determine the long-term sustainability of the food security system (Swaminathan, 2010).

The food insecurity atlas of M.S. Swaminathan Research Foundation & World Food Programme (2008) reveals that every State in the country has its strengths and weaknesses about the five major dimensions, viz. (i) availability of food, which is a function of production, access to food and they are related to the purchasing power; (ii) absorption of food in the body, which is determined by the availability of safe drinking water, environmental hygiene, primary healthcare, and primary education; (iii) vulnerability to transitory hunger, which is related to natural and man-made calamities and disasters; and (iv) sustainability of production, which is influenced by the extent of attention given to the ecological foundation essential for sustained advances in production. Further, the Atlas exhibits that non-food factors, like livelihood and income-earning opportunities, healthcare facilities, education, sanitation, and environmental hygiene are as important for food security at the individual level, availability of food grains at the market level, and access to clean drinking water at the societal level.

Policy Options for Achieving Food Security

To improve Food Security "a wide range of alternative policies can be pursued; there is not just one general, an optimal set of policies for improving food security. Characteristics of the food security problem and institutional capabilities need to be considered when making policy choices, as much economic and fiscal cost of desired actions.

It is possible in principle to distinguish two contrasting approaches to the removal of food insecurity. "One approach is to promote economic growth and take the best possible advantage of the potentialities released by greater general affluence, including not only an expansion of private incomes but also an improved basis for public support. Another alternative is to resort directly to wide-ranging public support in domains such as employment provision, income redistribution, healthcare, education, and social assistance to remove destitution without waiting for a transformation in the level of general affluence. The two approaches are connected, especially in the long run (Von Braun, 1992). Production-oriented programmes that aim to increase food production on the production of crops for sale or both can have favourable effects on food security if they increase or stabilize the real incomes of the people facing food insecurity. Growth in food supplied can have dual effects on food security by reducing food prices, which benefits food purchasing households in rural and urban areas, and depending on the nature of growth by promoting employment. As the incomes of poor households increase, their absolute expenditure on food consumption also increases, although the relative share tends to decrease (Von Braun, 1992). Besides policies and programmes oriented towards agricultural production, other programmes for generation and diversification of employment and income can reduce risks for food-insecure households. These programmes differ from programmes oriented towards food production. This type of programme is used to stimulate or stabilize demand for food but may not directly expand the food supply simultaneously. They include labour-intensive public work for food security and credit to the poor for consumption stabilization and self-employment.

Labor-intensive Public Works programmes can address, simultaneously, three central problems facing many low-income countries today—food insecurity, growing unemployment, and poor infrastructure (Dreze and Sen, 1989; Von Braun, Teklu, and Webb, 1992; IFPRI/BIDS, 1989). They are in general public programmes that provide employment and generate public goods such as physical and social infrastructure. Labour intensive public works go a long way towards direct and sustainable poverty alleviation and strengthening of self-help capacities. Food income transfers (food subsidies) are a widely used means of alleviating food insecurity. Policies intended to encourage growth in food production were expected to involve incentives to producers such as high prices for food and improved technology to lower production costs. Such policies would benefit many in the agricultural sector.

Conclusion

Achieving sustainable food security for all will depend on policy action and institutions that address the causes of food insecurity, malnutrition, and unsustainable management of natural resources within the context of the driving forces. Rapid pro-poor economic growth together with the empowerment of the poor and effective provision of public goods will be the backbones of any successful attempt to achieve sustainable food security for all. Policies and institutions should be designed and implanted to guide economic growth and public goods creation for the benefit of low-income people, and the excluded communities must be empowered through human resource development, access to productive resources, and participatory political systems.

Policies and institutions should facilitate effective contribution by civil society, including farmers' associations and local and national non-governmental organizations (NGOs). Socially excluded groups, such as, SC, ST, Minorities, Women etc., should be empowered to gain access to resources and decision-making processes, and social and cultural institutions and practices that prevent women from reaching their full potential should be reformed. Governments must assure that markets are not biased against small farmers, less-favoured areas, or poor consumers. The rural poor must have secure access to land and other productive resources and employment. Policies and institutions are needed to facilitate the access by poor rural families to inputs and appropriate technologies as well as non-farm employment.

So, within this changing environment, following steps should be followed to ensure food security. To begin with, rapid economic growth is essential for achieving sustainable food security for all by 2030. The challenge is to achieve that growth in a way that benefits the poor, that is, pro-poor economic growth. This kind of growth, together with the empowerment of the poor and effective provision of public goods, will be the foundation for addressing the problem of food insecurity among the excluded communities in India.

References

Journals

Adhikari, D. (2013). "Health and Human Security." *Human Security in Nepal: Concepts, Issues and Challenges*, *5*(2.9), 119.

Agarwal, B. (2018). "Gender equality, food security and the sustainable development goals." *Current opinion in environmental sustainability*, *34*, 26-32.

B.K., M.B. *Dynamics of Social Exclusion/Inclusion: Impact on Food Security.*

Boraiah, G.B. (2016). "Social Security—A Tool for Social Inclusion." *International Journal in Management & Social Science*, *4*(9), 115-121.

Campbell, B.M., Vermeulen, S.J., Aggarwal, P.K., Corner-Dolloff, C., Girvetz, E., Loboguerrero, A.M. & Wollenberg, E. (2016). "Reducing risks to food security from climate change." *Global Food Security, 11*, 34-43.

Dev, S.M. & Sharma, A.N. (2010). *Food Security in India: Performance, Challenges and Policies.*

DFID (2005): Reducing poverty by tackling social exclusion : A DFID Policy Paper, published by the Department For International Development, September.

Dreze, J. & Goyal, A. (2003). "Future of mid-day meals." *Economic and Political Weekly*, 4673-4683.

Drèze, J. & Sen, A. (1991). *Public Action for Social Security: Foundations and Strategy*, pp. 3-40, Oxford University Press.

EC-FAO (2007): Food Security information for Action Programme, Distance Learning to support Capacity Building and Training for National and Local Food Security Information Systems and Networks.

Eide, A. (1998). "The human right to adequate food and freedom from hunger." *FAO (1998). The Right to Food in Theory and Practice.* Rome: Food and Agriculture Organization of the United Nations, 1-5.

FAO (2009). *The State of Food Insecurity in the World—Economic Crisis—Impacts and Lessons Learned*, Rome.

Gurung, Y.B. (2008). "Migration from Rural Nepal. A Social Exclusion Framework." *Migration, 8*, 1-2012.

Hindle, R.E. (1990). "The World Bank approach to food security analysis." *IDS Bulletin, 21*(3), 62-66.

http://www.righttofood.org/new/html/WhatRighttofood.html

Huyer, S., Ouedraogo, M. & Chanana, N. (2021). *Overview of gender and social inclusion activities in AICCRA.*

Jha, M.K. (2009). "Food security in perspective: The significance of social action." *Community Development Journal, 44*(3), 351-366.

Kannan, E. (2012). "Rapporteur's Report on Food and Nutrition Security: Failure and Governance." *Indian Journal of Agricultural Economics, 67*(902-2016-67845).

Karan, R., DeLeon, T., Biradar, H. & Subudhi, P.K. (2012). "Salt stress induced variation in DNA methylation pattern and its influence on gene expression in contrasting rice genotypes." *PloSone, 7*(6), e40203.

Kompier, C., Prasad, A., Sajjad, H., Premchander, S., Katyar, S., Saheb, D. & Taware, S. (2013). "Labour Markets: Exclusion from decent work." *India Exclusion Report: 2013, 14*, 121-162.

Künnemann, R. (1999). *The Road to Freedom.*

Mander, H. (2012). "Food from the courts: the Indian experience." *IDS Bulletin, 43*, 15-24.

Martin, J.L. & Itzhak, Y. (2000). "7-Nitroindazole blocks nicotine-induced conditioned place preference but not LiCl-induced conditioned place aversion." *Neuro report, 11*(5), 947-949.

Maslow, A.H. (1943). "A theory of human motivation." *Psychological Review, 50*(4), 370.

Mittal, S. & Sethi, D. (2009). "Food Security in South Asia: Issues and Opportunities", No. 240. *Working Paper.*

Ruminska-Zimny, E. (1997). *Human poverty in transition economies: Regional overview for HDR 1997.* New York: Human Development Report Office, United Nations Development Programme.

Sachar, R. (2006). *Sachar Committee Report.* Government of India.

Sarangi, T.K. (2013). "Legalising Rights through Implementation of Forest Rights Act, 2006." *A Critical Review on Odisha and Jharkhand.*

Sen, A. (1981). "Ingredients of famine analysis: availability and entitlements." *The Quarterly Journal of Economics, 96*(3), 433-464.

Sen, A. (2000). *Social exclusion: Concept, application and scrutiny.*

Swaminathan, M. (2008). "Report on the state of food insecurity in rural India." *M.S. Swaminathan Research Foundation.*

Swaminathan, M.S. (2010). "Achieving food security in times of crisis." *New Biotechnology, 27*(5), 453-460.

Von Braun, J. (Ed.). (1992). *Improving Food Security of the Poor: Concept, Policy, and Programmes.* Intl Food Policy Res Inst.

Books

Das, M.B. & Mehta, S.K. (2012). *Poverty and social exclusion in India.*

Nathan, D. & Xaxa, V. (2012). *Social exclusion and adverse inclusion: Development and deprivation of Adivasis in India.* Oxford University Press.

Percy-Smith, J. (2000). *Policy Responses to Social Exclusion: Towards Inclusion?* Mcgraw-Hill Education (UK).

Ramaswamy, S. & Surulivel, L. (2019). *Food Security in India.* MJP Publisher.

Smith, D.M. & Smith, D.M. (2005). *On the margins of inclusion: Changing Labour Markets and Social Exclusion in London.* Policy Press.

11

Swachh Bharat Mission in Rajasthan

A Case Study of Chirawa Block in Jhunjhunu District

Cheruku Jeevan Kumar and *Rahul Kumar*

Introduction

Sanitation is a widely discussed and debated topic of policy in India. The Government of India launched Swachh Bharat Mission (SBM) under the leadership of Prime Minister Narendra Modi on October 2, 2014, on the occasion of the birth anniversary of Mahatma Gandhi. SBM is a mission that exclusively focuses on sanitation and cleanliness. The task aims to make India clean by October 2, 2019. SBM includes constructing toilets, solid and liquid waste disposal systems, and provision of safe and adequate drinking water supply to every family from the countryside to metropolitan cities (MDW&S 1). The driving features of SBM-Grameen are the elimination of open defecation (OD), providing subsidies for the constructionof individual households latrines (IHHLs), changing the behaviour of individuals and triggering the community to adopt practice sanitation and personal hygiene.

Implementation of SBM completed five years of its performance. During the 2014-2019 periods, there was a shift in monitoring, from looking for behaviour change to simply counting toilets. It has brought pressure on the village panchayats to reach the target date for announcing ODF status (October 2019). And the credibility of ODF declarations is questioned within the government, with the government reporting only that the village councils (Gram Panchayats) had declared themselves ODF (Mehrotra, 2021).

Literature Review

Sanitation denotes a comprehensive conceptual framework of a clean home, community, institutions for better health and a safe environment. Sanitation can be defined broadly as safe disposal of human waste, wastewater management, solid waste management, water supply, controlling vector-prone diseases, household and personal hygiene, and hygiene maintenance in food and housing. Moreover, safe, sanitary practice and personal hygiene are crucial indicators for qualifying improvement in living standards.

World Health Organisation (WHO) defines sanitation as "the provision of facilities and services for the safe disposal of human urine and faeces and literal meaning of word 'sanitation' also refers to the maintenance of hygienic conditions, through services such as garbage collection and wastewater disposal."

India cannot reach actual development if a significant proportion of the population lives in an unhygienic and unclean surroundings environment due to lack of access to hygiene and sanitation facilities. Hygiene and sanitation facilities have many repercussions for an extended period. There is a direct link between hygiene, sanitation, health and human well-being. Consumption of contaminated drinking water, improper disposal of human excreta, improper disposal of solid and liquid waste and lack of personal and household hygiene have been causing to birth and spread of diseases in India. It is estimated that around 30 million people suffer from illnesses related to it.

After independence, India has a considerable development in different areas of social and economic justice through poverty alleviation programme, rights to education, the guarantee of employment, abundance production in the agriculture sector, ample rising in Per Capita Income, technological developments but relative negligence of general discourse on the sanitation policies and laws could have adverse impacts on other dynamics of socio-economic policies like a burden on social health, finance, and poverty in society.

In the last couple of decades, policies discourse and policies developed at the international and national levels through Millennium Development Goals (MDGs), Total Sanitation Campaign (TSC) lead to new progress in sanitation. It also increased the attention of policymakers and the ordinary person to give more importance to sanitation as a separate field of legislation. WHO (WHO and UNICEF, 19-22) reported data shows that there is 79.2 crore (792 million) population pressed to live without access to toilet facilities or improved sanitation facilities whereas 59.7 crore (597 million) population practice open defecation in India.

According to Jacob Burckhardt (Burckhardt 315), "Cleanliness is an indispensable part of the modern notion of social perfection." Sanitation and cleanliness are the ideal contributing factors in human life after health and beauty. This is a virtue and divine quality of life that must practice by the human. Sanitation as an awareness programme began in the 1960s in different parts of the world as part of the environmental revolution. Later in the 1980s, it became a full-fledged condition of sustainable development (World Commission on Environment and Development). It also has relation to physical well-being and a healthy environment that constitutes socio-cultural and ecological dimensions.

The national figure Mahatma Gandhi once said, "Sanitation is more important part than independence." So, he made sanitation and cleanliness an integral part of the breathing pattern. He had the dream of 'total sanitation for all.' He emphasized cleanliness as the essential part of the physical well-being and sustainable ecology and environment. David Strachan, Professor of London University, put forth the 'Hygiene Hypothesis' (Strachman, 1259-60). According to this hypothesis, environmental microbes play crucial roles in developing the immune system and environmental cleanliness.

In India, the practice of Open Defecation in children is ingrained during their early childhood by their parents or relatives and accepts it as a persisted norm of daily life. Society does not accept the construction of toilets as their primary responsibility. The construction of toilets is still treated as a function of government. The disposal of human excreta is one of the most significant central issues of sanitation and cleanliness. As we know, that human being is an extensive reservoir of diseases that can destroy his health and incapacitate. Open disposal of an unhealthy and sick human excreta leads to the burden of disease on human civilization. The human faeces of an ill person are the first source of the infection. It carries the disease agents who lead the transmission of the disease through various hosts like water, soil, food and, hand and fingers etc. Figure 11.1 shows how the open disposal of human excreta leads to a cause of different illnesses, and UNICEF defines vector prone disease as the disease transmission cycle.

Channels of transmission of Disease from Excreta

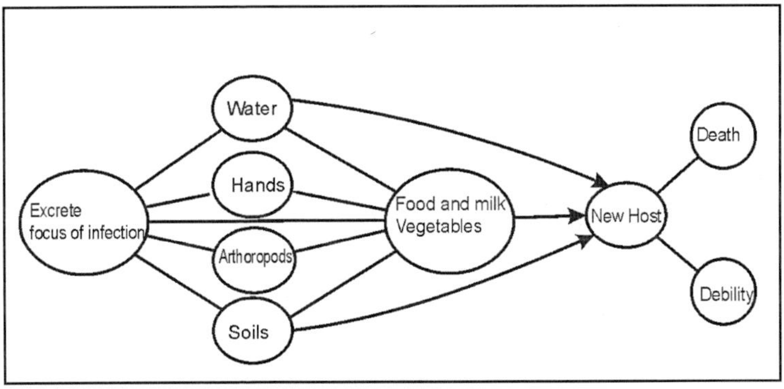

Fig. 11.1: Disease transmission route

Source: Peace Corps.

The cycle of disease transmission can be solved by providing the facility of sanitation and toilets at the community and households level and personal hygiene. In the absence of the causative agents, the chances of spreading diseases will be reduced, and the new host of illnesses will become lesser.

World Health Organization defines "sanitation as the maintenance of hygienic conditions, through services such as garbage collection and wastewater disposal" (WHO, 2015).

In the post-Independence period, sanitation has become more grievous with an uncontrolled increase of population and development of industrial growth. Poor sanitation affects freshwater resources, besides causing waterborne diseases like diarrhoea, cholera, polio, jaundice, viral fevers, dysenteries, hepatitis, typhoid etc. The Government of India made efforts to address sanitation and open defecation, particularly in rural areas. Accordingly, it has put up thousands of crore rupees in the rural water supply and sanitation sector since the First Five-year Plan. The campaign like 'Swachhta Pakhawara' at the national level, with the involvement of institutions like the educational institution, corporate social responsibility has accelerated the pace of sanitation. However, the outcome and achievements of SBM is not very effective.

Research Problem

Sanitation and cleanliness is the central problem in rural areas of the country. For instance, 52.1 per cent of the population in rural India practice open defecation. In Rajasthan, 62.7 per cent of the population practice open defecation (Swachhta Status Report, GoI, 2016). According to NSSO Report, 45.3 per cent of households in India have sanitary toilets, whereas, in Rajasthan, it is limited to 38 per cent only (NSSO, 2016: 67). In contrast to this, a report by MDWS revealed that Rajasthan has 99.71 per cent of households had a restroom. 24 out of 33 districts have been declared open defecation free (ODF) in Rajasthan, and 93.60 per cent of villages have been declared ODF (MDW&S, 2017).

Since October 2, 2014, SBM—Gramin began to be implemented in both Gram Panchayats of Chiwara Block of Jhunjhunu District, in Rajasthan, i.e. Kithana and Mohanpura. In the last two decades, all the programmes related to rural sanitation and rural development have been implemented in Gram Panchayats. Both Gram Panchayats worked on Total Sanitation

Campaign in 1998. In 2007-08, they were honoured by Nirmal Gram Puruskar. In 2012, the Nirmal Gram Abhiyan (NBA) was enacted in both villages with the help of MGNREGA. The researchers chose to investigate rural sanitation in these panchayats, precisely the prevalent behaviour of open defecation. The study assesses the impact of the Swachh Bharat Mission in addressing the problem of open defecation and individual's accessibility of toilets in rural areas.

Research Methods

Population

The researchers chose two villages (Kithana and Bhamarwasi) from Kithana and Mohanpura Gram Panchayats in Chiwara Block of Jhunjhunu District, Rajasthan. These villages constitute 1002 households with a population of around 5442. These households' members are permanent residents, out of which many were the direct beneficiaries of Individual Households Latrine (IHHL) schemes and participated in SBM-G programme. Researchers adopted random sampling. Sample was drawn from Kithana and Bhamarwasi. The sample size is 10 per cent of total households of both Gram Panchayats, i.e. 100 households. Respondents are distributed into two categories: individual member and household members; and Panchayat Raj Institutions officials.

Sample Size

Geography	Sample Size
Kithana	52 Households
Bhamarwasi	48 Households

Data Collection Methods

Primary data were collected through Interviews from officials and individual Household respondents, Gram Sevak and Paden Sachiv (new nomenclature of Village Development Officer) at GP level. The researchers adopted participatory observation.

Secondary data were collected from books, journals articles, reports published by departments and agencies of government and non-government bodies, and the internet.

Results and Discussion

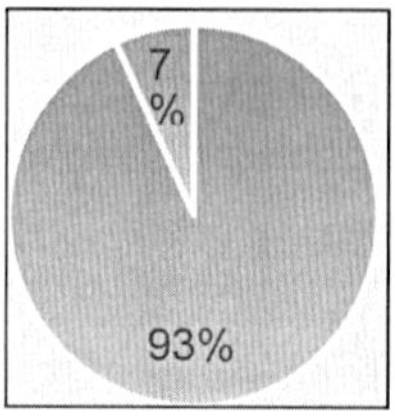

Fig. 11.2: Availability of and Accessibility to Toilets

Fig. 11.2 suggests that 93 per cent of households have access to toilets. The remaining seven per cent of households lack either own toilets or lack access to toilets. It can be inferred that a considerable number of families in both GPs have toilets and accessed toilet facilities.

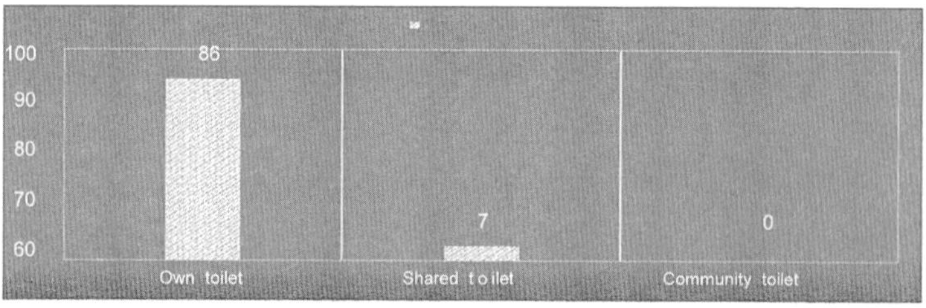

Fig. 11.3: Type of Toilets.

During the field visit, the researchers tried to understand the types of toilet facilities available to the respondents. Fig. 11.3 suggests three different types of toilets: own toilets within house premise shared toilets, and community toilets. 86 households have their toilet facilities within the premises. 7 per cent of homes are using shared toilet facilities. It is to be noted that respondents relatively have more freedom to access toilets.

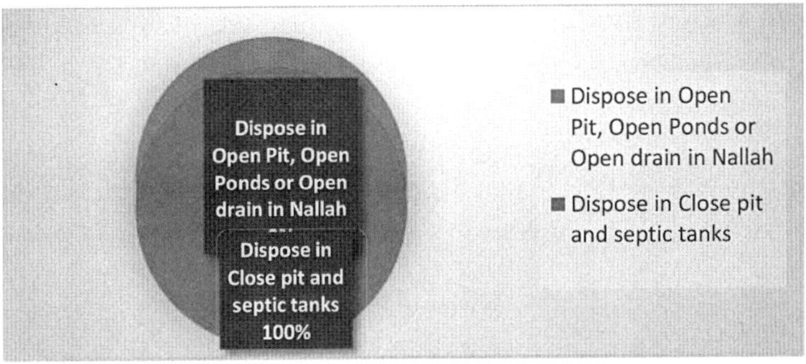

Fig. 11.4: Disposal of excreta in toilets

Fig. 11.4 suggests that all respondents have a connection to the close pit and septic tank. This shows that a hundred per cent of toilets are very safe in terms of secure disposal of the excreta. It means that there are lesser chances of contamination and infection.

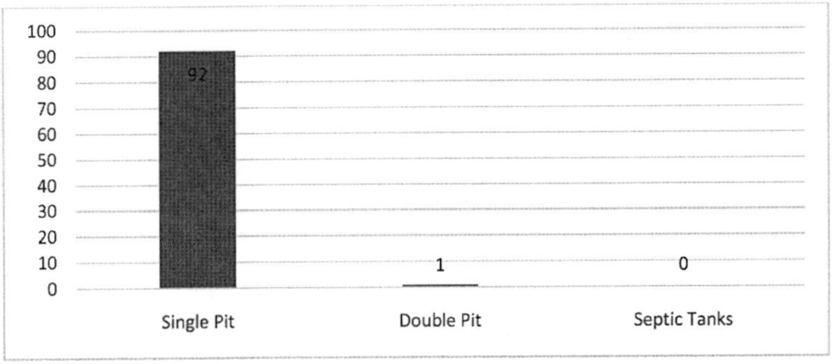

Fig. 11.5: Techniques or type of disposal attached to toilets

There are three kinds of pits: single pit, double pit and septic tanks. Figure 11.5 suggests that a total 92 of toilets were connected to a single pit for disposal of human excreta. 1 toilet was connected to double pit technique. It is to be noted that no toilet was connected to the septic tank.

Fly-proof toilets are more secure and safe, with lesser chances of fly infection. Figure 11.6 suggests that fly-proof facilities covered 92 per cent of toilets. 1 per cent toilet was lacking a proper facility of fly-proof. It is to be noted that a hundred per cent of households had the facilities of water and soaps for cleansing hands.

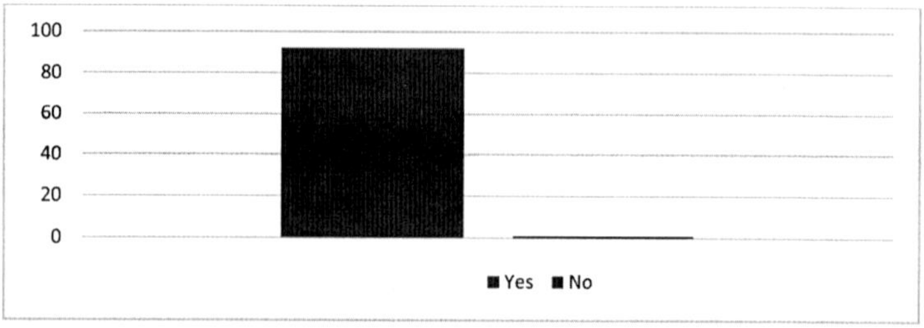

Fig. 11.6: Fly-Proof facility

Fig. 11.7 suggested that 48 per cent of households got a subsidy for the construction of IHHLs. In contrast to this, 45 per cent of total households did not get any subsidy for constructing the toilets, putting the financial burden on the respondents. Seven per cent of households neither did have facilities of toilet nor subsidies to build their own. In contrast to this, the government records show a hundred per cent coverage of the construction of toilets in the district. There is scope for the government's intervention to provide the financial subsidy.

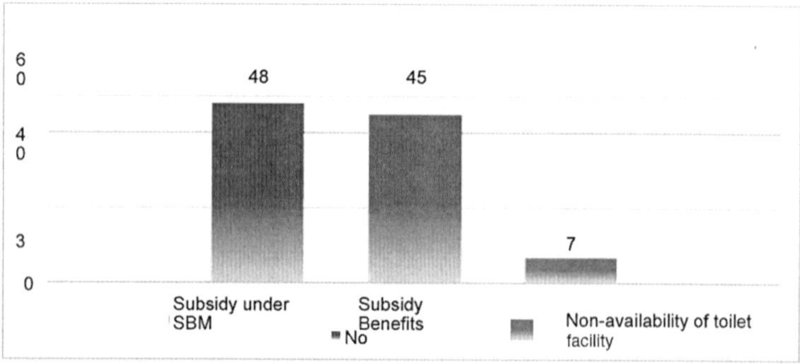

Fig. 11.7: Subsidy for toilet construction

Fig. 11.8 suggests the data about the impact of SBM in the study area. The households are divided into two categories: families with toilet facility; and households without toilet facilities. A total of twenty-one households practised the open defecation, out of which

14 homes practice open defecation occasionally though they have a toilet. Total seven families practised open defecation daily as they did not have any toilet facility.

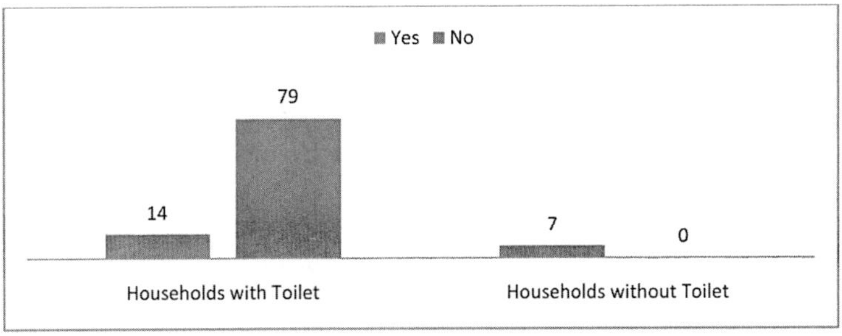

Fig. 11.8: Practice of open defecation

Implementation of SBM proved to have raised the dignity and safety of the women in the study area. In village Bhamarwasi, a man named Bhardwaj said:

> "It was the programme (SBM) and slogan which encouraged and motivated us to leave the practice of open defecation, and we are aware of the impact of the open defecation on the health of villagers."

In village Kithana, a woman, named Bhagawati, who was benefitted from the IHHL scheme under the SBM, said:

> "that now my whole family and I are regularly using the toilet for defecation. The construction of toilets developed a sense of security and dignity for me. I was compelled to go out for defecation due to lack of facilities of the toilet."

Conclusion

The study focused on the problem of open defecation and the implementation of SBM-Gramin in the study area. The analysis focused on some major components of the SBM-G like open defecation, financial subsidy provision for toilet construction, and availability of the CSC facility. Researchers adopted interview Schedules and observations. Though SBM was implemented in the study area by following SBM guidelines, there is still scope for effective implementation.

The data shows that approximately 79 per cent of households have access to toilet facilities and left the OD practice. But there are still some households lacking the facility of the toilet and compel to practice OD. There is a question on the sustainability of the official declaration of ODF status. One of the five households or members was practising OD despite having toilet facilities due to old habits and other reasons. There is the scope of complete ODF if we include those who prefer OD practice due to lack of a toilet. There is an immediate need to make aware and provide a toilet facility.

The facility of CSC is not available at the community level; people lack sanitation and toilets facilities. In the case of households that lack the facility of toilets could access the toilet at the community level. The CSC must follow an ideal structure designed by MDW&S. In case of lack of space to construct a toilet at the household level, and it is a better alternative to access the toilet facility. It helps to curb the problem of OD and sustainability of the ODF more viable. The most important is maintaining the sustainability of ODF. If awareness is created among the people about personal hygiene and sanitation practice, it is possible to leave the OD practice and achieve ODF status at the grassroots level.

References

Burckhardt, J. (2014). *The Civilization of the Renaissance in Italy.* Auckland, New Zealand: The Floating Press.

Mehrotra, Santosh (2021). *Monitoring India's National Sanitation Campaign (2014-2020)*, Institute of Development Studies, UK.

MDS&W (2015, August). *Archival.* Retrieved from www.mdws.gov.in: www.mdws.gov.in/guidelines-swachh-bharat-mission-gramin-11102017

MDW&S. (2017, December 31). *Swachh Bharat Mission—Gramin (All India).* New Delhi, India.

Peace Corps (1984). *Water Purification, Distribution and Sewage Disposal.* Washington DC, The USA: Information Collection and Exchange.

WHO and UNICEF. (2014). *Progress on Drinking Water and Sanitation.* Geneva: WHO Press.

WHO. (2015). *Sanitation.* Retrieved from http://www.who.int/topics/sanitation/en

https://sbm.gov.in/sbmReport/State.aspx

https://sbm.gov.in/sbmdashboard/IHHL.aspx

12

Demographic and Health Status of Scheduled Tribes in Andhra Pradesh

A Comparative Study of Visakhapatnam and Vizianagaram Districts

D. Pulla Rao

Introduction

The Scheduled Tribes are the segregated and isolated communities and are concentrated in the states of Orissa, Bihar, Madhya Pradesh, Andhra Pradesh, Maharashtra, Gujarat and Rajasthan where they constitute about 80 per cent of the Scheduled Tribe population of India. In some of the North Eastern states also they form more than 80 per cent of their population, and mostly live on the hillsides and forests. They are isolated from the rest of the society due to poor transportation and communication facilities and have remained as educationally, culturally, economically and socially disadvantaged sections. Scheduled Tribes have been considered to be lowest in the social hierarchy. Being mostly illiterate, they have been subjected to all kinds of exploitation—social, economic and political. They comprised 6.87, 6.82, 7.76, 8.08, 8.20 and 8.60 per cent of India's population in 1961,1971,1981,1991, 2001 and 2011 census respectively.

Low agricultural production and lack of an appropriate food distribution system are the reasons for low levels of the nutritional status. In addition to the low agricultural production, the nutritional status of the population is to be viewed as the problem of poor quality of food intake due to low literacy and lack of awareness. Food consumption expressed in kilocalories (kcal) per capita per day is a key variable used for measuring and evaluating the global and regional food situation. Shortage of food and nutrient inadequacies leads to ill-health of the tribal people.

The growth rates of Scheduled Tribe population in Andhra Pradesh are 5.47, 2.24, 6.50, 2.79, 3.01 and 1.67 for the years 1951, 1961, 1971, 1981, 1991, 2001 and 2011 respectively. From 1951 to 2011, the tribal population has increased by five times but for the general population it is only 2.3 times.

The Data and Methodology

The primary data comprise collecting information from the selected sample tribal households in the tribal areas of Visakhapatnam and Vizianagaram Districts of Andhra Pradesh by way of canvassing a structured schedule among them. In addition, the secondary data are also taken from the Chief Planning Officers of Visakhapatnam and Vizianagaram Districts. The primary data have been collected during the month of June and July of 2017.

A sample of 338 households is selected for the study. A Multi-stage random sampling technique is employed to select the sample households. In the first stage, two districts, viz. Visakhapatnam and Vizianagaram of Andhra Pradesh have purposively been selected for the study. Then, randomly two mandals were selected, one from each district, viz. Ananthagiri mandal from Visakhapatnam District and Pachipenta mandal from Vizianagaram District. In the third stage, four villages from each mandal were selected. In Visakhapatnam District, the four villages are Damuku, Ananthagiri, Chilakalagedda and Khambhavalasa. In Vizianagaram District, the four villages are Bobbilivalasa, Ammavalasa, Pindrangivalasa and Pachipenta. In the fourth stage, all the tribal households in the sample villages were interviewed with a pre-prepared schedule.

This chapter deals with the demographic and health status of the sample households like sex composition, age composition, castes and so on. The demographic features like the size of the family, sex ratio, size of the population, mean age at marriage, educational status, and occupational pattern of the sample households and the health status of the sample households based on disease prevalence rate, distribution of infected persons by sex and age groups and etc.

Table 12.1 explains the size of family and the average size of the family. Majority of the sample households at the aggregate and random levels are in the region of three to six members per household. The average size of the family is 4.22 in Visakhapatnam District and 4.23 in Vizianagaram District.

Table 12.1: Distribution of the sample households on the size of their family

Size of the family	Visakhapatnam	Vizianagaram	Total
1	1 (0.72)	1 (0.50)	2 (0.59)
2	16 (11.59)	27 (13.50)	43 (12.72)
3	27 (19.56)	39 (19.50)	66 (19.52)
4	43 (31.16)	56 (28.00)	99 (29.29)
5	21 (15.22)	39 (19.50)	60 (17.75)
6	22 (15.94)	28 (14.00)	50 (14.79)
7 & Above	8 (5.79)	10 (5.00)	18 (5.32)
Total Households	**138 (100.00)**	**200 (100.00)**	**338 (100.00)**
Total Sample Population	**583**	**846**	**1429**
Average Size of the family	4.22	4.23	4.23

*Figures in the parentheses indicate their percentages with their respective totals.

Table 12.2 denotes the gender-wise classification of the total sample population and sex ratio. In the Visakhapatnam District, out of the sample population of 583, 293 persons are males and the remaining 290 are females, pegging the sex ratio of around 990 females per 1000 males. Although it is less, it is better when compared to the national and state sex ratio.

In the District of Vizianagaram, out of the sample population of 846 persons, 438 persons are males and the remaining 408 are females, making the sex ratio to 932 females for one thousand males. This is quite disheartening because it is less when compared to the national and state sex ratio. With regard to the total sample population of 1429 persons, 731 are males and the remaining 698 are females, fixing the sex ratio at 955 males for one thousand males. In the child sex ratio, the Visakhapatnam District is farming well.

Table 12.2: Gender-wise Classification of the Total Sample Population

Gender	Visakhapatnam	Vizianagaram	Total
Male	293	438	731
	(50.26)	(51.77)	(51.15)
Female	290	408	698
	(49.74)	(48.23)	(48.85)
Total	**583**	**846**	**1429**
	(100.00)	**(100.00)**	**(100.00)**
Overall Sex Ratio	989.70	931.50	954.85
Child Sex Ratio	1080	834.50	920.56

*Figures in the parentheses indicate their percentage with their respective totals.

Table 12.3 gives the age specific and gender specific classification of the total sample population. In the Visakhapatnam District, out of the total sample population (583 persons), majority of the population is under the category of productive age group, i.e. 15 to 59 years, while the unproductive categories, i.e. below 14 years and above 60 years comprise 26 and 5 per cent of the total sample population respectively. With slight variations, same picture can be found in the case of Vizianagaram. The analysis indicates that the population under the productive age group and under the below 14 years age group is very high and in the category of above 59 years, it is very low.

Table 11.3: Age Specific and Gender Specific Classification of the Total Sample Population

Age Group	Visakhapatnam			Vizianagaram			Total		
	Male	Female	Total	Male	Female	Total	Male	Female	Total
0-14	75	81	156	139	116	255	214	197	411
	(25.60)	(27.93)	(26.76)	(31.74)	(28.43)	(30.14)	(29.27)	(28.22)	(28.76)
15-59	203	198	401	279	279	558	482	477	959
	(69.28)	(68.28)	(68.78)	(63.70)	(68.38)	(65.96)	(65.94)	(68.34)	(67.11)
60+	15	11	26	20	13	33	35	24	59
	(5.12)	(3.79)	(4.46)	(4.57)	(3.19)	(3.90)	(4.79)	(3.44)	(4.13)
Total	**293**	**290**	**583**	**438**	**408**	**846**	**731**	**698**	**1429**
	(100.00)	**(100.00)**	**(100.00)**	**(100.00)**	**(100.00)**	**(100.00)**	**(100.00)**	**(100.00)**	**(100.00)**

*Figures in the parentheses indicate their percentage with their respective totals.

Table 12.4: Mean age at marriage for the married women in the reproductive age

Age at Marriage	Visakhapatnam	Vizianagaram	Total
< 15 years	76 (62.81)	85 (46.96)	161 (53.31)
15 to 20 years	45 (37.19)	96 (53.04)	141 (46.69)
Total	**121 (100.00)**	**181 (100.00)**	**302 (100.00)**

*Figures in the parentheses indicate the percentage with their total.

Table 12.4 classifies the married women in the reproductive age based on their mean age at marriage. In the Visakhapatnam District, out of 121 women in reproductive age, 76 persons (63%) are married on or before they attained fifteen years of age. Even though, the child marriage is prohibited in India these tribal people are averse to change their way of life. Only 37 females are married in the age group of 15-20 years.

In the Vizianagaram District, 181 women are in the reproductive age group, among whom 85 persons (46.96%) were married on or before 15 years of age. Contrary to the Visakhapatnam District, higher percentage of married women in this area has married in the age group of 15-20 years. With regard to the overall sample, around 53 per cent are married before 15 years of age and the remaining are after 15 years of age.

In this regard, the government should initiate more motivational measures about the demerits of the early marriage, like infant mortality, maternal mortality, stillbirth, and early birth and to stop the child marriages.

Table 12.5: Age at first Conception for the Women in the Reproductive age

Age in ranges	Visakhapatnam	Vizianagaram	Total
≤15	21 (17.35)	41 (22.65)	62 (20.53)
15 to 20	89 (73.55)	130 (71.82)	219 (72.52)
20 to 25	1 (0.82)	0	1 (0.33)
In fecund	10 (8.26)	10 (5.52)	20 (6.62)
Total	**121**	**181**	**302**

*Figures in the parentheses indicate the percentage with their total.

Table 12.5 brings out the classification of the women in the reproductive age based on their age at first conception. This is an important indicator in the demographical development of any society. As already explained, the chances for infant mortality, maternal mortality and stillbirth are very high, when the women's age is very low. When going through the mean age at marriage, child marriages are still prevalent in these areas to much extent; giving chances for other consequences have been explained. In the district of Visakhapatnam, more than 17 women in reproductive age have conceived below 15 years. It is also interesting to see some in fecund women. With regard to the district of Vizianagaram, again around 23 per cent of the women in the reproductive age conceived before they attained the age of 15 years of age. The number of in fecund women existed here also. With regard to the overall sample, around 21 per cent have conceived on or before they attained the age of 15 years. In this context, it is imperative of the government to initiate some motivational measures to eradicate this social evil of child marriage, which brings out unhealthy citizens of the future, which brings down their health status and the level of their resistance towards some diseases.

Table 12.6: Sterilization for the Women in the reproductive age group

Whether sterilized	Visakhapatnam	Vizianagaram	Total
Yes	71 (58.68)	117 (64.64)	188 (62.25)
No	50 (41.32)	64 (35.36)	114 (37.75)
Total	**121 (100.00)**	**181 (100.00)**	**302 (100.00)**

*Figures in the parentheses indicate their percentage with their respective totals.

Table 12.6 classifies the women in the reproductive age based on whether they have undergone the family planning operation or not. This indicates the efforts made by the medical personnel working in these areas and the level of enlightenment of the couples in these areas regarding family planning.

With regard to the Visakhapatnam District, as the data indicate, out of the 121 women in the reproductive age as many as 58.68 per cent of the women are being sterilized. The number of non-sterilized women stands at 41 per cent. At this study, it is understood that more than 40 per cent of the eligible women are not sterilized. In the Vizianagaram District, out of the eligible women of 181, 117 women are sterilized. In addition, around 35 per cent of the sample is not sterilized.

With regard to the overall sample, around 62 per cent are sterilized and around 38 per cent are not sterilized. In this regard, this study appreciate the efforts of the medical personnel working with service motto in these areas, and their efforts in sterilizing the women in the reproductive age without bothering the terrain and the situations prevailing there, but more is left behind. Therefore, the Government should encourage the Non-Governmental Organizations in this area. These data clearly reveal that the family planning programme in Andhra Pradesh is a major success. Even among tribal families, family planning acceptance rate is more than 60 per cent, which is the target for the whole country.

Table 12.7: Any Abortions for the women in the Reproductive Age Group

Abortion	Visakhapatnam	Vizianagaram	Total
Yes	36 (29.75)	35 (19.34)	71 (23.51)
No	85 (70.25)	146 (80.66)	231 (76.49)
Total	**121 (100.00)**	**181 (100.00)**	**302 (100.00)**

*Figures in the parentheses indicate the percentage with their total.

Table 12.7 brings out the classification of the women in the reproductive age based on the information on whether they had experienced any abortions in their lifetime. This is also an important indicator of demography. In Visakhapatnam District, around 30 per cent of the eligible women experienced abortions in their life. In Vizianagaram District, around 19 per cent of the sample women experienced abortions in their life.

With regard to overall sample, the percentage of women who experienced abortions stands at around 24. Some of the causes are lack of proper medical attention (pre-natal care), and the immature handling done by the midwives in those areas. These are the outside causes. The main reason behind this is, the social evil of child marriage is widely prevalent here and lower age at first conception. In this regard apart from improving the services of the medical personnel, the government should enlighten the people about this problem.

Table 12.8: AIDS Awareness for the sample households

Awareness	Visakhapatnam	Vizianagaram	Total
Yes	87 (63.00)	164 (82.00)	251 (74.26)
No	51 (37.00)	36 (18.00)	87 (25.74)
Total	**138 (100.00)**	**200 (100.00)**	**338 (100.00)**

*Figures in the parentheses indicate their percentages with their totals.

Table 12.8 brings out the classification of the sample households based on their awareness regarding the Acquired Immune Deficiency Syndrome, notoriously called AIDS, a cureless disease prevailing in the world in general and India and Andhra Pradesh in particular. The advent of this disease to a person has no need to be explained. Keeping in mind the consequences of this disease, this question tends to enquire about their awareness of this disease. With regard to the Visakhapatnam District, it is interesting to see 63 per cent of the sample households are aware of this. Contrary to this, in the district of Vizianagaram, more than 80 per cent of the sample opined of having been informed about this problem and the consequences. With regard to the overall sample around 75 per cent of the sample expressed of having knowledge of this problem. In this context, the government should initiate the measures to enlighten them about this problem, its advent, its consequences and the preventive measures to be followed.

Table 12.9 brings out the classification of the sample households based on the age, sex and morbidity data collected during the reference before three months of the data collection, i.e. June 2007. The disease prevalence rate for the age groups is also presented in the table. The disease prevalence rate is high among the vulnerable groups of children and elder people. At the aggregate and individual levels, we can observe that women are the main victims of diseases in these regions.

Table 12.9: Distribution of the infected population on the basis of their Age and Sex

Range of age (in years)	Visakhapatnam Diseased persons		Vizianagaram Diseased persons		Total Diseased persons	
	Male	**Female**	**Male**	**Female**	**Male**	**Female**
0-14	19	18	30	30	49	48
	(27.94)	(21.95)	(38.46)	(25.00)	(33.56)	(23.76)
Disease Prevalence Rate	25.33	22.22	21.58	25.86	22.90	24.37
15-58	45	59	43	85	88	144
	(66.18)	(71.95)	(55.13)	(70.83)	(60.27)	(71.29)
Disease Prevalence Rate	22.17	29.80	15.41	30.47	18.26	30.19
59 & above	4	5	5	5	9	10
	(5.88)	(6.10)	(6.41)	(4.17)	(6.16)	(4.95)
Disease Prevalence Rate	26.67	45.45	25.00	38.46	25.71	41.67
Total	**68**	**82**	**78**	**120**	**146**	**202**
	(100)	**(100)**	**(100)**	**(100)**	**(100)**	**(100)**
Disease Prevalence Rate	23.21	28.28	17.81	29.41	19.97	28.94

*Figures in the parentheses indicate their percentage with their totals.

Table 12.10: Distribution of the afflicted population based on Sex and Type of Disease

Gender	Visakhapatnam				Vizianagaram			
	Gen. fev.*	**Mal.****	**Others**	**Total**	**Gen. fev.**	**Mal.**	**Others**	**Total**
Male	26	42	--	68	30	47	1	78
Female	20	60	2	82	28	91	1	120
Total	**46**	**102**	**2**	**150**	**58**	**138**	**2**	**198**

Gen. fev.*- General Fevers, Mal.**- Malaria.

Table 12.10 brings out the classification of the sick persons based on their gender and the type of disease from which they suffered from. In this area majority, there is a wide-spread of malaria attack and the others followed with lack of sufficient nutritional food and timely medical provisions, leading them to starve and wait for the outside help. That is the main reason for taking only some diseases in this regard. With regard to the Visakhapatnam District, out of the disease affected persons in the reference period, 46 persons suffered from general fevers and 102 persons suffered from malaria, viral fevers and some of its perpetuities, only two persons suffered from other diseases, such as gastric problems and others. Out of the 102, malaria affected persons; nearly 60 per cent are women, the vulnerable section in the society. In the Vizianagaram District, out of the 198 affected persons, 58 are with general fevers, 138 are with malaria, viral fevers and its perpetuities. Out of the persons affected with malaria and viral fevers more than 60 per cent are females. As a whole majority of the sick people are women, and that the majority of persons affected with malaria and viral fevers are females, they seem to be the vulnerable section of this society. So the government should take some proactive measures in this regard, such as, enlightening them on hygienic surroundings and drinking boiled water and using the modern medicine. In the process of data collection, it is observed that majority of the tablets given are simply set-aside in the house, and are not used for the intended purpose.

Table 12.11: Distribution of the patients on the basis of Sex and consulting a doctor

Gender	Visakhapatnam			Vizianagaram		
	Yes	**No**	**Total**	**Yes**	**No**	**Total**
Male	46	22 (43)	68	66	12 (30)	78
Female	53	29 (57)	82	92	28 (70)	120
Total	**99**	**51 (34)**	**150**	**158**	**40 (20)**	**198**

*Figures in the parentheses indicate their percentages with their totals.

Table 12.11 brings out the gender differential classification of the disease-affected persons in the sample households based on whether they consulted the doctor or not. In the tribal areas due to the inaccessible terrain and the non-supporting atmosphere, many of the government doctors do not wish to serve in these areas. Owing to ignorance many a number of tribals believe in the traditional medicine, that too the private and unqualified doctors who take up that activity for their employment, collect huge amounts of money and make the tribals believe that supernatural elements are the cause for the disease. Meanwhile, the disease becomes severe and leads to death of the person. That is why the question of whether they consulted the doctor arises.

With regard to the Visakhapatnam District, out of the affected 150 persons, 34 per cent of them did not consult the doctor. In that, 40 per cent are males and the remaining 57 per cent are females. With regard to the Vizianagaram District, out of the affected 198 persons, 20 per cent of them did not consult the doctor. In that, 30 per cent are males and 70 per cent are females. In this regard, it is observed that there exist the gender-differences in consulting the doctor. At this outset, it is imperative to understand that due to lack of sufficient money or due to ignorance they are unable to obtain proper medical attention to get rid of the disease. Therefore, the government should initiate proper measures in this regard. Proper motivational programmes are the need of the hour. If the tribal people approach the doctor, he or she may obtain proper medical attention for the disease. On the other hand, if the affected tribal people, by lack of money cannot reach or approach the doctor, in some particular seasons, the government should enable them to reach the hospital free of cost.

Table 12.12: Distribution of the patients on the basis of Sex and Type of Doctor Consulted

Gender	Visakhapatnam				Vizianagaram			
	G.D	P.D	Not. con.	Total	G.D	P.D	Not. con.	Total
Male	13	33	22	68	28	38	12	78
Female	19	34	29	82	43	49	28	120
Total	**32**	**67**	**51**	**150**	**71**	**87**	**40**	**198**

*Not.con: Not consulted the Doctor. * G.D—Government Doctor. * P.D—Private Doctor.

Table 12.12 brings out the gender differential classification of the disease-affected persons based on the question of what type of doctor they consulted. The doctors are taken in to two categories, government doctor and private doctor. As already explained, the tribal people approach the traditional superstitious healers and the unqualified doctors, who play with their lives. In this context, it is imperative to study the type of doctor they consult, when they are sick. In both the districts, it is understood at a glance that majority are approaching the traditional and unqualified natural healers. In this way, they themselves are allowing others to take them to the deathbed. In the same way in the Vizianagaram District also, the majority of tribal people are approaching the private doctors.

The government should encourage the tribal people to go for modern medicine. The private doctors should be discouraged in the sense they have to be replaced by experts from outside or train the local educated youth in this regard in providing timely help and also to motivate the unmotivated to take modern medicine and advice. This can go a long way in solving most of their problems. Instead of serving the Scheduled Tribes in the interior regions, the majority of the government doctors prefer to quit the job. Therefore, the government should take stringent action against the doctors who are reluctant to work in remote areas. It should also provide the Scheduled Tribes with anti-biotics; safe drinking water and free ration in the lean seasons so that they may not be afflicted with diseases.

Table 12.13: Distribution of the diseased persons by their Sex and Expenditure Incurred

Gender	Visakhapatnam (in Hundreds of Rs.)					Vizianagaram (in Hundreds of Rs.)				
	1 to 5	5 to 10	10 & above	NA*	Total	1 to 5	5 to 10	10 & above	NA	Total
Male	21	19	6	22	68	22	35	9	12	78
Female	20	20	13	29	82	38	39	15	28	120
Total	**41**	**39**	**19**	**51**	**150**	**60**	**74**	**24**	**40**	**198**

*Not applicable—Those who does not consult Doctor.

Table 12.13 brings out the gender differential classification of the disease-affected persons based on the amount of expenditure incurred in the process of getting rid of that disease. In the Visakhapatnam District, out of the 150 affected persons, 99 consulted the doctor, majority of them incurred expenditure more or less Rs. 1,000. Moreover a few persons that incurred more than Rs. 1,000. In the same way, the tribal people of Vizianagaram District also incurred more in the process of getting cured from the diseases. As a whole, it has been understood that the female's medical expenditure is too high. The government is providing medicines at free of cost. The government should initiate educating the tribal people in this regard. Corruption is prominent in each nook and corner of society. However, extending it to the tribal areas and using it on the illiterate and ignorant people is cynical. Their ignorance in this regard is playing perpetual role. From the above analysis, it can be observed that many a number of tribal patients are approaching the traditional and private healers without any knowledge and qualification. In the meantime, the latter making money on this indigenous people. The measures meant for the tribals should have the motivational programmes at the core, and then only they can succeed in their intention.

Table 12.14: Distribution of the sample households on their Annual Expenditure on Medical Care for the year 2006

Range (in Rs.)	Visakhapatnam	Vizianagaram	Total
0	23 (16.67)	12 (6.00)	35 (10.36)
1 to 500	42 (30.43)	117 (58.50)	159 (47.04)
500 to 2500	63 (45.65)	66 (33.00)	129 (38.17)
2500 to 4000 and above	10 (7.25)	5 (2.50)	15 (4.44)
Total	**138 (100.00)**	**200 (100.00)**	**338 (100.00)**

*Figures in the parentheses indicate their percentage with their totals.

Table 12.14 brings out the classification of the sample households based on their expenditure on the medical care. Medical care is necessary in these inaccessible areas. People in these areas suffer from many a type of epidemics and are prone to diseases because of the atmospheric conditions and bad hygiene.

With regard to the Visakhapatnam District, more than 75 per cent of the sample is spending much amount for the maintenance of their lives. That too, the remaining persons who do not spend are because of lack of money but not lack of sickness. Over the years, it is interesting to see the number of persons spending more money on medical care. With regard to the Vizianagaram District, more than 90 per cent of the sample is expending money for the maintenance of their health. Again, it is also disheartening to see more number of households expending more money for the sake of their health.

With regard to the overall sample also much percentage of the people are spending more amount for the sake of their health. In this regard, when asked for their immediate needs many voted for the providing of hospitals. This indicates that many are in need of health facilities. When visited the areas, much sophisticated medicines are provided for the tribal people, but due to the inaccessible terrain and lack of financial assistance and that much motivation in using the modern medicine, they are starving, in the sense this is due to the working of vicious circle of poverty. Therefore, it is advised that those measures that are intended for the welfare of the tribes must start with the motivation of their opinions with regard to the development.

Conclusion

The average size of the family in the study area is around 4.23. The sample households have good size of family, though it is more than national target of four persons per a family.

With regard to the sex ratio of the sample population, in Visakhapatnam it is 989.70 and in Vizianagaram it is 931.50. The child sex ratio is better in both the districts. The issue of sex ratio is quite bad in the sample of Vizianagaram District and the child sex ratio is also alarming. The child sex ratio in the total sample population is less when compared to state and national average figures. At the aggregate and disaggregate levels, the sex ratio of the sample households is not even comparable to their ratio itself.

The percentage of children in the sample population is high in Vizianagaram District. The percentage of working age group population in the sample is slightly higher in Visakhapatnam. In the total sample population, 48.84 per cent are females. The working age group population in the sample population is higher than the national average.

Visakhapatnam District has more married women that got married before attaining fifteen years of age. In the total sample population, 53.31 per cent of the married women got married before they attained fifteen years of age. The mean age at marriage for the sample population is not encouraging. It is very less, and may be the cause for high mortality rates in the Scheduled Tribes. As the mean age at marriage is low, the age at first conception for the eligible sample women is also very low.

Vizianagaram District has more eligible households who have their first conception before they attain fifteen years of age. On an average, both the districts have 72 to 73 per cent of women who have their first conception in the age group of 15-20 years. In fecund women are of six per cent of the total eligible sample married women. More than 58 per cent of the sample women in the reproductive age group in the Visakhapatnam District have undergone the family planning operation. This percentage is more than 64 for Vizianagaram District. More than 62 per cent of the total eligible sample women who are in the reproductive age group have undergone family planning operation.

More than 23.51 per cent of the sample women who are in the reproductive age group have abortions in their lifetime. Visakhapatnam District has more percentage of sample women who have abortions in their lifetime. It is interesting to see more than 74 per cent of the sample households are aware of AIDS.

The family planning programme in the study area is a good success, and it has the ratio which is the target for the nation as a whole. Having abortions in the lifetime for women is not an abnormal issue, but having more number of women in this ambit needs much attention. Having more households aware of AIDS is a good sign but increasing that to the cent per cent level is must for that notorious disease.

The disease prevalence rate for females in the total sample is around 29 per cent. That is for every 100 females in the society of Scheduled Tribes 29 are affected with diseases. But this for males is only 20 per cent; even this is more when compared with the general population. The disease prevalence rate is high among the children and elders. Malaria and general fevers are widely prevalent in these sample areas. In Visakhapatnam, out of the affected 150 persons, 102 are from malaria and around the same results exist in the Vizianagaram District. In this aspect also females are worst hit. Most of the Scheduled Tribes do not agree for modern medicine, and they are reluctant to accept it. In this regard, it is observed the existence of gender differentials in consulting a doctor. Most of the women did not consult a doctor when necessary. Most of the sample tribal households are approaching the private unqualified doctors when they are sick. More than 40 per cent of the sample households are spending more than rupees 500 on medical care. In this regard, the government should initiate motivational programmes elucidating the importance and usefulness of modern medicine.

References

Anima Guha (1986). "Folk Medicine of Boro-Kacharis", in *Tribal Health: Socio-cultural Dimensions*, edited by Chauduri *et al.*, Inter-India Publishers, New Delhi.

Bairathi Shashi (1991). *Tribal Culture, Economy and Health,* Rawat Publishers, Jaipur.

Dey, A.S. (2003). "A comprehensive study of fertility and contraceptive practices among the scheduled tribes of Madhya Pradesh", in Adak (ed.) *Demography and Health Profile of the Tribes*, Anmol Publications, New Delhi.

Dey, D. (2003). "The status of Reproductive and child health among the scheduled tribe population in Madhya Pradesh—An observation from NFHS 1992-1998-1999", in Adak (ed.) *Demography and Health Profile of the Tribes*, Anmol Publications, New Delhi.

Gopal Rani K. (1996). *Tribals and their Health Status,* APH Publishing Corporation, New Delhi.

Hema Malini (2005). "The sensitivity of disease incidence in the tribal zones of Visakhapatnam District", in Dr. B.S. Vasudeva Rao (ed.) *Tribal Developmental Studies,* Associated Publishers, Ambala Cantonment, Ambala.

Meera, A., Nangia, P. and Roy, T.K. (2003). "The reproductive behaviour of tribal women in Madhya Pradesh", in Adak (ed.) *Demography and Health Profile of the Tribes,* Anmol Publications, New Delhi.

Mukherjee, D.P. and Nandy, S.K. (1986). "Tribal Health of Asurs in the Netrahut Plateau", in *Tribal Health: Socio-cultural Dimensions* edited by Chauduri *et al.,* Inter-India Publishers, New Delhi.

Nanda, S. (2003). "Household factors affecting infant mortality in the scheduled tribes of Madhya Pradesh", in Adak (ed.) *Demography and Health Profile of the Tribes,* Anmol Publications, New Delhi.

Pandey *et al.* (2003). "Fertility differentials in Khairwars of Madhya Pradesh", in Adak (ed.) *Demography and Health Profile of the Tribes,* Anmol Publications, New Delhi.

Roy Burman, B.K. (1961). *Demographic and Social Profile of the Hills of N.E. India,* Monograph series. New Delhi: Census of India.

Sachidanand (1978). "Social structure, status and Morbidity patterns: the case of tribal women." *Man in India,* Vol. 58, No. 1, January-March.

Sharma, A.N. (2003). "Trends of morbidity among Bharias of Patalkot, Madhya Pradesh", in Adak (ed.) *Demography and Health Profile of the Tribes,* Anmol Publications, New Delhi.

13
Inclusive Development in Rural Areas through PRIs
A Comparative Study of Two Districts in Odisha

Manas Behera

Introduction

The democratic governance, decentralisation and inclusive development are interlinked. The PRIs have a decisive role to play in reducing poverty in rural areas and this can be possible through a decentralised democratic governance structure. These institutions must be self-sufficient and should be successful, effective in the delivery of services. People's involvement in the process of governance of these PRIs is vital not only for democracy but also to have inclusive development. But sustained participation of the people, particularly of the marginalised is the biggest challenge before democracy, particularly for a democratic system that functions in an environment of inequalities and oppression in rural areas. The spirit of PRIs is to create and sustain democratic space for the masses at the grassroots level so that both democracy and development will be inclusive and decentralised. But this has not happened so far. The consistency of anti-democratic forces is not matched by the democratic forces. Panchayati Raj Institutions not only have the potential for decentralised, democratic, inclusive governance and development at the grassroots level but have the strength to influence the democratic process at the state and national level. It can unleash democratic forces that will have a decisive impact on the democracy of the nation. To understand the dynamics of this process one has to understand the political economy of the rural areas. The functioning of the PRIs needs to be situated in the context of the power structure, power relations and power struggles in the rural areas. The multiple forms of inequalities, social, economic and cultural that exists in rural societies actually obstruct democratisation of the society and governance structures and stifle the voices of the marginalised. There is a link between the performance of the institutions of decentralised democracy and the level of discriminations in a particular state or geographical area. Decentralisation encourages realignment of power in terms of class, gender, caste etc. and obviously invites resistances from the hegemonic groups. To achieve inclusive Development, the democratic structures at the grassroots level need to be inclusive. This chapter is an empirical and comparative study of the PRIs of two districts: Jajpur and Sundergarh of Odisha from the context of inclusive Development.

Inclusive Development

Inclusive development is concerned with the human centred and broad based development creating equal opportunities for all to participate fully and freely in different activities, i.e. economic, social, political, cultural and spiritual. The Oxford Dictionary defines the term inclusive as not excluding any sections of the society. In the words of Mahbub-ul-Huq, the architect of the first Human Development Report, the central thesis of human development is that it is people who matter, beyond the confusing maze of GNP numbers, beyond the curling smoke of industrial chimneys, beyond the endless fascination with budget deficits and balance of payment crisis—it is people who matter. People must be at the centre of our development debate—what really counts is how they participate in economic growth and how they benefit from it. Production processes are indispensible but they cannot be allowed to obscure human lives (Quoted in N. Gupta, 2008: 8). While the stated agenda of development is inclusion, people at the lowest level could be experiencing exclusion, deprivation and marginalisation.The resistances to the growing inequalities and deprivations, particularly of the marginalised sections of the society have to be addressed by the liberal, democratic state. These considerations served as the ground for official introduction of the trope of inclusive development (Planning Commission, 2008: 11). And for the dispossessed living in rural areas, the institutions of grassroots democracy are arenas of struggle for inclusion. Inclusive development brought changes in the political discourses in India. Identity and regional politics are very often getting reduced to demands for inclusion in the distributional network of the state. State governments headed by regional political forces are being held accountable by the electors for their performance with respect to different social programmes of inclusion. This means the issue based local politics as well as politics and its processes in general are becoming state centric and groups are struggling to get assimilated into the conduits of inclusive development. This competition over resources and politics based on it is reshaping the democratic politics in the country today. The growing demand for socially and economically inclusive policies is creating reactions among the capitalist class who talk of fiscal deficiency and fiscal management to reign in these socially inclusive policies and to maximize capital accumulation. These are termed as unproductive in the neo-liberal capitalist discourse and these voices become more pronounced during capitalist crisis and fall in the growth rate. The existence, functioning and strengthening of the PRIs and the project of inclusive development through these institutions and through inclusive policies to be implemented by these institutions of local governance needs to be situated in the above context of contradictions between the neo-liberal policies and the policies of inclusion for the marginalised. The PRIs has a stake in inclusive development project because this will not only help in strengthening PRIs but also the deprived voices in its democratic spaces.

The Objectives of the Study

The objective of this study is to identify the strength and weaknesses of the PRIs objectively and to find out the means through which their performances can be improved to achieve inclusive development, decentralised, democratic and accountable governance. It aims at analysing the functioning of the PRIs and the representatives in an environment of inequality, exclusion, deprivation and dominance. How the factors of class, caste, gender are affecting the process of democratisation and inclusive development in the rural areas is important to develop a strategy for inclusive development. It is relevant to know how the space created out of the institutional arrangement of the PRIs is actually occupied, particularly by the marginalised. It studies the implementation of the poverty alleviation programmes and hindrances in their implementation in a transparent manner. The study aims to map the deficits in achieving inclusive rural development so that inclusive policies can be designed.

Methodology

An objective methodology is critical for quality research to make it more scientific. For the purpose of the present study, there has been a combination of methods like behavioural, survey method, comparative analysis, historical and political economy methods. The study has been based on both primary and secondary sources. The primary sources include collection of data through survey, questionnaire, and interviews. The secondary sources include books journals, articles etc. The field study was carried out in the selected districts of Jajpur and Sundergarh. The districts of Sundergarh and Jajpur have been selected for study because of their diversity and differences in terms of demographic, social and economic features. Two districts belong to two different parts of the state of Odisha, coastal and western and are widely varied in terms of language, culture, development pattern etc. A meaningful comparative research can be done on the basis of data out of the survey conducted. Sundergarh is tribal dominated district and has huge natural resources like coal and Jajpur has also natural resources like iron ore. The development index in terms of per capita income, education, health etc. is widely different in these two districts. Both are rich in natural resources but different in parameters of development. So a comparative study will be relevant and more objective.

Limitations

The present study is limited in many respects like any empirical research. It is limited by time, money and human resources. Again convincing the respondents about the objectives of research was a difficult task. The wide linguistic and cultural variations of the selected blocks were also challenging. Winning the confidence of the respondents was a limitation in the way of finding data. Travelling far off places from one part of the state to another was also difficult and a major limitation. The common people were cooperative but sometimes have doubts on the intention of the research.

Poverty Alleviation Programmes

Poverty has been the biggest challenge for the country in post-Independence times and there have been many plans and designs to eradicate poverty. There is a consensus in the country that if poverty alleviation programmes can be implemented through institutions of democratic decentralisation, then it will be effective and fruitful. Various programmes can be divided into programmes of wage, self-employment and housing. PRI system has a decisive role in bringing inclusive development for the common people, particularly the marginalised sections living in rural areas through poverty alleviation programmes implemented by Central as well as State governments from time to time. The delivery of services and successful implementation of the programmes is completely dependent on the key functionaries like Sarpanches, Panchayat Samiti members, Zilla Parishad members, ward members etc. First they have to believe in the capacity of these programmes for poverty alleviation otherwise there will be no commitment on their part to implement them sincerely and honestly and they may be reduced to bureaucratic routine exercises. Table 13.1 studies the perception of the respondents regarding the objectives and efficacy of the various poverty alleviation programmes in eradicating poverty and achieving inclusive development. 70 per cent of the respondents have faith while 27.5 per cent are in the negative. Only 2.5 per cent somehow believe in the capacity of these programmes. This means there is no confusion and there is a clear perception of the respondents. Both the districts present similar perceptions in both positive and negative category. The percentage of the people who are half-hearted and confused is very negligible. Majority of them believe that these poverty alleviation programmes and other schemes of the government targeting the poorer sections of the society have the capacity to empower them and ameliorate their living conditions towards better. They can be included in the development process through implementation of these programmes. Food security, housing, drinking water, primary health, primary education, loans, old age allowance, widow allowance, connectivity etc. were areas on which there are many programmes of both Central and State government implemented by PRIs from Gram Sabha to Zilla Parishad. Questions were asked in interviews on the capability of these programmes to bring changes in the life of the marginalised and deprived sections in the rural areas. The development indicators in the state and in these districts point to the fact that the majority of the population living in rural areas still do not have access to basic needs like safe drinking water, food security, housing, education, livelihood, employment etc. The PRIs are the accessible democratic institutions available near them to air their grievances democratically and the programmes of the state will be implemented by these PRIs. If the leadership of the PRIs have confidence in these programmes, this will be the first step towards the successful working of these pro-people empowerment strategies. Those who expressed their opinion in negative (27%) might have been influenced by factors of corruption, bureaucratic bottlenecks, and limitations of the programmes in transforming beneficiaries into owners of resources.

Table 13.1: Perception of the elected representatives on objectives and capability of the poverty alleviation programmes (N=120)

Poverty alleviation programme for the rural poor	Lephri-para	Balisan-kara	Total	Binjhar-pur	Bad-chana	Total	Grand Total
Yes	22	16	38	25	21	46	84 (70%)
No	05	14	19	05	09	14	33 (27.5%)
Somehow possible	03	00	03	00	00	00	03 (2.5%)
Total	**30**	**30**	**60**	**30**	**30**	**60**	**120**

Satisfaction Level on Service Delivery to the Beneficiaries

Various services were provided to the common people through PRIs and their proper and effective delivery is most crucial for inclusive development. If the delivery mechanism is found to be defective then the beneficiaries will be deprived of their due and the very purpose of different schemes and programmes will be meaningless. Respondents were asked questions on the delivery of rice at subsidised prices, kerosene, wheat, food for the children in *Anganwadi* centres, medicine to pregnant and lactating mothers, allowance to old people and widows and other benefits. As the respondents are key persons to see and look after these very significant programmes, their perception is crucial to analyse them from the perspective of inclusive development. It is expected that as they are part of the system particularly the sarpanches and ward members, they will not be able to divulge the correct picture. Still their opinion is crucial as they have a crucial role to play in this regard and they are accountable to their voters. There cannot be any conclusion or observation in this regard without the opinion of the elected representatives. Table 13.2 aims at studying the satisfaction level of the respondents at the delivery of services and benefits which are aimed at bringing development for the marginalised sections of the society. The respondents were honest enough to give their views in this regard after thorough discussions with them on the objectives of research. Only 14 per cent of the respondents expressed their full satisfaction on the delivery of services to the beneficiaries. 65 per cent of the respondents are satisfied to some extent which means delivery of services are there but they are not being delivered properly. There may be leakages, lapses, corruption etc. and these factors have cropped up during discussions with them. 41 per cent of the respondents are not satisfied with the delivery of services and they are not a negligible number. They are almost equivalent to the half of the respondents. If their position and responsibility is to be taken into account then this is a frustrating picture. The leaders of the programmes who are to bring inclusive development through effective implementation of various programmes are themselves not satisfied and that to the tune of 41 per cent, and then there are lapses in the system which cannot be called inclusive.

Table 13.2: Satisfaction level on service delivery to the beneficiaries by elected representatives (N=120)

Perception level	Lephri-para	Balisan-kara	Total	Binjhar-pur	Bad-chana	Total	Grand Total
Highly satisfied	03	02	05	05	04	09	14 (11.6%)
Satisfied to some extent	19	18	37	16	12	28	65 (54.1%)
Not satisfied	08	10	18	09	14	23	41 (34.16%)
Total	**30**	**30**	**60**	**30**	**30**	**60**	**120**

Source: Primary Data.

Opinion of Elected Representatives on MGNREGA

Employment generation is the biggest challenge in rural areas and lack of employment is the major reason of rural distress. Agriculture in rural areas no longer sustains employment for the rural poor. As both these districts are largely agricultural, agricultural labourers constitute a significant section and in terms of both caste and class they belong to the marginalised section. The neo-liberal reforms have led to a condition of jobless growth accentuated in the drastic squeeze in the purchasing powers of the rural poor resulting in demand constrained system (Pattnaik, 2005). In this background, MGNRGEA came a flagship programme of the Central Government to provide employment to the rural poor and to provide them basic livelihood security. This Act owes its origin to a radical shift in policy framework of the state while inheriting the major features of all the entitlement based previous wage employment programmes. NREGA which came in 2005 was renamed as Mahatma Gandhi National Rural Employment Guarantee Act in 2008 and it aims at providing 100 days of guaranteed wage employment in a financial year to every household whose adult members are willing to do the unskilled manual work. This Act is considered as a powerful tool to achieve inclusive development in rural areas and it will have positive impacts on social security, participatory governance, decentralisation and empowerment of the marginalised. It has three aspects—protective, preventive and promotive (Mathur, 2007). It shields the rural poor from vulnerabilities by providing them demand based employment. It prevents risks associated with agricultural investment and forced migration of the rural poor. It brings in resurgence in rural economy through increased demands for consumption. It has the potential to bring in radical changes in the life of the rural poor, if implemented perfectly. GPs and other PRIs are to play a crucial role in the implementation of this employment guarantee Act. Planning and implementation are to be decided in the Gram Sabha by the people. This Act has a bottom-up, people centred, demand driven structure and the responsibility of its successful implementation largely lies with Gram Panchayats, Gram Sabhas and the wage-seekers. Thus this is unprecedented in its reach and scope so far as inclusive development, particularly of the rural areas is concerned. Today the survival of the most distressed and disposed in the rural areas is dependent on MGNREGA. Any programme of inclusive development cannot afford to take the risk of its dilution or deviation etc. The most important agency for its successful and effective implementation is the PRIs, particularly the Gram Panchayat. The elected representatives at the GP level like the sarpanch, ward members, PS members etc. Their experiences, perceptions and opinions are vital to study and measure the success of this employment guarantee scheme in these selected blocks. Table 13.3 analyses the opinions of the elected sarpanches on the functioning of MGNREGA in these four blocks and selected panchayats. This is very crucial in the tribal dominated Sundergarh and particularly in Balisankara Block where trafficking of women is a serious problem as discussed earlier. Only 25 per cent of the respondents have expressed their satisfaction over the functioning of this employment guarantee scheme. Almost equal percentage of respondents, 24.1 per cent have categorically expressed their opinion in the negative. Half of the respondents that are 50 per cent are somehow satisfied and not fully satisfied. In a comparative analysis of two districts, it is revealed that less numbers (9.1%) are satisfied in Sundergarh whereas a higher number (16.6%) are satisfied. The migration and distress is higher in Sundergarh which is reflected in this perception. A higher number (15%) in Sundergarh is dissatisfied than Jajpur whose percentage in this category of dissatisfied is (9.1%). Respondents under the Categories of 'satisfied to some extent' is almost same in terms of percentage (25.8%) and (24.1%) of both the districts. Overall analysis of the data shows that the performance of this employment generation programme is not satisfactory up to expectations. The tribals are the most vulnerable sections of the society and their representatives at the grassroots level do not express full satisfaction over the results of MGNREGA in generating employment. This corroborates to the fact of massive trafficking of tribal girls in Balisankara block of Sundergarh district. This is the result of severe distress of the tribal families and the responsibility of earning fall on the girls of those families. The district of Jajpur, though advanced than Sundergarh in many indicators has also the same problem. A majority of the respondents are not fully satisfied with the performance of this employment generation programme. If the key persons with the responsibility of implementing this programme cannot express their satisfaction then the programme cannot be termed as successful, not to talk of being effective.

Table 13.3: Opinion on employment of rural poor (MGNRGA) (N=120)

Opinion on MGNREGA	Lephri-para	Balisan-kara	Total	Binjhar-pur	Bad-chana	Total	Grand Total
Satisfactory	08	03	11 (9.1%)	11	09	20 (16.6%)	31 (25.8%)
Not satisfactory	06	12	18 (15%)	06	05	11 (9.1%)	29 (24.1%)
To some extent	16	15	31 (25.8%)	13	16	29 (24.1%)	60 (50%)
Total	**30**	**30**	**60**	**30**	**30**	**60**	**120**

Source: Primary Data.

Perception of Elected Representatives on Corruption in PRIs

Corruption is a major handicap in any development strategy. This is regarded as a stumbling block in the way of empowering marginalised sections as their benefits are taken away by others on the way and strengthen the already rich and empowered. It helps in sustaining the inequalities and injustice that is already there. Many consider corruption as an inevitable phenomenon and do not take it seriously. But in the environment of limited resources in developing societies like India and Odisha and with heavy demands for state-led programmes for the welfare and development of the deprived and the poor, corruption will defeat the very purpose of these programmes. So there cannot be any justification for corruption under any pleas. The goal of inclusive development has a stake in a transparent and honest governance system and in the effective delivery of benefits and services to the poor. The perception of the key persons in the PRIs like the elected representatives on corruption is vital to assess the governance as well as the development programme undertaken by the PRIs. As all the major programmes implemented at the PRI level and by PRIs aim at the poor and the deprived sections, any kind of corruption, even negligible in terms of size, will affect the beneficiaries because they are already deprived and are getting the minimum for their sustenance etc. So prevention of corruption at the grassroots level development programmes is a major challenge for both Inclusive Development and for Good Governance at that level. Table 13.4 tries to assess the perception on corruption of those who are the real leaders in implementing projects of Good Governance and Inclusive Development. On the question, whether corruption is inevitable, 39 per cent of the respondents agreed to it. This means they accept that corruption is there and it is inevitable. This is out of their experience in PRI governance. Almost same percentage of respondents (38%) expressed their inability to say on this. This is because they are directly involved in the process of governance as elected representatives. Only 22.5 per cent of them denied clearly that there is no corruption at PRI level. The number of 'Cannot say' category is higher in Sundergarh than in Jajpur. This may be due to unwillingness of the tribal representatives to have a categorical opinion on this issue. Thus, if we put the categories of 'a' and 'c' together for analysis, it is found that majority of the respondents believe that corruption is there. The categorical rejection of the factor of corruption is much less.

Again on the questions of the causes of corruption in local governance, almost half of the respondents (46.6%) identified elections as the major cause. This means as elections to the PRIs have become expensive and elections have been corrupted, it lays the basis of future corruption in the PRIs. Only 17 respondents (14%) from Sundergarh consider elections as the cause of corruption in PRIs whereas 39 respondents from Jajpur (32.5%) agree to this. This implies that elections to PRIs are different in both these districts. While elections in Jajpur is an expensive affair it is not so in Sundergarh comparatively. This may be reason for differences in responses of both these districts regarding elections as the cause of corruption. Bureaucracy has been identified as the second most important reason of corruption in the PRIs (35%). This has implications for the fact that bureaucracy has a powerful role in the governance of the PRIs. The PRIs and their governance and their role in inclusive development are under the shadow of bureaucracy. The data has been presented in Table 13.4.

Table 13.4: Perception on corruption (N=120)

Corruption	Lephripara	Balisankara	Total	Binjharpur	Badchana	Total	Grand Total
Is corruption inevitable							
Yes	10	12	22	11	14	25	47 (39%)
No	05	06	11	07	09	16	27 (22.5%)
Cannot Say	15	12	27	12	07	19	46 (38%)
Total	**30**	**30**	**60**	**30**	**30**	**60**	**120**
Causes of Corruption							
Elections	07	10	17	19	20	39	56 (46.6%)
Bureaucracy	12	11	23	11	08	19	42 (35%)
No awareness	05	05	10	00	02	02	12 (10%)
Cannot Say	06	04	10	00	00	00	10 (8.3%)
Total	**30**	**30**	**60**	**30**	**30**	**60**	**120**

Source: Primary Data.

Primary health and education are two basic conditions necessary for a civilised living. These are vital for inclusive development. Majority of people do not have access or limited access to these services in rural areas. Both Central and State governments have many programmes like NRHM (National Rural Health Mission) and SSA (Sarva Shiskha Abhiyan) for increasing accessibility of the marginalised in these two sectors. There cannot be any thinking on inclusive development without Primary Health and Education. But the ground reality has to be studied to assess the actual situation. There cannot be better persons than the elected representatives in the PRIs because they have close interaction with the marginalised in rural areas and because they are the first persons accessible to these people for their grievances and difficulties. Again they are the real leaders in the implementation of various inclusive policies and they have real and practical understanding of the situation. Their perception and opinion is vital to have an objective study. The tables aim at studying the opinions and perceptions of the elected representatives on two major sectors—Primary Health and Education and sectors have been divided into two tables. Firstly, the satisfaction levels of these representatives on education and health in general have been attempted to be studied. Secondly, the specific problems in these two sectors have been presented through questions to make the study more scientific and objective. The specific problems of quacks and witch-hunting in Sundergarh have been put as questions because these are serious problems in the tribal area.

Health Services

34.1 per cent of the respondents are not satisfied with the health services available and provided to the people in their area whereas 28.3 per cent have expressed their satisfaction. 37.5 per cent of the respondents are somehow satisfied with the health services available to the people. The lack of proper infrastructure in government run hospitals, non-availability of doctors, other technical staff and even doctors are there, their non-availability in the headquarters etc. are some of the common problems relating to health services in rural areas. In a comparative analysis of the two districts, it is found that the situation in the tribal district of Sundergarh is worse than in Jajpur. Only 6.6 per cent out of the total respondents are satisfied in Sundergarh whereas 25 per cent are not satisfied. But 18.3 per cent of the total respondents are somehow satisfied in Sundergarh. This means a clear majority of the local leaders and representatives are not satisfied with the health system available for them and obviously they reflect the opinion of their voters, the common masses. In Jajpur, 21.6 per cent of the total respondents are satisfied with the services whereas 9.1 per cent are satisfied. 19.1 per cent of the total respondents are somehow satisfied with the health services. If the categories of not satisfied and somehow satisfied are put together then in Jajpur also it is 34 out of 60 which is 56.6 per cent. And this is 52 out of 60 in Sundergarh that is 86.6 per cent. Though Jajpur reflects somewhat a better situation than Sundergarh but in overall scenario Health system is not inclusive in the rural areas.

Table 13.5: Health Services (N=120)

Health Services	Lephri-para	Balisan-kara	Total	Binjhar-pur	Bad-chana	Total	Grand Total
Satisfied	05	03	08 (6.6%)	12	14	26 (21.6%)	34 (28.3 %)
Not satisfied	14	18	32 (25%)	06	05	11 (9.1%)	41 (34.1%)
Somehow satisfied	11	09	20 (18.3%)	12	11	23 (19.1%)	45 (37.5%)
Total	**30**	**30**	**60**	**30**	**30**	**60**	**120**

Source: Primary Data.

Table 13.6 on health system (5) have data on the details of health services.54.1 per cent of the total respondents have admitted that there is no access of the people, particularly the poor to the government hospital services due to distance of hospitals, non-availability of doctors and other necessary staff in hospitals and also for other reasons. Even hospitals are there, services are not available, opined 65.8 per cent of the total respondents. Jajpur is somehow better than Sundergarh. The problem of quacks is specific to Sundergarh. In the absence of an effective and accessible health system, the space is being occupied by the quacks and the life and health of the majority of the tribals are in the hands of these quacks. 65 per cent of the respondents from Sundergarh confirmed the existence and service of these quacks. Witch-hunting is another major area of concern specific to Sundergarh as people believe in the existence of witches and think that witches are reasons behind ill-health, diseases etc. Instead of going to hospitals they are after the witches. 61.6 per cent of the respondents from Sundergarh accepts the existence of this phenomenon. This is not a problem in Jajpur. A nation aspiring to be modern and developed cannot afford to accept the existence of quacks and the phenomena of witch-hunting in such large scale in a tribal area like Sundergarh with big industries and urbanisation. It is a failure of the state to provide health services that is accessible to the poor. However, the provisions of good roads and vehicles are giving opportunities to go to district hospitals.

Table 13.6: Health Services-2 (N=120)

Availability of health services	Lephri-para	Balisan-kara	Total	Binjhar-pur	Bad-chana	Total	Grand Total
Hospital accessibility							
Yes	07	08	15	19	21	40	55 (45.8%)
No	23	22	45	11	09	20	65 (54.1%)
Total	**30**	**30**	**60**	**30**	**30**	**60**	**120**
Service availability							
Yes	07	05	12	14	15	29	41 (34.1%)
No	23	25	48	16	15	31	79 (65.8%)
Total	**30**	**30**	**60**	**30**	**30**	**60**	**120**
Dependent on quacks							
Yes	19	20	39 (65%)	01	00	01	40 (33%)
No	11	10	21	29	30	59	80 (66.6%)
Total	**30**	**30**	**60**	**30**	**30**	**60**	**120**
Fact of witch-hunting							
Yes	20	17	37 (61.6%)	00	00	00	37 (30.8%)
No	10	13	23	30	30	60	83 (69.1%)
Total	**30**	**30**	**60**	**30**	**30**	**60**	**120**

Source: Primary Data.

Primary Education

Education is a pre-condition of inclusive development today. Everybody across the ideological divide accepts this. Any nation trying to be developed cannot afford to neglect education, particularly, primary education. Education is the most powerful weapon today for the marginalised for upward mobility and to break the chains of caste, class, gender, language, region etc. Lack of access to education is considered equivalent to lack of fundamental right in today's discourses of development. Even small underdeveloped nations give stress on primary education today. It is unfortunate that India after six decades of independence have not been able to eradicate illiteracy from the country. PRIs are the most crucial institutions to bring quality primary education to the people, particularly the deprived sections of the society. There are so many programmes by the Central and State governments to ensure primary education to the learners living in rural areas and under conditions of deprivation. The opinion of the elected representatives of the local institutions of decentralisation is most important to form a scientific and objective view on this because they are the people with first-hand experience on this phenomenon. Table 13.7 reflects the level of satisfaction of these representatives on the availability and quality of primary education in these surveyed areas. Only 19.1 per cent of the total respondents have expressed their satisfaction over the primary education in their areas while 39.1 per cent of the respondents are not satisfied. 41.6 per cent, that is about half of the respondents are somehow satisfied, not fully satisfied over the state of affairs in the primary education sector in these 4 blocks of the two sample districts. The situation in the district of Jajpur is somehow better in a comparative perspective as 18 of the total sixty respondents of that district have expressed satisfaction while only 5 out of 60 respondents from Sundergarh have expressed their satisfaction. The level of dissatisfaction is almost equal in case of the districts, 24 and 23 in Sundergarh and Jajpur respectively. If the categories of not satisfied and somehow satisfied are put together to mean, they are not fully satisfied with the existing state of affairs then it will be a huge 80 per cent. This means the availability of quality primary education is insufficient to bring any kind of inclusive development for the common masses living in rural areas.

Table 13.8 reflects the opinion on existence of schools, availability of working toilets, of the teachers, of the required teaching hours, on the functioning of Village Education Committees, on the role of the elected representatives themselves in this area and on drop-outs of the students. All these are relevant factors for any system of quality education. Government through various schemes have ensured Concrete buildings for schools and working toilets. Toilets, particularly for the girls are a major factor to prevent their drop-outs. The elected representatives have a bigger role in ensuring the proper functioning of the schools as well as the availability of teaching-learning environment in these schools. They need to be concerned and aware of their roles in this regard. Likewise, the village education committees have an important role in this regard. Drop-out is a major problem today, particularly for the deprived children. Despite various measures like MDM, free cycles, school dresses etc. the phenomena is still there. Keeping all these factors in mind, relevant questions were put to elected representatives. 86 per cent of the total respondents are of the opinion that there are school buildings in villages for primary education. 57.5 per cent of the total respondents said that teachers are available in schools whereas 42.5 per cent are in negative in this regard. This is not a negligible opinion. Teacher non-availability is a major problem. Without teachers schools are nothing but concrete buildings. More than 50 per cent of the respondents from Sundergarh accepted the fact of non-availability of teachers. So in a comparative analysis this is problem more in Sundergarh than in Jajpur. 85 per cent of the total respondents said that toilets are not functioning properly in schools. This is a major problem in both the districts. Almost 80 per cent (79.1%) of the respondents admitted that there are drop-outs in schools and this has not been checked. More than half of the respondents (52.5%) are of the opinion that Village Education Committees are not functioning properly. They are crucial in ensuring education to the learners. They are democratic and have a stake in primary education in the villages.

55.8 per cent of the respondents felt that they do not have a role in the functioning of primary education system in the rural areas. It seems that they are either not aware of their roles in the primary education sector or they have priorities in other areas. Their non-commitment to the primary education will have a negative impact on its effective functioning. Primary Education, though one of the pre-conditions of inclusive development has not taken place in the prior agenda of the elected representatives and this is unfortunate thing from the perspective of inclusive development in the rural areas. There cannot be real empowerment of the impoverished unless the children belonging to these sections are provided with quality primary education. Both the PRI system and the civil society organisation of village education committees appear to have failed in discharging their responsibilities in this vital area necessary for inclusive development. A large majority of the rural poor are unable to afford private education for their children at a higher cost. Any problem or deficiency in the public-funded education system amounts to the denial or at least squeezing of their opportunities and rights to basic education. Education creates awareness and without awareness the poor people cannot assert and enjoy their legal rights and benefits. In a situation of limited access to basic education, the project of inclusive education cannot go ahead.

Primary Education and PRIs

Table 13.7: Primary education (N=120)

Primary Education	Lephri-para	Balisan-kara	Total	Binjhar-pur	Bad-chana	Total	Grand Total
Satisfied	03	02	05	08	10	18	23 (19.1%)
Not satisfied	11	13	24	12	11	23	47 (39.1%)
Somehow Satisfied	16	15	31	10	09	19	50 (41.6%)
Total	**30**	**30**	**60**	**30**	**30**	**60**	**120**

Source: Primary Data.

Table 13.8: Primary education availability (N=120)

Primary Education	Lephri-para	Balisan-kara	Total	Binjhar-pur	Bad-chana	Total	Grand Total
Schools in Villages							
Yes	25	24	49	26	29	55	104 (86.6%)
No	05	06	11	04	01	05	16 (13.3%)
Total	**30**	**30**	**60**	**30**	**30**	**60**	**120**
Teachers available							
Yes	16	12	28	20	21	41	69 (57.5%)
No	14	18	32	10	09	19	51 (42.5%)
Total	**30**	**30**	**60**	**30**	**30**	**60**	**120**
Working Toilet							
Yes	04	02	06	07	05	12	18 (15%)
No	26	28	54	23	25	48	102 (85%)
Total	**30**	**30**	**60**	**30**	**30**	**60**	**120**
Drop-outs							
Yes	28	29	57	20	18	38	95 (79.1%)
No	02	01	03	10	12	22	25 (20.8%)
Total	**30**	**30**	**60**	**30**	**30**	**60**	**120**
VEC Working							
Yes	09	11	20	19	18	37	57 (47.5%)
No	21	19	40	11	12	23	63 (52.5%)
Total	**30**	**30**	**60**	**30**	**30**	**60**	**120**

(*Contd.*)

Primary Education	**Lephri-para**	**Balisan-kara**	**Total**	**Binjhar-pur**	**Bad-chana**	**Total**	**Grand Total**
Your Role							
Yes	11	12	23	14	16	30	53 (44.1%)
No	19	18	37	16	14	30	67 (55.8%)
Total	**30**	**30**	**60**	**30**	**30**	**60**	**120**

Source: Primary Data.

Opinion of the Beneficiaries and the Participants

The best judge of any programme or benefit is said to be its beneficiary. The opinions of the elected representatives need to be situated in the context of the environment and connectedness in which they are working. While giving their opinions on the functioning of institutions which they are heading or they are an integral part of the structures and governance of these institutions, they might not be interested to have a critical opinion. So to have an objective understanding of the various inclusive policies and programmes as well as of the institutions of local governance engaged in implementing these programmes, the opinion of the beneficiaries and of the participants in the democratic process at the Gram Sabha level has been sought in this study. Care has been taken to seek opinion of the most deprived sections of the society so that the reach of the inclusive policies can be assessed correctly. The respondents in this category either have got some benefits under various schemes like MGNREGA, NRLM, MO KUDIA, PRADHAN MANTRI AWAAS YOJANA, BPL RICE, KEROSINE, education, health etc. or have participated in the Gram Sabha. Their perception is necessary to see the actual working of the programme of inclusive development and good governance in rural areas. Also the purpose of selecting this sample is to compare their opinions with the opinions of the elected representatives so that a correct picture will emerge. 56 per cent of the respondents in Jajpur belong to the age group of 36 to 50 whereas 26 per cent belong to 25 to 35. The numbers of young respondents in the age group of 25 to 35 is higher in Sundergarh, that is 38 per cent than Jajpur. 18 per cent in Jajpur are the category of 50 plus whereas this category is 25 per cent in Sundergarh. The respondents in the age group of 36-50 dominate the scene. As they are active and more experienced than the young their opinion will be matured. 73 per cent of the respondents from Sundergarh belong to the category of tribals whereas 11 per cent are OBCs and 8 per cent each are from SCs and General category. This sample size reflects the demography of Sundergarh, particularly of the rural areas. The categories of unreserved and SCs in Jajpur are almost equal, 35 per cent and 37 per cent respectively. OBCs constitute 28 per cent in Jajpur whereas they are only 11 per cent in Sundergarh. SCs and STs taken together constitute more than half of the sample size making it inclusive. 60 per cent of the respondents fall within the educational category between intermediate and graduation. 35.5 per cent of the respondents from both the districts are within the qualification of 10th while only 4.5 per cent are above graduates. Respondents from Jajpur are ahead of their counterpart in Sundergarh in terms of educational qualifications. 75 per cent from Jajpur are between intermediate and graduation while this percentage in Sundergarh is 45 per cent. In terms of gender females dominate the scene as their numbers out of the total numbers of the respondents is 115 which are 57.5 per cent. The percentage of the males is 42.5 per cent. In district-wise comparison females dominate the sample size of the districts, 51 per cent in Jajpur and 64 per cent in Sundergarh.

Opinion on the Objectives and Capabilities of the Poverty Alleviation Programmes

As the opinion of the elected representatives are studied on the objectives and capabilities of various poverty alleviation programmes in reducing poverty and in achieving inclusive development, so the opinions of the beneficiaries and participants in this regard is very much necessary to compare them and arrive at a conclusion. Table 13.9 shows that 30.5 per cent of the total respondents believe in the capacity of the poverty alleviation programmes and other inclusive policies to eradicate poverty whereas 34 per cent respondents are in the negative opinion in this regard. A majority of 35.5 per cent believe that somehow this is possible. This kind of perception underlines the fact that these people have faith in the policies but they are somehow dissatisfied either with their objectives or implementation etc. In district-wise analysis more respondents (36%) from Sundergarh have faith in these policies whereas in case of Jajpur it is only 25 per cent. This may be due to the positioning of the respondents in Sundergarh as they do not have alternative and may be in their severe distress these policies are helpful to them. Also the implementation of these policies might be better than Jajpur for which the level of satisfaction is higher. More people are in negative in Jajpur (42%) than Sundergarh which is only 26 per cent. This may be due to the above reasons. The numbers of respondents belonging to the third category of somehow possible, in both these districts, are close to each other, 38 per cent and 33 per cent. The perceptions of the respondents on the capabilities of the inclusive programmes in bringing inclusive development shows that majority, taking the categories of both yes and somehow possible together, believe in these policies and programmes. Their negative opinion is out of the problems in their implementation, corruption etc.

Table 13.9: Perception of the beneficiaries and participants on objectives and capability of the poverty alleviation programmes (N=200)

Poverty alleviation programme for the rural poor	**Lephri-para**	**Balisan-kara**	**Total**	**Binjhar-pur**	**Bad-chana**	**Total**	**Grand Total**
Yes	19	17	36	11	14	25	61 (30.5%)
No	11	15	26	25	17	42	68 (34%)
Somehow possible	20	18	38	14	19	33	71 (35.5%)
Total	**50**	**50**	**100**	**50**	**50**	**100**	**200**

Source: Primary Data.

Opinion on the Satisfaction Level on Service Delivery to the Beneficiaries

PRIs, particularly the GPs work at the grassroots level with direct interaction with the common masses. All the beneficiaries are in touch with the institutions and representatives of the PRIs.Various services and benefits are being provided by the Government to achieve inclusive development in the rural areas and to bring the excluded into the development process through these benefits and services. So, delivery of services and benefits to the beneficiaries is crucial for the success of these schemes, otherwise the purpose of these will fail. The best judges in this regard are the beneficiaries themselves and the common people living in those areas, because any kind of lapses will be reflected in their opinion. Table 13.10 reflects the data on the opinion of the participants at the Gram Sabha level and of the beneficiaries who have received any kind of benefits like, subsidised rice, kerosene, houses under PAY, MO KUDIA, loans, self-employment schemes, employment under MGNREGA etc. 53.5 per cent of the respondents expressed their dissatisfaction over the delivery of services and benefits given to the beneficiaries whereas 37 per cent of them expressed that they are somehow satisfied. Only 9.5 per cent of them said that they are highly satisfied. In the district-wise analysis all categories have similar results. The categories under not satisfied is 53 per cent in

Table 13.10: Satisfaction level on service delivery to the beneficiaries (N=200)

Perception level	Lephri-para	Balisan-kara	Total	Binjhar-pur	Bad-chana	Total	Grand Total
Highly satisfied	06	04	10	03	06	09	19 (9.5%)
Satisfied to some extent	20	17	37	18	19	37	74 (37%)
Not satisfied	24	29	53	29	25	54	107 (53.5%)
Total	**50**	**50**	**100**	**50**	**50**	**100**	**200**

Source: Primary Data.

Sundergarh and 54 per cent in Jajpur. Similarly, categories under somehow satisfied is 37 per cent for both the districts. The highly satisfied group is 10 per cent in Sundergarh and 9 per cent in Jajpur. Thus in the overall analysis majority of the respondents are not satisfied with the services and benefits provided to the people at the grassroots level.

Opinion on Employment of Rural Poor (MGNREGA)

The opinion of the elected representatives on various schemes implemented by them has its own limitations and it is self-explanatory. This is why the opinions of the beneficiaries and people living in the villages are significant to formulate an objective view regarding the functioning of the PRIs in the context of inclusive development. The MGNREGA is the only programme to give guaranteed employment for hundred days in a year to the poor. There are many studies on this programme in the country which have highlighted its drawbacks. As this is one of the major tools of inclusive development in the rural areas, there cannot be a comprehensive study of the inclusive development without the study on this programme. So the opinions of the beneficiaries as well as of the common people were reflected in Table 13.11 on the benefits, success and deficiencies of MGNREGA in this surveyed area. 44.5 per cent of the respondents expressed their dissatisfaction over the implementation and benefits of this flagship programme.

Table 13.11: Opinion on employment of rural poor (MGNRGEA) (N=200)

Opinion on MGNREGA	**Lephri-para**	**Balisan-kara**	**Total**	**Binjhar-pur**	**Bad-chana**	**Total**	**Grand Total**
Satisfactory	12	10	22	16	17	33	55 (27.5%)
Not satisfactory	25	28	53	19	17	36	89 (44.5%)
To some extent	13	12	25	15	16	31	56 (28%)
Total	**50**	**50**	**100**	**50**	**50**	**100**	**200**

Source: Primary Data.

28 per cent of the respondents are somehow satisfied while 27.5 per cent are satisfied. In the district-wise analysis, 56 per cent respondents from Sundergarh are not satisfied while 36 per cent from Jajpur are dissatisfied. There is a huge gap in this category between two districts. This may be due to the trafficking problem in Balisankara block where MGNREGA is unable to check this through providing employment to the poor there.

Perception on Corruption

Corruption is a major hurdle in the way of inclusive development as the benefits are leaked on the way to others other than the beneficiaries. All the beneficiaries have their perceptions on corruption in getting the benefits and services under the PRIs. Their opinion on corruption is crucial because as beneficiaries they may be encountering corruption or may not be encountering. On the basis of their opinion conclusions can be drawn if the delivery of services and the processes involved are transparent and free of corruption. The respondents were asked questions whether they believe that there are corruption at the local governance level. Those who clearly agreed that there is corruption in the delivery of services etc., they were again asked to identify the causes of corruption out of three options, elections in the PRIs, Bureaucracy and Lack of Awareness among the people. As lot of money is involved in elections, people think that corruption is the way to compensate that and this is the reason of corruption. Some others think that bureaucracy is the reason of corruption while some others think that lack of awareness is the reason behind corruption. 54 per cent of the respondents believe that there is corruption in the local governance while only 19.5 per cent clearly denied it. 26.5 per cent did not have a clear opinion and they expressed their inability to say yes or no in this regard. In the district-wise comparison, 58 per cent from Jajpur and 50 per cent from Sundergarh accepted the existence of corruption. On questions of the causes of corruption, 54 per cent of the respondents identified the money and resource involved in the elections to the PRIs is a major reason behind corruption at the local level of governance. Another 31.6 per cent of the respondents made bureaucracy responsible for corruption in the PRIs. Only 14.5 per cent respondents think that due to lack of awareness among the people corruption is there in the governance of the PRIs. One thing is crystal clear that majority of the respondents believe that there is corruption and the reasons mentioned are all relevant. They might have experienced some kind of corruption in their engagement with PRIs for some services or benefits for which they have categorical opinions on this. Inclusive development cannot be successful in a system afflicted with corruption. Governance and development under the PRIs need to be transparent to make them inclusive and accountable. The reasons of corruption are relevant here to make PRIs free of corruption in future. Table 13.12 reflects the perceptions of the respondents on issues of corruption. The second part, that is causes of corruption studies the opinion of only those who said that there is corruption. The entire data has been presented also in a pie-chart form for better appreciation.

Table 13.12: Perception on corruption (N=200)

Corruption	Lephri-para	Balisan-kara	Total	Binjhar-pur	Bad-chana	Total	Grand Total
Is corruption there in local level							
Yes	22	28	50	24	34	58	108 (54%)
No	10	11	21	12	06	18	39 (19.5%)
Cannot Say	18	11	29	14	10	24	53 (26.5%)
Total	**50**	**50**	**100**	**50**	**50**	**100**	**200**
Causes of Corruption							
Elections	10	14	24	10	22	32	56 (54.3%)
Bureau-cracy	08	10	18	11	10	21	32 (31.6%)
No awareness	04	04	8	03	02	05	15 (14.5%)
Total	**22**	**28**	**50**	**24**	**34**	**58**	**103**

Source: Primary Data.

Analysis of the Findings of the Study

The study finds that inclusive development through PRIs, particularly for the marginalised is not inclusive. Here inclusive development is understood to be development in the rural areas by the PRIs through various development programmes and schemes of both the Central and State Governments. Various studies were taken and opinions have been presented in tabular form. The basic indicators of any development are health, education, employment, housing, food etc. All these important categories have been taken into account while seeking the opinions of the respondents, both the elected representatives and the beneficiaries. Then their opinions have been compared. Opinions were sought from the respondents on the availability of primary education, primary health, housing, subsidised rice, essential items under PDS, loans, employment under MGNREGA; corruption etc.10 tables exhibit the primary data on these issues. 34.1 per cent respondents are not satisfied with the delivery of services and they are somehow or other involved in this delivery of services. 54.1 per cent are somehow satisfied. This means 88 per cent of the respondents are not fully satisfied with the delivery of essential services to the deprived sections by the PRIs. This scenario cannot be defined as conducive for inclusive development. 24.1 per cent of the respondents are dissatisfied with the functioning of the MGNREGA and 50 per cent are somehow dissatisfied. The overall lack of full satisfaction amounts to 74 per cent. 39 per cent of the respondents feel that corruption is inevitable. This reflects the grip of corruption on the system. 46.6 per cent of them think elections in PRIs as the causes of corruption while 37.5 per cent of them feel bureaucracy to be the reason behind corruption. One thing is clear that corruption is a fact in the governance of PRIs. This is in direct contradiction to the concept of inclusive development.

Two important preconditions of inclusive development have been taken for study, health and education. 34 per cent of the respondents are not satisfied with the primary health available in their GPs while 37.5 per cent of them are somehow satisfied, not fully. The situation in this critical sector is not inclusive. 54 per cent have negative opinion on the access to health services and regarding availability of health services 65.8 per cent have a negative opinion. The existence of quacks (33%) and Witch hunting (31%) in Sundergarh is a big question mark on the available health services and its inclusive character. This means the critical component of inclusive development that is primary health is not available to the people, particularly, the marginalised sections living in rural areas neither to their satisfaction level nor to the satisfaction level of their representatives. Regarding another important component of development, primary education, while 39.1 per cent of the elected representatives are not satisfied with the conditions in the primary education sector, 41.6 per cent are somehow satisfied with this. Regarding availability of teachers in schools 45.6 per cent are not satisfied while 85 per cent are not satisfied with the toilets in schools. 79.1 per cent agree to the fact of drop-outs in primary education. Regarding questions on their role in improving the conditions of primary education, 55.8 per cent feel that they do not have a role in this. This situation is totally negative so far as inclusive development is concerned. On the other hand, 44.5 per cent beneficiaries are not satisfied with the performance of MGNREGA. 54 per cent of the beneficiaries are of the opinion that there is corruption in the governance of the PRIs and same percentage of beneficiaries feel elections as the cause of corruption. The question on the level of satisfaction were put to the categories of beneficiaries combining all major services and benefits including primary health and education. 53.5 per cent of them expressed their dissatisfaction over this. And this is more than half. Thus, the scenario as emerged from the primary data on this issue of inclusive development contradicts to the successful existence of such development, particularly for the marginalised.

Conclusion

Various right based movements are deepening the democratic consciousness among the marginalised which is creating a democratic base that will help in the journey towards inclusion of the excluded in development as well as in governance of the structures of local democracy. In Jajpur district movement of the agricultural labourers demanding increase in wages and for share in the crop have showed dividends in challenging the hegemony of the caste because almost all the agricultural labourers in that area (Hasanpur GP of Binjharpur block) are *dalits*. Even in one GP, a candidate belonging to Scheduled Caste could win in an unreserved seat for two times. This is due to the influences of the left led struggle of agricultural labourers. In the district of Sundergarh in Balisankara block the anti-liquor movement of women had a positive influence on checking trafficking of girls. Inclusive development is a complex and long term process in which the crucial component is the delivery of benefits and services to the actually needy persons, specifically to those who are excluded so far from the fruits of development. The state of Odisha suffers from multiple forms of exclusions and deprivations in terms of caste, class, gender, region etc. The goal of inclusive development is more relevant here. But the scenario that emerges from this study cannot be termed as conducive for inclusive development.

The nature and functioning of the PRI system is not independent of the socio-economic and political system in which it operates. The broader policies at the national and state level influence these institutions and their functioning. The neo-liberal paradigm of development advocates aggressively for privatisation of the public face. The rationale of inclusive development does not sit comfortably with neo-liberalism (Chakrabarthy, 2016: 293). In such a situation, the role and relevance of the grassroots democratic institutions like the PRIs assumes significance and more relevance. If the democratic space in the rural areas can be expanded and deepened, then it will have the positive impact on the state for interventions in favour of inclusive development. In the struggle between neo-liberal ideas and a welfare state, the cause of inclusive development can be strengthened through this democratic process through PRIs.

The state itself recognises the limitations of neo-liberal globalisation in putting an end to exclusion and achieving inclusive development. "The truth is that, while markets have a natural propensity to deliver on efficiency, they do not have any innate propensity for equity and equality. Hence, it is true that for eradicating poverty and creating a more equitable and inclusive society, there is need for purposive action by Governments—central, state and local. The view we take is that Government should play an enabling role *vis-a-vis* the market, facilitating trade, exchange, and enterprise. On the other hand, when it comes to distribution and mitigation of poverty, Government has to be more proactive with policy interventions (Economic Survey, 2011). But the state interventions for inclusive development will not come automatically, particularly in an environment dominated by neo-liberal ideas. Pressure has to be made on the state and this can be possible if the democratic action at the grassroots level prove PRIs as the efficient institutions of inclusive development. Democracy has a long and difficult road to go. The silver lining is that these excluded, dispossessed, marginalised people have a stake in Democracy than others. They want democracy, they believe in democracy, they sacrifice for democracy. The PRIs are the best available institutions of democracy for the marginalised, despite their limitations and deficiencies. They need to be strengthened at any cost in the interests of democracy and in the interests of inclusive development. There is no alternative to it.

References

Chakarbarti, A. and others (2016). *The Indian Economy in Transition*, Cambridge, New Delhi, p. 293.

Huq, M. (2008). Quoted in "Democracy and Human Development in India" by N. Gupta, Publications Division, Government of India, New Delhi, p. 8.

Mathur, L. (2007). "Employment Guarantee so far" in *Economic and Political Weekly*, December 29, 2007.

Pattnaik, P. (2005). "On the Need for Providing Employment Guarantee", *Economic and Political Weekly*, January 2015, p. 206.

Planning Commission (2008). *Prime Minister's Foreword to the 11th Five Year Plan* (2007-12), Planning Commission, GoI, New Delhi, p. 11.

14

Financial Literacy and Personal Financial Decision among Households

Anjali, C.M. and *B. Johnson*

Introduction

Financial Literacy: Financial literacy refers to the knowledge and understanding in financial resources which helps them to analyse and understand the financial matters. It means the understanding about the various financial products and services and the skill and ability to manage it well. Lack of proper financial literacy may lead to negative consequences in one's financial position.

OECD has defined financial literacy as follows: "a combination of awareness, knowledge, skill, attitude, and behaviour necessary to make sound financial decision and ultimately achieve individual financial well-being."

Personal Financial Decision: The heart of personal financial success is sound personal financial decision. That means having proper personal financial decision will help one to achieve what they want to achieve in their life irrespective of what life throws at them. A good decision taken reduces the difficulties in their financial goal achievement. Personal financial decision involves various financial areas like money management, investment decision, tax planning, retirement planning, and credit decision.

Significance of the Study

Today, in this cashless economy, financial opportunities are abundant, our economy is getting more and more progressed in every minute, and the credit opportunities are available in our doorsteps, even in a single touch. A proper management of these financial aids can help the individuals to achieve their financial goal as soon as possible and at the same time the mismanagement of these aids can lead to easy accumulation of debt and thereby to utter financial failure. It is always important to know the financial understanding of households and their attitude in personal financial decision making as the future of our country is in the hands of each household.

Objectives of the Study

The broad objective of the study is to analyse financial literacy and its influence over personal financial decisions of households in Kozhikode district. The specific objectives of the study are:

- To assess the level of financial literacy of the households,
- To study the influence of demographic factors of households on financial literacy, and
- To examine the relationship between financial literacy and personal financial decision of the households.

Hypotheses

Based on above objectives, following hypotheses have been formulated:

- H01: There is no relationship between gender and financial literacy.
- H02: Age and financial literacy are not related.
- H03: There is no relationship between income and financial literacy.
- H04: Educational qualification and financial literacy are not related.

- H05: There is no relationship between occupation and financial literacy.
- H06: There is no influence of financial literacy on personal financial decisions.

Conceptual Model of Financial Literacy and Personal Financial Decision

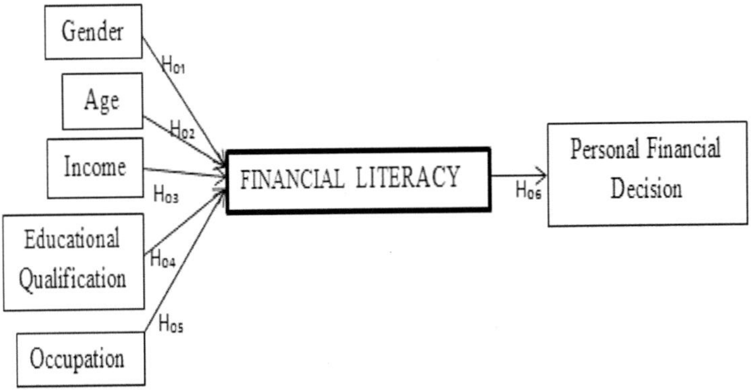

Methodology

The study is a descriptive and analytical one based on secondary as well as primary data. Secondary data required for the study were collected from various published sources like survey reports of Standard and Poor's Rating Services Survey, Financial literacy annual report by Consumer Financial Protection Bureau, Census report of Government of India 2011, books, journals, newspapers, articles, magazines and reports related to the topic.

The study is mainly based on primary data. The investigators collected the primary data directly from the 90 sample income earning members of the family who is denoted as households, from different parts of Kozhikode district through a properly structured questionnaire. Non-probability convenient sampling is chosen. The reason of choosing this method over the others is primarily to have flexibility and freedom in selecting sampling units as per convenience. The analysis of data was carried out by using Statistical Package for Social Sciences (SPSS) version 20. The tools are

Arithmetic Mean, Standard Deviation, Percentage, Mann-Whitney U test, Kruskal Wallis Test and Regression.

Results and Discussion

Demographic Characteristics of the Respondents

A brief description about the demographic details of the respondents is given in Table 14.1.

Table 14.1: Demographic characteristics of respondents

	Classification	Number	Perc. (%)
Gender	Male	51	56.7
	Female	39	43.3
Age	18-25	16	17.8
	25-35	16	17.8
	35-55	47	52.2
	Above 55	11	12.2
Monthly Income	Below 10,000	24	26.7
	10,000-20,000	36	40.0
	20,000-40,000	8	8.9
	Above 40,000	22	24.4
Educational Qualification	SSLC	18	20.0
	UG	32	35.6
	PG	7	7.8
	Professional Qualification	33	36.7
Occupation	Professional	33	36.7
	Businessman	9	10.0
	Government job	7	7.8
	Household	18	20.0
	Other	23	25.6

Source: Primary data.

It is evident from the documented studies conducted outside and/or in different states of India that demographic factors are co-related to the individual's financial literacy. For the purpose of the study each demographic variables like gender age and income are analysed with financial literacy.

Analysis of Financial Literacy

The respondents were given different components related to the terminology financial literacy to measure their level of knowledge. Twenty statements were given to measure their attitude among which each five statements belong to measure financial knowledge, financial attitude, financial planning and financial control.

Table 14.2: Financial Literacy Variables—Descriptive Statistics

			Statistic	**Std. Error**
Financial knowledge		Mean	18.2333	0.52314
	95% Confidence Interval for Mean	Lower Bound	17.1939	
		Upper Bound	19.2728	
	5% Trimmed Mean		18.2593	
	Median		20	
	Variance		24.63	
	Std. Deviation		4.9629	
	Minimum		11	
	Maximum		25	
	Range		14	
	Interquartile Range		10.25	
	Skewness		-0.345	0.254
	Kurtosis		-1.355	0.503
Financial attitude		Mean	21.0556	0.22367
	95% Confidence Interval for Mean	Lower Bound	20.6111	
		Upper Bound	21.5	
	5% Trimmed Mean		21.1049	

(*Contd.*)

			Statistic	Std. Error
	Median		21.5	
	Variance		4.502	
	Std. Deviation		2.12191	
	Minimum		15	
	Maximum		25	
	Range		10	
	Interquartile Range		2	
	Skewness		-0.363	0.254
	Kurtosis		0.414	0.503
Financial planning	Mean		17.0556	0.3961
	95% Confidence Interval for Mean	Lower Bound	16.2685	
		Upper Bound	17.8426	
	5% Trimmed Mean		17.0185	
	Median		17	
	Variance		14.12	
	Std. Deviation		3.75772	
	Minimum		10	
	Maximum		24	
	Range		14	
	Interquartile Range		8	
	Skewness		0.157	0.254
	Kurtosis		-1.204	0.503
Financial control	Mean		17.8444	0.40221
	95% Confidence Interval for Mean	Lower Bound	17.0453	
		Upper Bound	18.6436	
	5% Trimmed Mean		17.7963	
	Median		18	
	Variance		14.56	

(*Contd.*)

		Statistic	Std. Error
	Std. Deviation	3.81573	
	Minimum	12	
	Maximum	25	
	Range	13	
	Interquartile Range	5	
	Skewness	-0.178	0.254
	Kurtosis	-0.935	0.503

Source: Primary data.

In this analysis, financial attitude is the highest with mean score of 21.05. The second highest mean is for financial knowledge with 18.36. Then financial planning and financial control has the least mean with 17.5 and 17.84 respectively. The highest mean is for financial attitude and the lowest mean is for financial planning. Financial knowledge and financial control is in the middle stage. This is not an appropriate condition. This will affect their financial situation. The financial control must increase to enhance the financial planning. If the financial control is going in a proper way, they can get the proper financial planning also. It will lead their standard of living into a stable and smooth way.

Financial Literacy and Demographic Characteristics

It is evident from the documented studies conducted outside and/or in different states of India that demographic factors are correlated to the individual's financial literacy.

Table 14.3: Financial Literacy and Demographic Characteristics—Mean rank

	Financial Literacy	N	Mean Rank	Test statistics (Mann—Whitney U test/ Kruskal Wallis Test)
Gender	Male	51	53.3	0.001101
	Female	39	35.29	
	Total	**90**		

(Contd.)

	Financial Literacy	N	Mean Rank	Test statistics (Mann—Whitney U test/ Kruskal Wallis Test)
Age	18-25	16	64.22	0.002995
	25-35	16	52.81	
	35-55	47	38.12	
	Above 55	11	39.18	
	Total	**90**		
Income	Below 10,000	24	42.13	0.000308
	10,000-20,000	36	34.29	
	20,000-40,000	8	61.56	
	Above 40,000	22	61.68	
	Total	**90**		
Educational Qualification	SSLC	18	44.58	0.015656
	UG	32	54.56	
	PG	7	55.71	
	Professional qualification	33	35.05	
	Total	**90**		
Occupation	Professional	33	33.45	0.000104
	Businessman	9	64	
	Government employee	7	79.07	
	Household	18	46.11	
	Other	23	44.85	
	Total	**90**		

Source: Primary data.

The gender-wise analysis of financial literacy states that there is a high difference in the level of financial literacy in connection with gender. The mean value for male literacy is 53.3 while for female it is only 35.29. The test statistics (Mann-Whitney U test) shows 0.001101 level of significance which strongly infers that there is significant level of relationship between gender and financial literacy.

There is significant difference in the mean rank for various age groups. Age group between 18-25 that is independent life age having good mean rank 64.22, age group 25-35 that is early family life stage have mean rank 52.81, and between the age of 35-55—empty nest life stage it is 38 and for age group above 55, retirement life stage, the mean rank is 39.18. The test value is 0.002995 and since it is less than .05, it is concluded that there is significant level of relationship between financial literacy and age. The income group below 10,000 having mean rank 42.13 and income group between 10,000-20,000 having mean rank 34.298. Level of significance is .05 and since the test value is 0.000308, there is significant relationship between income and financial literacy. While considering educational qualification, the highest mean rank is for the post-graduation degree and then for undergraduation and SSLC *vice versa*. Mean rank for professionally qualified people is 35.05. The significant test value is 0.015656 and hence there is significant relation between educational qualification and financial literacy. As regard to the mean rank based on occupation, it is revealed that government employees are having the highest rank 79.07 followed by businessman with a rank of 64, households 46.11 and professional 33.45. The Kruskal Wallis Test value for this test is 0.000104 and it concludes that there is significant relationship between occupation and financial literacy.

Source of Collecting Financial Information

The mean score of each variable is calculated as per the number assigned to the different category of responses. Towards the influence of variables, points are assigned on a Likert scale ranging from 1-5, with 1 showing the least influence and 5 showing the most significantly influence are given to the respondents.

Table 14.4: Score of Variables Preference towards Source of Information

			Statistic	Std. Error
Certified financial planner	Mean		2.37	0.134
	95% Confidence Interval for Mean	Lower Bound	2.1	
		Upper Bound	2.63	
	5% Trimmed Mean		2.31	
	Median		2	
	Variance		1.606	
	Std. Deviation		1.267	
	Minimum		1	
	Maximum		5	
	Range		4	
	Interquartile Range		3	
	Skewness		0.358	0.254
	Kurtosis		-1.234	0.503
Financial adviser/ broker	Mean		2.31	0.117
	95% Confidence Interval for Mean	Lower Bound	2.08	
		Upper Bound	2.54	
	5% Trimmed Mean		2.28	
	Median		3	
	Variance		1.228	
	Std. Deviation		1.108	
	Minimum		1	
	Maximum		5	
	Range		4	
	Interquartile Range		2	
	Skewness		0.112	0.254
	Kurtosis		-1.182	0.503
	Mean		2.51	0.113

(*Contd.*)

			Statistic	Std. Error
Rating agency reports	95% Confidence Interval for Mean	Lower Bound	2.29	
		Upper Bound	2.74	
	5% Trimmed Mean		2.49	
	Median		3	
	Variance		1.152	
	Std. Deviation		1.073	
	Minimum		1	
	Maximum		5	
	Range		4	
	Interquartile Range		1	
	Skewness		0.026	0.254
	Kurtosis		-0.807	0.503
Family member or friends	Mean		4.19	0.093
	95% Confidence Interval for Mean	Lower Bound	4	
		Upper Bound	4.37	
	5% Trimmed Mean		4.29	
	Median		4	
	Variance		0.784	
	Std. Deviation		0.886	
	Minimum		1	
	Maximum		5	
	Range		4	
	Interquartile Range		1	
	Skewness		-1.475	0.254
	Kurtosis		2.864	0.503
Annual reports	Mean		2.91	0.132
	95% Confidence Interval for Mean	Lower Bound	2.65	
		Upper Bound	3.17	
	5% Trimmed Mean		2.9	

(*Contd.*)

			Statistic	Std. Error
	Median		3	
	Variance		1.565	
	Std. Deviation		1.251	
	Minimum		1	
	Maximum		5	
	Range		4	
	Interquartile Range		2	
	Skewness		-0.146	0.254
	Kurtosis		-0.903	0.503
Financial papers and newspapers	Mean		3.77	0.091
	95% Confidence Interval for Mean	Lower Bound	3.59	
		Upper Bound	3.95	
	5% Trimmed Mean	3.82		
	Median	4		
	Variance	0.743		
	Std. Deviation	0.862		
	Minimum	1		
	Maximum	5		
	Range	4		
	Interquartile Range	0		
	Skewness	-1.142	0.254	
	Kurtosis	1.642	0.503	

Source: Primary data.

Among the various sources of information, the most preferred source of information is the information from family member or friends (mean 4.19). Individual provides importance to other sources of information like financial paper and newspaper (mean 3.77), Annual reports (mean 3.17), agency reports (mean 2.51), financial advisor or broker (mean 2.31) and finally, certified financial planner with mean 2.37.

Analysis of Personal Financial Decisions

The five aspects of personal financial decision are analysed along with financial literacy to know how financial literacy influences these financial decisions.

Table 14.5: Personal financial decision factors and financial literacy—ANOVA

Model		Sum of Squares	df	Mean Square	F	Significance level
Money Management						
1	Regression	11.716	1	11.716	5.312	0.023528
	Residual	194.073	88	2.205		
	Total	**205.789**	**89**			
Investment Decision						
1	Regression	1667.62	1	1667.62	13.556	0.000399
	Residual	10825.54	88	123.017		
	Total	**12493.16**	**89**			
Retirement Planning						
1	Regression	136.382	1	136.382	55.373	0.00000
	Residual	216.741	88	2.463		
	Total	**353.122**	**89**			
Credit Decision						
1	Regression	5.435	1	5.435	4.625	0.034317
	Residual	101.065	86	1.175		
	Total	**106.5**	**87**			
Tax Planning						
1	Regression	8.271	1	8.271	11.5	0.003729
	Residual	11.507	16	0.719		
	Total	**19.778**	**17**			

The test value significance is 0.023528 for money management. So financial literacy will be an influencing factor for cash management. Level of significance is 0.000399 for investment management, so financial literacy is an important factor influencing investment decision. Level of significance 0.000000 indicates the influence of financial literacy on retirement planning. Financial literacy and their level of influence on credit decision is established by the significant level of 0.000034317. Tax planning in considered to be an important factor of personal financial decision in which financial literacy have a crucial role with significant level of 0.003729.

Personal Financial Decision and Financial Literacy

Keeping in mind all the components analysed above, financial literacy have been again studied with overall personal financial decision to know the impact.

Table 14.6: Personal finance decision—Model Summary

Model	R	R Square	Adjusted R Square	Std. Error of the Estimate
1	.271a	.373	.062	2.84289

Source: Primary data.

The impact of financial literacy on credit decision will be 37.3 per cent.

Table 14.7: Personal financial decision and financial literacy—ANOVA

Model		Sum of Squares	df	Mean Square	F	Sig.
1	Regression	54.937	1	54.937	6.797	0.010760
	Residual	695.052	86	8.082		
	Total	**749.989**	**87**			

Level of significance is 0.010760, financial literacy is an influencing factor on personal financial decision.

Financial literacy is a highly influencing factor for personal financial decision. In simple words it is based on level of financial literacy the personal financial decisions will be taken. The financial literacy's impact on personal financial decision is 37.3 per cent and there are significant influences of financial literacy on personal financial decisions are evident.

Conclusion

The present chapter enriches the understanding of personal financial planning in Kozhikode and how the development might be influenced by financial literacy level of the households. It also showed that individuals who are more financially literate focused more on personal financial planning pre-empt adverse impact that poor financial planning might have on their lives, *vice versa.* This goes on to confirm that financial literacy is a useful indicator of personal financial planning decision. Individuals who are thinking to opt and map their ways to financial well-being have to increase awareness of the multiple areas of financial planning and be geared up with the required financial knowledge. To this effect, the education level attained by the individuals provides a strong foothold for such progression. Financial planning professionals in practice would need to engage effective communication and education when delivering their services to clients who come with differing financial literacy level. This would enable more of the public to reap the benefits of personal financial planning. When effective financial planning becomes widespread in the country, economic growth will be stimulated and social problems arising from poverty and criminal activities can be minimised.

References

Betina Greimel, Fuhramann, Maria Antoinette (2002). "Analyzing the gender gap in financial literacy", *African Journal of Business Management.*

Yuksek Usta, Fatma Tezel, "Financial Literacy in the Early Childhood Period", *Current trends in preschool education*-1.

Mandell, Lewis (2008). "Financial literacy of high school student", *Handbook of Consumer Finance Research.*

Tullio Jappelli (January 2009). "Economic Literacy: An International Comparison", *The Economic Journal.*

Tabea, Bucher Koenen, A. Lusardi (October 2011). "Financial literacy and retirement planning in Germany", *Research Gate.*

Anna Maria Lusardi, Olivia Mitchell (March 2014). "The Economic Importance of Financial Literacy: Theory and Evidence", *Journal of Economic Literature, 52*(1): *5*(44).

Oscar Anstem Stopler, Andreas Walter (March 2017). "Financial literacy, financial advice, and financial behaviour", *Journal of Business Economics,* p. 87.

Sunil Karve & Hema Deogharkar, "A study on financial planning need and analysis", *International Journal of Arts, Humanities and Management Studies,* ISSN No. 2395-0692.

Walker, B. Robert, Walker, P. Kristy, *Personal Finance,* McGraw-Hill.

Indian Journal of Accounting, Vol. XLVIII(1), June 2016.

http://www.FinLit.MHFI.com

www.rbi.org

http://digitalcommons.ilr.cornell.edu/cahrswp

http://econpapers.repec.org/paper/abnwpaper/

www.palgrave.journals.com

15

Thematic Plan for Youth in the Rural Economy

Skill Development and Employment

Anthony Rodrigues and *Alok Kumar Chakrawal*

Introduction

"Skill development is critical for economic growth and social development. The demographic transition of India makes it imperative to ensure employment opportunities for more than 12 million youth entering working age annually. It is estimated that during the seven-year period of 2005-2012, only 2.7 million net additional jobs were created in the country. To enable employment ready workforce in the future, the youth need to be equipped with the necessary skills and education.

The country presently faces a dual challenge of severe paucity of highly-trained, quality labour, as well as non-employability of large sections of the educated workforce that possess little or no job skills. The skill development issue in India is thus pertinent both at the demand and supply level. To meet the demand side challenge, consistent efforts are being made towards expansion of economic activities and creation of large employment opportunities. On the supply side, a simple look at the projected youth population provides a fair reason to believe that India has the strength to cater to this demand. However, the employability quotient is questionable and remains a major area of concern. Already huge gaps exist between the industry requirements and the level of skills of workers due to varied reasons including inadequate training infrastructures, inappropriate mix of skills and education, outdated curricula, limited industry interfaces, limited standards etc.

The skill development ecosystem in India is skewed towards a formal education system with limited vocational training. While the vocational training is a dismal state both qualitatively and quantitatively, the higher education system itself is grappling with issues related to scale and quality.

Moreover, there is a disconnection between the formal education system and work requirements, compounding the challenges related to the skill gap. A concerted action is thus required on the supply side to ensure sustained employability of the Indian youth. Extensive efforts to skill the workforce are required, both in quantity and quality. Transforming the skill development ecosystem and makes it responsive to the needs of both industry and citizens requires a scalable, efficient and comprehensive vocational training ecosystem to meet future requirements.

The areas that have been taken into account are Tiswadi, Mormugao and Salcete. The types of employment opportunities in rural communities are the factors influencing youth and acquisitions to get engaged in employment opportunities.

Due to these factors, "the rural individuals are mostly engaged in minority jobs. The primary sector by promoting employment opportunities among them is the agricultural sector. Apart from agriculture and farming practices, they are involved in production of handicrafts, food items, pottery making, silk weaving, and animal husbandry and so on" (FICCI Report, Skill Development in India, 2015).

Literature Review

Varun Dhamija, Arun Dhamija (2016) in the article "Employment for All: Empowering the Rural Youth" state that India has been a country that celebrates knowledge and intellect. However, skills are not celebrated. The Skill India Mission is, therefore, trying to make a significant dent with the objective to raise social awareness about the values of skills and vocational education. Different schemes have been introduced under Skill India Mission to bridge the gap between unemployment and employment in rural youth."

Swadesh Singh (2016) in his article "Empowering Rural Youth: Challenges and Opportunities" states that India has a maximum number of working population. The challenge is to make this population a human resource and it is possible with education and skill development. The author states that, the rural youth faces many challenges to compete in the modern market and hence, the government is trying its best to engage, educate, employ and make rural youth entrepreneur.

Sayantan Mandal (2016) in the article "Development of Education and Skills for Rural Youth" states that a large section of youth and soon to be youth live in villages. They see good education and employment as their right, which would make a difference in their lives. With low literacy rate and less skills they find it difficult to find employment. To help the rural youth, the government has encouraged to set up Skill Development Centres which would enhance the skills of the rural youth and hence enable them to fetch employment. However, improving the skills and education of rural youth is a matter of detailed discussion.

P. Srivatsa (2016) in the article "Importance of Skill Development among Rural Youth" states that a large population lives in villages and their household depends on small and marginal farms. The youth is searching for employment and the industries are suffering from inavailability of skilled workers. Most of the educated youth in the rural areas are not getting their desired jobs as per their educational qualification.

In this chapter, the author gives probable solutions to the unemployment in rural India.

Jatinder Singh (2018) in the article "New-age skills—Generating opportunities for youth" states that, the more the youth will join mainstream through education and skilling, the more will be the skilled labour surplus by 2030 in India. The Central and State governments are working towards youth so that the youth can use this opportunity and gain employment. Initiatives like Make in India, Skill India, Start-up India, Stand-up India and Digital India are various opportunities for youth.

A. Srija, Shamim has conducted a study on skill and entrepreneurship development for rural India. India is home to world's youngest population as half of its population is below the age of 25. To encourage rural youth including women, start-up village entrepreneurship programme (SVEP) is being implemented. In view of the foregoing this article provides an overview of labour market conditions, major Skilling and entrepreneurship programme available for youth and Union Budget announcement to strengthen Skilling and entrepreneurship programme in India.

H.L. Sharma (2019) in the article "Innovative Entrepreneurship among rural youth" realises the importance of rural youth in the process of economic development, Government of India has taken various steps and launched various schemes to empower them through developing their innovative entrepreneurial skills to achieve the motive of continuous and sustainable income and employment generation in rural India.

Anupriya Chadha (2019) in her article "Education Initiatives for Rural Youth" states that this 'demographic dividend' offers a great opportunity. However, in order to capture this demographic dividend, it is essential that the economy has the ability to support the increase in the labour force and the youth have the appropriate education, skills, health awareness and other enablers to productivity contribute to the economy. This demands the commitment of the entire nation to all-round development of the youth of India so that they can realize their full potential and contribute productivity to nation building process. Some of these schemes are National Service Scheme, Deen Dayal Upadahyay, Grameen Kaushal Yojana, Skills India etc.

Jai Prakash Pandey (2016) in the article "Skill, Education and Jobs for Rural India" states that, Skill development is main trust of NDA government since it took office in May 2014. Unemployment has been a major concern. Country has to channelize one crore unemployed youth in productive activities. Immense growth can be achieved through skill development. Rs. 1804 crore has been allocated for this. With the help of this fund, 1500 multi-skilling training institutes will be set up in coming years to promote skill development with the help of other ministries. Pradhan Mantri Kaushal Vikas Yojana to impact skill to 1 crore youth over next 3 years from current 24 lakh. National Board for Skill Development Certification is also proposed to be set up in 2016-17. This board will be set up in partnership with the industry and academics. Skill development has to be in congruence with industry to reap its full benefits.

Barna Ganguli (October 2014) in the study, "Rural Employment —A Challenging Task" aims at knowing the performance of the rural economy in terms of growth and employment which have strong influence on the rural poverty. She concluded that the rural youth are in the dire need of appropriate and satisfying jobs within the villages. Further added that rural people should be provided inputs of credit, marketing facilities etc. which will enhance their income generating capital and strengthen their entrepreneurial capacity.

Arpita Sharma (February 2013) in the article "Government Initiatives in Rural Employment" aims to discuss the success of the employment generation, government schemes and scope of employment generation in the organized and unorganized sectors. In the article it was concluded that in the past, a number of schemes have provided temporary employments, public on work programmes at the government discretion, but the present-day scenario brings with it legislation and rights—based approach for implementing pro-people development policies in the country.

A. Srija (June 2018), studied about the "Skill Development And Employment For Rural Youth", in the study it was found that, according to the word bank, about 13 million people enter the working age every year but only 3 million new jobs are created every year. The need of the hour is to improve the skill set of the labour force such that they are productively engaged in the job roles emerging from digital India, rural road connectivity etc.

Swadesh Singh (May 2017) in the article "Transforming Rural India through Skill Development" aimed to know whether the transforming rural India is an imperative to make India. A developed nation and in this process the youth have a special role to play. He stated that the government has been successful in creating an ecosystem for skill development but still, there is a need to make efforts in a sustained manner. He also added that with "make in India" as a national dream and acceptance of skill development as a priority for the next decade, reforms will come true for the government, education system and the Indian industry.

R. Sasikalapushpa, B. Ramaswamy (October 2018) conducted a study on "Employment generation through MSMEs." For future growth in Indian economy and GDP increase, the share of MSME contribution would increase the current 8 per cent to 15 per cent by the year 2020. This would be replaced by the growth of the new wave MSME led by entrepreneurship focused in innovation, creating opportunities for women entrepreneurs and developing skill resources.

A. Srija (January 2019) has conducted a study on a topic "Empowerment of Youth through Skilling." According to her study, for long term employment of rural youth it is necessary to ensure that they should at least complete the required schooling for pursuing skill development courses which will lead to sustainable development. The institutional reform will lead to improvement in quality and market relevance of skill development programmes that would enhance the value of vocational education and will increase skilled manpower.

Narendra Singh Tomar (January 2019) conducted a study on the topic "Empowerment of Rural Youth". According to him, empowerment of rural youth is directly related to the empowerment of villages. The population of youth comprises 40 per cent of the total population of India. Unskilled workers are required to be given skill-training in our country after economic reforms, the country's rural areas have witnessed a rapid transformation and in this era of technological revolution, the youth of rural areas has access to communication and other facilities.

Sabita Kumari (October 2014) in her study "Rural Employment Schemes in India", her objective is to increase the wage earning capacity of artisans and contribute to increase in the growth rate of rural and urban employment. Also generates employment opportunities in rural as well as urban areas through setting up a new self-employment. It was found that the majority of the poor in rural areas of the country depend mainly on the wages they earn through unskilled labour.

Pawan Kumar Sharma (January 2019) conducted a study on "Empowering Rural Youth for Nation Building". 'Strength is life and weakness is death', the youth need to have strong internal will-power and the strength of internal clarity this will give the youth confidence and courage to face all challenges that come in their way and ability to resolve problems. Rural youth are yet to unleash their full latest talent. Instead of merely depending on government jobs, the youth should show their indifference to the system and work towards improving constitutional provisions.

Pravakar Sahoo, Abhirup Bhunia (March 2019) have conducted a study on "Initiatives to Empower Rural Youth". The growth potential through demographic dividend depends upon shifting labour force from agriculture. The need of the hour is Skilling large number of young labour force to benefit from the changing market and production structure. India can be the hub for other countries for their outsource work and manufacturing provided India improves its education system imparting right training and skill to the labour force.

Amitabh Kant (August 2019) conducted a study on "Fostering Youth to take Opportunities of the Futures". Encouraging the youth and preparing them for the future livelihood opportunities through skill development, mentoring and support for research and development is the key to the nation advancement. This budget reiterates government commitment to empower the youth to take challenges of the future and top opportunities brought forth by changes in technologies and other transformation in the local and global economic situation. India is all set to foster its youth to take every challenges head on and emerge as future leaders in their communities as well as on the global stage.

Statement of the Problem

From the literature review, reveals that unemployment is one of the biggest problems among the rural youth. The reason for unemployment is due to lack of encouragement and secondly, lack of awareness regarding the various schemes and programmes initiated by the State and Central Governments.

An attempt is being made in this study to identify the factors for unemployment of the rural youth and the difficulties and problems faced by them in availing any government schemes initiated by the government to encourage and support self-employment and development of the youth.

Objectives of the Study

- To analyse and assess the unemployment in selected rural areas.
- To create awareness regarding various schemes of the government.
- To study and identify the various opportunities and facilities available for the rural youth.
- To identify the problems faced by rural youth and suggesting solutions for the same.
- To identify Opportunities (government sector, private sector and self-employed).
- Exploring, examining and analysing the various problems faced by educated unemployed youth.

Research Methodology

Primary

The data is collected from the youth through a questionnaire and also from Employment Exchange and Skill Development and Entrepreneurship in order to conduct a study on the topic "Thematic plan for youth in the rural economy: Skill Development and Employment."

Secondary Data

The information is obtained from various magazines, journals, and websites.

Scope

We decided to work on the topic "Thematic plan on youth in the rural economy: Skill development and employment." Study is conducted in selected Talukas of Goa.

Period of the Study

Period of study is the period of data collected.

Limitations of the Study

1. Time was the major constraint.
2. In some cases respondents failed to reply.
3. Information is considered as secret and confidential, and denied.
4. Couldn't cover all the Talukas and Panchayats of Goa.
5. Study is confined to only three Talukas of the state of Goa, so the results may not apply to the other Talukas of Goa.

Meaning of Skill Development

Skill Development is the development of a particular skill with proper professional training. A trained person can get employment easily than non-skilled labour.

Table 15.1: Employment Scenario in Goa (2014-15)

Taluka	**Age**											
	21		**22**		**23**		**24**		**25**		**26**	
Status	**X1**	**X2**	**X1**	**X2**	**X1**	**X2**	**X1**	**X2**	**X1**	**X2**	**X1**	**X2**
Bardez	14	433	32	474	99	436	119	371	127	312	130	313
Bicholim	10	390	24	442	39	429	67	388	69	308	59	268
Canacona	1	149	3	156	11	176	12	143	14	121	15	85
Dharbandora	1	92	5	108	11	90	9	75	15	81	7	64
Mormugao	8	183	29	229	29	29	65	189	63	152	64	122
Pernem	10	266	21	267	47	296	54	247	67	221	47	204
Ponda	8	338	30	433	77	432	113	350	114	345	115	279
Quepem	4	181	8	256	29	236	33	186	35	193	39	136
Salcete	9	289	36	368	95	397	112	334	103	291	103	213
Sanguem	3	129	3	138	10	161	15	129	17	109	17	107
Satari	4	366	22	425	34	418	30	328	28	278	38	246
Tiswadi	13	259	29	354	74	331	95	270	85	249	103	206
Grand total	**85**	**3075**	**242**	**3650**	**555**	**3606**	**734**	**3010**	**737**	**2660**	**737**	**2243**

Source: Goa Employment Exchange, Government of Goa.
X1= EMPLOYED.

X2= UNEMPLOYED.

1. Suppose the government opens new schools to educate people, the teachers will be required to run the school.
2. A study conducted by the Planning Commission estimates that nearly 20 lakh jobs can be created in the education sector alone.
3. Similarly, if we have to improve the health situation, we need many more doctors, nurses, health workers etc., to work in various parts of our country.

Skill development is the process of:

- Identifying your skill gaps. and
- Developing the existing skills.

It is important as your skills determine your ability to execute your plans and enables the person to achieve his/her goals.

Skill development is the most important aspect for the development of India. For that, the Government should focus on the skill development sector in order to make the Skill India campaign a successful model by achieving the mission of "Koushal Bharat, Kushal Bharat".

The Self-employment Programmes Initiated by the Government for Skill Development and Employment

National Apprenticeship Promotion Scheme (NAPS)

It was launched on the 19th August, 2016, with the objective of providing Apprenticeship Training to 50 lakh youth by 2020. Under this scheme, the Government will share 25 per cent of the prescribed stipend, subject to a maximum of Rs. 155 per month per apprentice with the employers. The government also shares up to a maximum of Rs. 7,500 per fresher apprentice (without any formal trade training), the cost of basic training with Basic Training Providers.

National Skill Development Corporation (NSDC)

NSDC has entered into a strategic partnership with Facebook

to empower youth and entrepreneurs with digital skills in India. The partnership, signed in Bhubaneswar, Odisha, will enable The Ministry of Skill Development and Entrepreneurship (MSDE) to incorporate Facebook's training on Digital Marketing Skills in its courses, besides providing trainees with access to local, domestic and international markets. The programme includes courses on digital marketing, online safety and financial literacy in regional languages with Facebook imparting training to people nominated by the NSDC. This will up-skill job seekers and increase their prospects of employment.

Start-up Village Entrepreneurship Programme

The Government is implementing the Start-up Village Entrepreneurship Programme with the objective of helping the rural poor including artisans and weavers to set up enterprises at the village level in non-agricultural sectors. Start-up Village Entrepreneurship Programme (SVEP), is a sub-scheme under the National Rural Livelihoods Mission (NRLM) was launched with the objective of helping rural poor by helping them set-up sustainable enterprises.

National Employability Enhanced Mission

The objective of National Employability Enhanced Mission (NEEM) is to offer on-the-job practical training to enhance employability of person either pursuing his or her graduation/ diploma in any technical or non-technical stream or discontinued studies of degree or diploma course to increase their employability. Till date, 29 NEEM Agents have registered under NEEM scheme. The training modules under NEEM training are NSQF complainers. NEEM Agents are persons who have linkage with small industry etc., who have knowledge of the demand for skills and hence can play a role in sourcing the requisite persons with appropriate skills. In 2017-18, the NEEM Agents have been able to provide industry apprenticeship for more than 43,000 candidates.

Table 15.2. Incremental Human Resource Requirement across Sectors by 2022

Sl. No.	Sector	Employment Base in 2013 (million)	Projected Employment by 2022 (million)	Incremental Human Resource Requirement (2013-22)
1	Auto and Auto Components	10.98	14.88	3.9
2	Beauty and Wellness	4.21	14.27	10.06
3	Food Processing	6.98	11.38	4.4
4	Media and Entertainment	0.4	1.3	0.9
5	Handlooms and Handicrafts	11.65	17.79	6.14
6	Leather and Leather Goods	3.09	6.81	3.72
7	Domestic Help	6	10.88	4.88
8	Gems and Jewellery	4.64	8.23	3.59
9	Telecommunication	2.08	4.16	2.08
10	Tourism, Hospitality & Travel	6.96	13.44	6.48
11	Furniture and Furnishing	4.11	11.29	7.18
12	Building, Construction and Real Estate	45.42	76.55	31.13
13	IT and ITES	2.96	5.12	2.16
14	Construction Material and Building Hardware	8.3	11	2.7
15	Textile and Clothing	15.23	21.54	6.31
16	Healthcare	3.59	7.39	3.8
17	Security	7	11.83	4.83
18	Agriculture	240.4	215.6	24.8
19	Education/skill development	13.02	17.31	4.29
20	Transportation and Logistics	16.74	28.4	11.66

(*Contd.*)

Sl. No.	Sector	Employment Base in 2013 (million)	Projected Employment by 2022 (million)	Incremental Human Resource Requirement (2013-22)
21	Electronic and IT Hardware	4.33	8.94	4.61
22	Pharma and Life Sciences	1.86	3.58	1.72
23	BFSI	2.55	4.25	1.7
24	Retail	38.6	55.95	17.35
	Grand Total	**461.1**	**581.89**	**120.79**

Source: Ministry of Skill Development & Entrepreneurship.

Schemes for Skill Development and Employment

Prime Minister's Employment Generation Programme (PMEGP)

"Prime Minister's Employment Generation Programme (PMEGP) is a credit-link subsidy programme introduced by the Government of India in 2008. PMEGP is a merger of two schemes, namely Prime Minister's Rojgar Yojana and Rural Employment Generation Programme. This programme focuses on generating self-employment opportunities through micro-enterprise establishment in the non-farm sector by helping unemployed youth and traditional artisans.

Mahatma Gandhi National Rural Employment Guarantee Scheme (MGNREGS)

The Mahatma Gandhi National Rural Employment Guarantee Scheme (MGNREGS) aims at social inclusion through the creation of productive assets as well as enhance livelihood security by providing at least 100 days of guaranteed wage employment in a financial year to every adult member of a household who volunteer to do unskilled manual work. In recent years, emphasis is on the construction of rural infrastructure through convergence with MGNREGA such as Individual Household Latrines (IHHL) for PMAY-G beneficiaries, infrastructure for agricultural and allied activities etc. During 2017-18, 4.63 crore households were provided employment in 163 lakh works and in the process, 182 crore person-days of employment was generated.

The Ministry of Micro, Small & Medium Enterprises (MSME) is implementing the Prime Minister's Employment Generation Programme (PMEGP), which is a major credit-linked subsidy programme aimed at generating self-employment opportunities through the establishment of microenterprises in the non-farm sector by helping traditional artisans and unemployed youth.

Deen Dayal Upadhyaya Grameen Kaushalya Yojana (DDU-GKY)

The DDU-GKY is a placement linked skill-training programme to empower rural poor youth with employable skills and facilitate their participation in the labour market. As of October 2017, the DDU-GKY has over 566 Training Centres in 674 Projects, in partnership with over 310 Project Implementing Agencies conducting training across 39 sectors, covering 329 job roles spread across 28 States. Against a target of Skilling 2 lakh candidates during 2017-18, over 83,745 candidates have already been trained, of which over 46,654 candidates have been placed in jobs. The Ministry has selected 12 new Champion Employers and entered into an MoU with them for high quality training and placements.

Deen Dayal Antyodaya Yojana (DAY)

"Deen Dayal Antyodaya Yojana (DAY) with an aim to uplift the urban poor folks by enhancing sustainable livelihood opportunities through skill development. Keeping in view the objective of Make in India, Skill Development is essential for socio-economic betterment. Deen Dayal Antyodaya Yojana was launched under the Ministry of Housing and Urban Poverty Alleviation (HUPA). Government of India has provisioned Rs.500 crore for the scheme.

The scheme is the integration of the National Urban Livelihood Mission (NULM) and The National Urban Livelihood Mission (NRLM).

The National Urban Livelihood Mission (NULM) is renamed as Deen Dayal Antyodaya Yojana (DAY-NULM) and in Hindi as—Rashtriya Shahri Aajeevika Mission. Under the scheme urban areas extend the coverage to all the 4041 statutory cities and towns, thereby covering almost the entire urban population. Currently, all the urban poverty alleviating programmes covered only 790 towns and cities.

Pradhan Mantri Mudra Yojana (PMMY)

Pradhan Mantri Mudra Yojana (PMMY) is a flagship scheme of Government of India to "fund the unfunded" by bringing such enterprises to the formal financial system and extending affordable credit to them. It enables a small borrower to borrow from all Public Sector Banks such as PSU Bank, Regional Rural Bank and Cooperative Banks, Private Sector Banks, Foreign Banks, Micro Finance Institutions (MFI) and Non-Banking Finance Companies (NBFC) for loan up to Rs. 10 lakh for non-farm income generating activities. The scheme was launched on 8th April, 2015 by the Hon'ble Prime Minister.

Pradhan Mantri Rojgar Protsahan Yojana Scheme (PMRPY)

The Pradhan Mantri Rojgar Protsahan Yojana or PMRPY Scheme is aimed at incentivising employers to generate employment, where the Government pays the employers' Employee Pension Scheme share of 8.33 per cent, for new employees for the first three years of their job.

There is also a proposal to make this applicable for those who are unemployed but are semi-skilled and unskilled as well. The Ministry of Labour has implemented the same scheme and has been in operation since August 2016.

The PMRPY scheme was announced during the 2016-17 Budget with the primary purpose of promoting the generation of employment with INR 1000 crore having been made.

The scheme targets workers who earn wages less than INR 15,000 on a monthly basis. It encourages employers of Small and Medium Enterprises and Micro Businesses to avail the benefits of this project.

Pradhan Mantri Kaushal Vikas Yojana (PMKVY)

The Pradhan Mantri Kaushal Vikas Yojana, the flagship scheme on Skilling was launched in 2015 to provide industry relevant skill training to the youth to enable them secure a better livelihood. The scheme provides short-term training to the job seekers as well as Recognition of Prior Learning (RPL) to the existing workforce through accredited and affiliated training partner/training centres and ensures placement. The scheme runs across 252 job roles related to 35 Sector Skill Councils. The PMKVY was first launched in 2015-16 and owing to its success, the scheme was re-launched as PMKVY 2.0 for the period 2016-2020.

Rural Self-Employment Training Institutes (RSETIs): not in Goa

The Ministry of Rural Development has been implementing the Rural Self-Employment Training Institutes (RSETIs) for the rural youth, which seeks to diversify household income of the rural poor. RSETI is a three-way partnership amongst the Ministry of Rural Development, State Government and Banks. There are 31 participating banks, which have set up 586 RSETIs in the country. RSETIs provide training in agriculture, process, product and general entrepreneurship development programmes (EDP) courses to candidates leading to self-employment wage employment. Against a target of skilling 3.97 lakh candidates during 2017-18, 2.35 lakh candidates have been trained and 1.55 lakh have been settled.

Pradhan Mantri Yuva Udyami Vikas Abhiyan (PM-YUVA)

The scheme aims to create an enabling ecosystem for entrepreneurship development through entrepreneurship education and training across the country in select Institutes of Higher Learning (Universities, Colleges and Premier Institutes), schools, Industrial Training Centres (ITIs) and Entrepreneurship Development Centres (EDCs) for over a period of five years (2017-18 to 2021-22). Additionally, students will get easy access to a robust network of peers, mentors, incubators, funds and business services through an online platform. So far, 239 Institutes of Higher Learning have been empanelled to impart entrepreneurship education and entrepreneurship courses have started in more than 200 Institutes of Higher Learning.

Data Analysis and Findings

The survey was conducted to know about the problems faced by rural youth and the reasons behind unemployment. Whether the youth are aware about the various schemes and facilities available in Goa by the Directorate of Skill Development and Entrepreneurship and also to know whether the youth are interested in taking up the Self-employment schemes to create employment opportunities for themselves and others.

Table 15.3: Position of Unemployed Youth

Taluka	Frequency	Per cent	Valid Per cent
Mormugao	146	47.6	47.6
Salcete	38	12.4	12.4
Tiswadi	123	40.0	40.0
Total	**307**	**100.0**	**100.0**

Source: Primary Data.

Table 15.3 shows that Mormugao has the highest number of unemployed youth resulting in 47.6 per cent, followed by Tiswadi which shows 40.1 per cent unemployed youth and Salcete with 12.4 per cent unemployed youth.

Table 15.4: Gender-wise Position of Unemployed Youth

Gender	Frequency	Per cent	Valid Per cent
Male	161	52.4	52.4
Female	146	47.6	47.6
Total	**307**	**100.0**	**100.0**

Source: Primary Data.

Table 15.4 reveals that 52.4 per cent are male unemployed and 46.6 per cent are female unemployed.

Table 15.5: Awareness about Government Employment Schemes

Schemes	Frequency	Per cent	Valid Per cent
PMEGP	139	18.00	18.00
MGNREGS	62	8.00	8.00
DDU-GKY	29	4.00	4.00
DAY-NULM	94	13.00	13.00
PMMY	95	13.00	13.00
PMRPY	101	13.00	13.00
PMKVY	119	16.00	16.00
RSETIs	60	8.00	8.00
PM-YUVA	55	7.00	7.00
Total	**307**	**100.00**	**100.00**

Source: Primary Data.

Table 15.5 shows that there are total nine popular schemes for the youth and for employment. Out of the schemes, PMEGP is known and utilised by the maximum youth resulting in 18 per cent followed by PMKVY whereas DDU-GKY was the least known resulting in 4 per cent awareness.

Table 15.6: Status for Government Schemes Applied

Schemes	Frequency	Per cent	Valid Per cent
PMEGP	53	14.00	14.00
MGNREGS	20	5.00	5.00

(*Contd.*)

Schemes	Frequency	Per cent	Valid Per cent
DDU-GKY	0	0	0
DAY-NULM	0	0	0
PMMY	0	0	0
PMRPY	0	0	0
PMKVY	11	3.00	3.00
RSETIs	0	0	0
PM-YUVA	0	0	0
Not Applied for Schemes	297	78.00	78.00
Total	**307**	**100.00**	**100.00**

Source: Primary Data.

Table 15.6 shows the status of government schemes applied and reveals that only expect PMEGP (14%), PMKVY (3%) and MGNREGS (5%) rest 78 per cent respondents have never applied for any of the schemes above.

Table 15.7: Unemployability

	Frequency	Per cent	Valid Per cent
Self	130	42.3	42.3
Education	40	13.0	13.0
Family	12	3.9	3.9
Government	125	40.7	40.7
Total	**307**	**100.0**	**100.0**

Source: Primary Data.

Table 15.7 reveals that the reason for not getting a job and reflects that 42.3 per cent respondents blames for self, followed by 40.7 per cent blames for the government whereas only 13 per cent respondents blames for the education.

Problems faced by Rural Youth

Table 15.8: Lack of Education

	Frequency	Per cent	Valid Per cent
No	164	53.4	53.4
Yes	143	46.6	46.6
Total	**307**	**100.0**	**100.0**

Source: Primary Data.

Table 15.8 shows that 53.4 per cent respondents find that no problem as far as education is concerned whereas 46.6 per cent respondents faced problems. With regard to finance, 62.5 per cent rural youth lack in finance required to acquire knowledge which reflects that the financial problem faced by them. As far as job availability is concerned 60.6 per cent youth faced problems whereas 39.4 per cent respondents were confident about availability of jobs. They are highly correlated to employment and skill development of rural youth.

Table 15.9: Lack of finance to acquire knowledge

	Frequency	Per cent	Valid Per cent
No	115	37.5	37.5
Yes	192	62.5	62.5
Total	**307**	**100.0**	**100.0**

Source: Primary Data.

Table 15.10: No jobs available

	Frequency	Per cent	Valid Per cent
No	121	39.4	39.4
Yes	186	60.6	60.6
Total	**307**	**100.0**	**100.0**

Source: Primary Data.

Correlation Matrix

		Lack of education	Lack of finance to acquire know-ledge	No jobs available	Decrease in employ-ment opport-unities
Corre-lation	Lack of education	1.000	.170	.058	.031
	Lack of finance to acquire knowledge	.170	1.000	.009	.109
	No jobs available	.058	.009	1.000	.233
	Decrease in employment opportunities	.031	.109	.233	1.000

Communalities

	Initial	Extraction
Lack of education	1.000	.569
Lack of finance to acquire knowledge	1.000	.595
No jobs available	1.000	.632
Decrease in employment opportunities	1.000	.611

Extraction Method: Principal Component Analysis.

Total Variance Explained

Compo-nent	Initial Eigen Values			Extraction Sums of Squared Loadings		
	Total	% of Variance	Cumulative %	Total	% of Variance	Cumulative %
1	1.311	32.784	32.784	1.311	32.784	32.784
2	1.096	27.388	60.172	1.096	27.388	60.172
3	.868	21.710	81.883			
4	.725	18.117	100.000			

Extraction Method: Principal Component Analysis.

Component Matrix[a]

	Component	
	1	2
Lack of education	.459	.599
Lack of finance to acquire knowledge	.508	.580
No jobs available	.613	-.506
Decrease in employment opportunities	.683	-.380

Extraction Method: Principal Component Analysis.
a. 2 components extracted.

Component Score Coefficient Matrix

	Component	
	1	2
Lack of education	.350	.547
Lack of finance to acquire knowledge	.387	.530
No jobs available	.468	-.462
Decrease in employment opportunities	.521	-.346

Extraction Method: Principal Component Analysis.

Table 15.11: Other alternative means of job than the government job

	Frequency	Per cent	Valid Per cent
No	123	40.1	40.1
Yes	71	23.1	23.1
Maybe	113	36.8	36.8
Total	**307**	**100.0**	**100.0**

Source: Primary Data.

Chi-Square Tests

	Value	Df	Asymp. Sig. (2-sided)
Pearson Chi-Square	9.300[a]	3	.026
Likelihood Ratio	11.389	3	.010
Linear-by-Linear Association	9.207	1	.002
N of Valid Cases	307		

a. 1 cells (12.5%) have expected count less than 5. The minimum expected count is 2.21.

Symmetric Measures

		Value	Asymp. Std. Error[a]	Approx. T[b]	Approx. Sig.
Interval by Interval	Pearson's R	.173	.050	3.076	.002[c]
Ordinal by Ordinal	Spearman Correlation	.172	.051	3.057	.002[c]
N of Valid Cases	307				

a. Not assuming the null hypothesis.
b. Using the asymptotic standard error assuming the null hypothesis.
c. Based on normal approximation.

Table 15.11 shows the other alternative means of job than the government job which reveals that 40.1 per cent respondents found that there is no other alternative whereas 23.1 per cent respondents strongly believe that there are lots of alternative means of job than the government job while 36.8 per cent respondents have mixed reaction.

Table 15.12: Self-Employment Program-Assistance

	Frequency	Per cent	Valid Per cent
No	40	13.0	13.0
Yes	267	87.0	87.0
Total	**307**	**100.0**	**100.0**

Source: Primary Data.

Chi-Square Tests

	Value	Df	Asymp. Sig. (2-sided)
Pearson Chi-Square	7.756[a]	2	.021
Likelihood Ratio	8.397	2	.015
N of Valid Cases	307		

a. 1 cells (16.7%) have expected count less than 5. The minimum expected count is 4.95.

Table 15.12 shows that 87 per cent respondents were positive for self-employment programmes if they were given whereas 13 per cent were not in favour of it.

Table 15.13: Youth tried for Self-Employment Schemes

	Frequency	Per cent	Valid Per cent
No	239	77.9	77.9
Yes	68	22.1	22.1
Total	**307**	**100.0**	**100.0**

Source: Primary Data.

Chi-Square Tests

	Value	Df	Asymp. Sig. (2-sided)
Pearson Chi-Square	4.130[a]	2	.127
Likelihood Ratio	4.250	2	.119
N of Valid Cases	307		

a. 0 cells (.0%) have expected count less than 5. The minimum expected count is 8.42.

Table 15.13 reveals that 77.9 per cent respondents never tried any self-employment schemes whereas 21 per cent respondents made an attempt to make use of them.

Factor Analysis for Problems Faced by Youth of Self-Employment

Table 15.14: Lack of skill

	Frequency	Per cent	Valid Per cent
No	209	68.1	68.1
Yes	98	31.9	31.9
Total	**307**	**100.0**	**100.0**

Source: Primary Data.

Table 15.15: Lack of finance

	Frequency	Per cent	Valid Per cent
No	124	40.4	40.4
Yes	183	59.6	59.6
Total	**307**	**100.0**	**100.0**

Source: Primary Data.

Table 15.16: Lack of support

	Frequency	Per cent	Valid Per cent
No	125	40.7	40.7
Yes	182	59.3	59.3
Total	**307**	**100.0**	**100.0**

Source: Primary Data.

Table 15.17: Lack of confidence

	Frequency	Per cent	Valid Per cent
No	131	42.7	42.7
Yes	176	57.3	57.3
Total	**307**	**100.0**	**100.0**

Source: Primary Data.

Table 15.18: Lack of awareness about government/state promotional schemes

	Frequency	Per cent	Valid Per cent
No	130	42.3	42.3
Yes	177	57.7	57.7
Total	**307**	**100.0**	**100.0**

Source: Primary Data.

Correlation Matrix

		Lack of skill	**Lack of finance**	**Lack of support**	**Lack of confidence**	**Lack of awareness about government/ state promotional schemes**
Correlation	Lack of skill	1.000	-.020	-.030	-.003	-.064
	Lack of finance	-.020	1.000	.223	.189	.128
	Lack of support	-.030	.223	1.000	.197	.189
	Lack of confidence	-.003	.189	.197	1.000	.074
	Lack of awareness about government/ state promotional schemes	-.064	.128	.189	.074	1.000

Communalities

	Initial	Extraction
Lack of skill	1.000	.788
Lack of finance	1.000	.439
Lack of support	1.000	.485
Lack of confidence	1.000	.430
Lack of awareness about government/state promotional schemes	1.000	.393

Extraction Method: Principal Component Analysis.

Component Matrix[a]

	Component	
	1	2
Lack of skill	-.132	.878
Lack of finance	.646	.150
Lack of support	.696	.034
Lack of confidence	.577	.311
Lack of awareness about government\state promotional schemes	.514	-.359

Extraction Method: Principal Component Analysis.
a. 2 components extracted.

The problem of self-employment were classified as lack of skill, lack of finance, lack of support, lack of confidence and lack of awareness of government/state promotional schemes. Study reveals that 31.9 per cent respondents feel that self-employment is not possible due to lack of skill, alternatively 68.1 per cent have no problem regarding skill, 59.6 per cent respondents face problem of self-employment due to lack of finance which is considered as a major constraint for self-employment. 40.4 per cent feel that there is no problem as regards to finance. Rural youth expect lot of support from the family, government, banks etc. which is revealed from Table 15.16 resulting in 59.3 per cent respectively faced problem for self-employment due to lack of support. As far as youth's self-confidence is concerned for self-employment, study reveals that

57.3 per cent respectively lack confidence, whereas 42.7 per cent have a positive and confident approach. Majority of rural youth are not aware about government and state promotional schemes for self-employment which can be seen from the study resulting in 57.7 per cent which is a major concern factor for youth self-employment as a result most of the schemes of the government remains on paper only. The factors are highly correlated to self-employment of the rural youth.

Satisfaction Regarding Rules, Regulations and Formalities for Availing Government Schemes

Table 15.19: Lengthy and complex registration process

	Frequency	Per cent	Valid Per cent
No	120	39.1	39.1
Yes	187	60.9	60.9
Total	**307**	**100.0**	**100.0**

Source: Primary Data.

Table 15.20: Government licences and NOCs

	Frequency	Per cent	Valid Per cent
No	155	50.5	50.5
Yes	152	49.5	49.5
Total	**307**	**100.0**	**100.0**

Source: Primary Data.

Table 15.21: Lack of seed money

	Frequency	Per cent	Valid Per cent
No	169	55.0	55.0
Yes	138	45.0	45.0
Total	**307**	**100.0**	**100.0**

Source: Primary Data.

Level of satisfaction of the rural youth regarding rules, regulation and formalities for availing government schemes shows that 60.9 per cent rural youth has to face lengthy and complex registration process, while almost 50.5 per cent of the respondents face no problem regarding Licence and NOCs from government while for seed money is concerned 55 per cent rural youth has problem while 45 per cent has no problem.

Table 15.22: Utilisation of Schemes for Self-Employment

	Frequency	**Per cent**	**Valid Per cent**
No	71	23.1	23.1
Yes	68	22.1	22.1
Not sure	168	54.7	54.7
Total	**307**	**100.0**	**100.0**

Source: Primary Data.

Table 15.22 shows that 54.7 per cent respondents are not sure about the utilisation of various schemes properly whereas 22.1 per cent respondents say that they are aware about.

Table 15.23: Educated Unemployed are ready to take up schemes for employment

	Frequency	**Per cent**	**Valid Per cent**
No	174	56.7	56.7
Yes	133	43.3	43.3
Total	**307**	**100.0**	**100.0**

Source: Primary Data.

Table 15.23 reveals that 56.7 per cent respondents are not interested in taking up the schemes whereas 43.3 per cent has shown interest in taking up government schemes.

Table 15.24: Role of government in solving educated unemployment problems

	Frequency	**Per cent**	**Valid Per cent**
No	112	36.5	36.5
Yes	50	16.3	16.3
Partially trying to solve	145	47.2	47.2
Total	**307**	**100.0**	**100.0**

Source: Primary Data.

Table 15.24 shows the government's seriousness in solving educated unemployment problems. 36.5 per cent respondents feels that governement is not serious whereas 47.2 per cent respondents partially agreeing while 16.3 per cent respondents feels that government is serious in solving educated unemployment problems.

Table 15.25: Future of Educated Unemployed

	Frequency	Per cent	Valid Per cent
Increase	169	55.0	55.0
Remains the same	26	8.5	8.5
Decrease	34	11.1	11.1
I have no idea	78	25.4	25.4
Total	**307**	**100.0**	**100.0**

Source: Primary Data.

Table 15.25 reveals that 55 per cent respondents feels that the educated unemployment will increase in near future whereas 11.1 per cent has a strong opinion that it will decrease while 25.4 per cent have no idea about this main issue.

Challenges in Skill Development

Lack of Entrepreneurship Skills

While the government expected that some of the PMKVY-trainees would create their own enterprise, only 24 per cent of the trainees started their business. And out of them, only 10,000 applied for MUDRA loans.

Workforce Challenge

In Goa, the first challenge is about the workforce. Youth needs to be trained across four levels, from the 'White Collar' workers to the 'Rust Collar' workers, linking them to job opportunities and market realities.

Skill Challenges

The skills challenge for India considering that the country has a large portion of its population below 25 years of age. This young population can be transformed into a productive workforce giving the Indian Economy a 'Demographic Dividend'.

Mismatch of Skill and Job

"The skills *versus* jobs mismatch often leads to economically inactive working age group people. This not only impacts the economy, it also has serious consequences for the society at large" (FICCI Report, Skills Development).

Conclusion

It is often said that you cannot do things the same way and expect different results. In order to see changes, one needs to do things differently. Industries shall not expect to see growth if they do not invest in Skill Development. Therefore, investing in Skill Development beneficial to the industries as much as to it is to employees. Skill Development always leads to competitive advantage. In order to be the best, an individual needs to have something that nobody else has. Hence, skill development helps in grooming and shaping an individual into a leader.

Among the three Talukas, Mormugao has the majority of unemployed youth followed by Salcete since there is no exposure of other opportunities and facilities available for youth, very few training centres, and no awareness. As compared to female, male are the more unemployed since they are less educated, hence there is low employability. Various schemes are available but youth are not fully aware of all the schemes except for PMEGP, PMKVY, and PMRPY.

Almost 80 per cent of youth have not applied for the schemes because of the long procedural issues, tedious paper work etc. Youth wants to take up self-employment jobs but are somehow not able to because of lack of education, fear if failure, low self-confidence, fears of criticism, low personal morale, lack of finance etc. Most of the youth feel that if they are given assistance for self-employment, they can take up self-employment schemes. Very few made an attempt to make use of self-employment schemes. More preference is given to formal education rather than Skilling; hence educated unemployed youth are not ready to avail for the schemes. Youth feel that in the near future the level of educated unemployed will increase since the level of competition in job market is increased.

Therefore, youth should take up Skill Development courses and keep upgrading their profile and their skills in order to succeed and attain employability and contribution to the nation and thus reduce unemployment in the state as well as in the country.

Suggestions

The Central Government and State government should provide funding support to state government institutions to make skills trainer a lucrative career option. This fund support shall not only allow the state governments to retain the trainers for the schools and other institutions but also invite participation of many more people into the training industry.

Since youth are not educated or less educated, this is the reason for low employability. In order to increase employment, youth should be educated as well as their skill should be given more importance so that they could succeed in whichever field they are interested in.

Government should encourage the youth to go for skill-based courses through various schemes and provide them with proper facilities and opportunities which will lead the youth to be employed. Awareness should be created about the schemes available for employment and ensure that youth are taking up the schemes. The procedure for applying for the schemes should be in simplest possible manner.

A policy can also be introduced for youth, i.e. 'EARN WHILE YOU LEARN'. This can further reduce the level of unemployability. Youth will also be benefited by it so that they can earn and get educated simultaneously.

Government should create more awareness regarding availability of self-employment schemes and emphasize on promoting self-employment by arranging seminars, campaigns, giving them confidence and support and provide them with financial back-up and facilities.

Equal importance should be given to formal education and skilling the youth which will help in bridging the gap between the unemployment and employment. To lower down the problems of educated unemployed youth, skill-based courses should be introduced and promoted.

Government should encourage more on entrepreneurship development, so that youth can start their own business and create employment opportunities for others.

Engaging Multi-National Corporations to provide skills solutions that transpose the models and practices. Greater interaction should be encouraged among industry, academia and skills providers to narrow the gap between the demand and supply of skilled manpower.

References

Journal

A. Srija, Ara Shamin (2019). "Skill and Entrepreurship Development for Rural India." *Kurukshetra*, Vol. 67, No. 10, p. 56.

A. Srija (January 2019). "Empowerment of Youth through Skilling." *Kurukshetra*, Vol. 67, No. 3, p. 11.

A. Srija (June 2018). "Skill Development and Employment for Rural Youth." *Kurukshetra*, Vol. 66, No. 8, pp. 11-15.

Chadha, Anupriya (January 2019). "Education Initiatives for Rural Youth." *Kurukshetra*, Vol. 67, No. 3, pp. 15-16.

Dhamija, Varun, Dhamija Arun (June 2016). "Employment for all: Empowering the rural youth." *Kurukshetra*, Vol. 64, No. 8, pp. 29-32.

Ganguli, Barna (October 2014). "Rural Employment—A Challenging Task."*Kurukshetra*, Vol. 62, No. 12, pp. 32-35.

Kant, Amitabh (August 2019). "Fostering Youth to take Opportunites of the Futures." *Yojana*, Vol. 63, p. 17.

Kumari, Sabita (October 2014). "Rural Employment Scheme in India", *Kurukshetra*, Vol. 62, No. 12, pp. 41-46.

Mandal, Sayantan (August 2016). "Development of Education and Skills for rural youth." *Kurukshetra*, Vol. 64, No. 10, pp. 14-18.

Pandey, Jai Prakash (April 2016). "Skill Education and Jobs for Rural India." *Kurukshetra*, Vol. 64, No. 6, p. 17.

Pravakar Sahoo, Abhirup Bhunia (March 2019). "Initiatives to Empower Rural Youth." *Kurukshetra*, Vol. 67, No. 5, p. 33.

R. Sasikalapushpa, B. Ramaswamy (October 2018). *Kurushetra*, Vol. 66, No. 12, p. 37.

Sharma, Arpita (February 2013). "Government Initiatives in Rural Employment." *Kurukshetra*, Vol. 71, No. 4, pp. 3-7.

Sharma, H.L (January 2019). "Innovative Entreprenuership among rural youth." *Kurukshetra*, Vol. 67, No. 3, p. 48.

Sharma, Pawan Kumar (January 2019). "Empowering Rural Youth for Nation Building." *Kurukshetra*, Vol. 67, No. 3, p. 51.

Singh, Swadesh (August 2016). "Empowering Rural Youth: Challenges and Opportunities." *Kurukshetra*, Vol. 64, No. 10, pp. 10-12.

Singh, Jatinder (June 2018). "New-age skills—Generating opportunities for youth." *Yojana*, Vol. 62, pp. 33-36.

Singh, Swadesh (August 2016). "Empowering Rural Youth: Challenges and Opportunities." *Kurukshetra*, Vol. 64, No. 10, pp. 10-12.

Srivatsa, P. (August 2016). "Importance of Skill Development among Rural Youth." *Kurukshetra*, Vol. 64, No. 10, pp. 27-30.

Tomar, Narendra Singh (January 2019). "Empowerment of Rural Youth." *Kurushetra*, Vol. 67, No. 3, p. 5.

Web-based Data:

https://www.kas.de/en/web/indien/single-title/-/content/skill-development-in-india

https://cleartax.in/s/pm-employment-generation-programme

https://en.m.wikipedia.org/wiki/National_Rural_Employment_Guarantee_Act,_2005

https://en.m.wikipedia.org/wiki/Deen_Dayal_Upadhyaya_Grameen_Kaushalya_Yojana

https://www.india.gov.in/spotlight/deen-dayal-antyodaya-yojana

http://vikaspedia.in/social-welfare/financial-inclusion/pradhan-mantri-mudra-yojana

https://cleartax.in/s/pradhan-mantri-rojgar-protsahan-yojana

http://vikaspedia.in/social-welfare/rural-poverty-alleviation-1/schemes/rural-self-employment-training-institutes

http://vikaspedia.in/social-welfare/entrepreneurship/pradhan-mantri-yuva-yojana

https://pmjandhanyojana.co.in/kaushal-vikas-yojana-pmkvy/

http://ddugky.gov.in/content/enrol

https://pradhanmantriyojana.co.in/yuva-yojna-pmmy/
http://www.nacer.in/eligibility_criteria.html
http://ficci.in/sector/74/Project_docs/SectorProfile.pdf
https://personalexcellence.co/blog/skills-development/

16

Political Empowerment of Women through Self-Help Groups in Karnataka with Special Reference to Kodagu District

Kavya, C.T. and *Midatala Rani*

Introduction

India is a land of multiple hierarchies rooted in caste, class and gender. Patriarchal hierarchies rank men above women in most spheres of life and, put very simply, assign them different social roles and responsibilities: Men are the heads of the family, bread-winners and decision-makers in the public realm; women are responsible for reproductive tasks and everything that has to do with the domestic domain; and her behaviour impinges directly on the honour of her family, in spite of several constitutional provisions in favour of women development.

The early 1990s witnessed four key events that are now regarded as marking a watershed in the development of post-colonial India.

(1) The introduction of the recommendations of the Mandal Commission on reservations for OBCs in 1990.
(2) The introduction of economic reforms and liberalisation from 1991.
(3) The rise of Hindu nationalism.
(4) The introduction of reserved seats for women in village and municipal councils in 1992.

While all four events have undoubtedly had significant consequences for everyday lives of women, we will here concern ourselves mostly with examining the impact of economic and political reforms in the wake of new economic policy—Liberalisation, Privatisation and Globalisation.Politically, the reservation for women of one-third of all seats in village and municipal councils has had a major impact on women's participation in public life. Although more than 20 years have now passed, we are only just beginning to see the contours of the changes which are considered to be potentially revolutionary to portray women at political forefront.

The 1995 Fourth World Conference on Women in Beijing marked a significant turning point in setting the agenda for women empowerment. The *Beijing Declaration and the Platform for Action*, adopted unanimously by 189 countries, is an agenda for women's empowerment and considered the key global policy document on gender equality. It sets strategic objectives and actions for the advancement of women and the achievement of gender equality in 12 critical areas of concern:

- Women and poverty,
- Education and training of women,
- Women health and hygiene,
- Violence against women,
- Women and armed conflict,
- Women and the economy,
- Women in power, politics and decision-making,
- Institutional mechanism for the advancement of women,
- Human rights of women, women and the media,
- Women and the environment, and
- The rights of girl-child.

Literature Review

United Nations Decade for Women was adopted December 15, 1975, by the *United Nations General Assembly* by *Resolution 31/136*. UN Women is the United Nations entity dedicated to gender equality and the empowerment of women. A global champion for women and girls, UN Women was established to accelerate progress on meeting their needs worldwide. In July 2010, the United Nations General Assembly created UN Women, the United Nations Entity for Gender Equality and the Empowerment of Women, to address challenges of women development and sustainable economic goals across the globe. In doing so, UN Member States took an historic step in accelerating the Organization's goals on gender equality the empowerment of women and women development. The first UN Women's Conference, held in Mexico City in 1975, designated 1975–85 as the UN Decade for Women, and five months later the UN General Assembly launched that programme. The second UN Women's Conference was held in Copenhagen in 1980, and the third UN Women's Conference was held in Nairobi in 1985. The participants at these meetings discussed issues such as pay equity, violence against women, landholding, and basic human rights. The UN Decade for Women concentrated mainly on women and development and promotion of equal rights and opportunities for women around the world. The UN Decade for Women and its conferences helped establish the legitimacy of women's issues regarding their roles as workers in the home and outside it. The decade also brought the many inequalities women face in education, healthcare, and work to the attention of national leaders and among the general public. The UN decade for women 1976-85 focused on the improvement of economic status of women and their effective participation in the development of their respective countries. The integrity and peace in any of the country largely depends on the extent to which women are empowered in the spheres of public participation followed by social and economic freedom.

The UN women decade for addressed the issues related to right to equality and social justice. Equality referred the prevalence of ideal social systems to promote right to status treatment of women irrespective of gender biases.The World Plan of Action from the meeting in Mexico (1975) recognised the importance of communication and information in improving women's status. Paragraphs 83 to 91 establish measures regarding education and the spread of information. These include a special emphasis on the sexist way in which women are portrayed, focusing on the importance of active participation by women in decision-making within the media. Finally, it is pointed out that there is a need to create educational programmes to eradicate the prejudices that restrict women's participation in society.

The Women Conference at Copenhagen, 14 to 30th of July, 1980 approved the legislation with the following recommendations:

- Guaranteeing women the right to vote to be eligible for election or appointment to public office and to exercise public functions on equal terms with men—wherever such legislation does not already exist. In particular, political parties should be encouraged to nominate women candidates to positions that give them the possibility equally with men to be elected.
- To promote the right to freedom and develop the ability to communicate through the eradication of illiteracy, while at the same time upgrading functional skills and basic information about employment and health related matters as well as their political, economic and social and healthcare rights.
- The legislation has proposed to start with a radio communication channel to sensitise women on literacy, healthcare, and empowerment in the sense of financial economic freedom.

UN women works globally to make the vision of the Sustainable Development Goals a reality for women and girls and stands behind women's equal participation in all aspects of life, focusing on four strategic priorities:

- Women lead, participate in and benefit equally from governance systems,
- Women have income security, decent work and economic autonomy, and
- All women and girls live a life free from all forms of violence.

UN women exclusively focus on,

- Division for the Advancement of Women (DAW),

- International Research and Training Institute for the Advancement of Women (INSTRAW),
- Office of the Special Adviser on Gender Issues and Advancement of Women (OSAGI),
- United Nations Development Fund for Women (UNIFEM), and
- Through which women empowerment is made a reality.

Professor Seema Singh *et al.* (2020) critically analysed the women empowerment in India and its various dimensions. It is identified that there are five dimensions of women empowerment viz., Cognitive, Psychological, Economic, Political and Physical dimensions. The critical explanation for each dimension and its associates are presented in the study.

Women Empowe-rment		Explanation	Parameters
1	Cogn-itive	Women having an understanding of the conditions and causes of their subordinationat the micro and macro levels. It involves making choices that may go against cultural expectations and norms.	• Raising self-esteem and self-confidence of women. • Elimination of discrimination and all forms of violence against women and girl child. • Building and strengthening partnership with civil society particularly women organisations. • Enforcement of constitutional and legal provisions and safeguarding rights of women. • Building a positive image of women in the society and recognising their contributions in social, economic and political sphere. • Developing ability among women to think critically. • Fostering decision-making and collective action. • Enabling women to make informed choices. • Ensuring women's participation in all walks of life. • Providing information, knowledge, skills for self-employment.
2	Psycho-logical	Belief that women can act at personal and societal levels to improve their individual realities and the society in which they live.	
3	Econo-mic	Women have access to, and control over, productive resources, thus ensuring some degree of financial autonomy. However, she notes that changes in the economic balance of power do not necessarily alter traditional gender roles or norms.	
4	Politi-cal	Women have the capability to analyse, organise and mobilise for social change.	
5	Physi-cal	Element of gaining control over one's body and sexuality and the ability to protect oneself against sexual violence to the empowerment process.	

Runi Datta (2019) analysed the Dr. B.R. Ambdkar's viewpoint on women empowerment in the Indian context. It is noted that the plight of women in India was overwhelmingly good during the pre-Vedic and initial stages of Vedic culure and its practices. The plight of women got worsen due to the *Manusmriti* and its stringent patriachial intentions to undermine the women development and treating women as the secondary citizens of the society.

Initially, women used to enjoy freedom, autonomy and rights in Indian society. Women were considered important in the pre-Vedic period when societies were found to be matriarchal. With the advent of the Aryan or Vedic culture, the matriarchal society got replaced by patriarchal society. However, women still enjoyed autonomy and variegated rights and had access to all kinds of learning. They had significant roles to play in religious ceremonies and in choosing their life partners. They could study the Vedas and dare to annul a marriage or go for a remarriage. Widow Remarriage was also permissible. However, the position of women deteriorated in the later Vedic period because of gender differentiation. Manu, in his book *Manusmriti*, codified all the social evils as social ethos instead of their eradication worsened the state of affairs relating to women empowerment.

Under the influence of *Manusmriti*, women had to face various deprivations in matters of acquiring property, education and studying religious scriptures. The notion that women should not be given freedom and be made subservient to male domination got deep-rooted. The Muslim invasion of our country and malpractices such as *purdah* system, polygamy and *Talaque* further worsened the situation.

Ambedkar's much reputed journals *Mook Nayak* and *Bahishkrit Bharat* became the forums to raise voice against gender inequality and the need for women's rights. There were three phases of women's movement under the aegis of Ambedkar: women's participation in the movements of the 1920s, along with men, such as the temple entry movements, building of autonomous organizations for women in the 1930s and politically organizing women under the All India Depressed Classes Mahila Federation in the 1940s.

It is equally worth mentioning the efforts of Swami Vivekananda and Raja Ram Mohun Roy who put on a hard effort to abolish *Sati* and supported widow remarriage. Jyotiba Phule dedicated his entire life for the education of women. Ishwar Chandra Vidyasagar and Mahatma Gandhi had also fought for women's cause by challenging the evil practices of *Manusmriti* against women, their social dignity and the equal right to empowerment and social justice.

Constitution of India supports that everything becomes meaningless and fruitless, be it unity, education or agitation, without the involvement of women.

Mrs. Farha Khan *et al.* (2018) analysed The Role of SHG and NGOs for Promoting Living Standard of Poor and Slum Area People in Bhopal. It is observed that the Self Help Group is an important initiative scheme used to by the government to promote poor and needy people. It is noted that SHGs are driving their best to create awareness of women empowerment and the associated factors like social, monetary, political, personal, familial, and cultural at various spheres of community well-being. The study is based on the following conceptual framework of Self Help Groups and Women Empowerment.

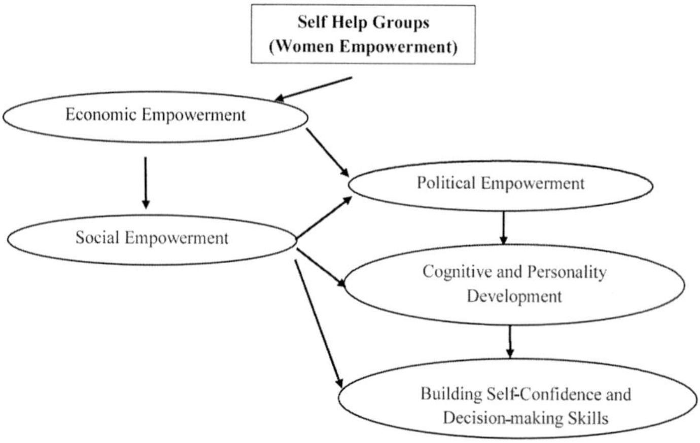

Conceptual model of Political Empowerment of Women

Naresh Rout (2016) describes the Role of Women in Ancient India and the multiple dimensions of Women Empowement during the ages of Vedic and Pre-Vedic period.The author is of the opinion that women are the gift to the society. During ancient period of India, women played a significant role followed by high status in society. It is mentioned that the role of women in Ancient Indian Literature is immense. Ancient India had many learned ladies. There were two types of scholarly women—the *Brahmavadinis*, or the women who never married and cultured the Vedas throughout their lives; and the *Sadyodvahas* who studied the Vedas till they married. Panini mentioned of female students studying Vedas.

It is concluded that the women occupied a very important position, in the ancient Bharat Varsha, in fact far superior position to the men of the time. "Shakti" a feminine term means "power" and "strength." Literary evidence suggests that kings and towns were destroyed because the rulers troubled a single woman. For example, *Valmiki Ramayana* teaches us that Ravana and his entire kingdom were wiped out because he abducted Sita. Veda Vyasa's *Mahabharata* teaches us that all the Kaurvas were killed because they humiliated Draupadi in public. Therefore, it is implied that women empowerment and best regards to the women at all levels of statecraft, administration and societal role it is treated as women empowerment is nothing but adding value to the overall well-being and upliftment of the community and the state.

Tam O'Neil *et al.* (2014) addressed the issues relating to Progress on women.

It is observed that :

- Women's empowerment is a process of personal and social change through which they gain power, meaningful choices and control over their lives.
- There are many pathways to women's empowerment but important enabling conditions include women's collective action, constitutional and legal reform, social and economic policy measures, and changes in socio-cultural norms.

- Empowerment is not something that can be done to or for women. Women are the agents of their empowerment.
- To contribute to progress on women's empowerment, the international community must support the political actions of women and their allies to change gender and other Power hierarchies.

The study highlights that power, politics and women empowerment are tuned together which implies that Power over, power to, power with and power within are the major dimensions of political empowerment of women.

Power over—the ability to control others. Changes in the distribution of power (e.g. when women gain power over men) are usually met with resistance and can result in new forms of domination and injustice.

Power to—the ability to exercise choice and change external conditions. Increasing women's individual capabilities is necessary if they are to contest and change power hierarchies (i.e. alter others' power over them).

Power with—the power that comes from collective action. Collective action increases women's solidarity and their ability to contest and change power structures.

Power within—increased critical consciousness and self-respect. A women's awareness of socially constructed identities and hierarchies, and her acceptance of herself and others as equals, are the basis of her desire for personal and structural change.

Mamta Mokta (2014) presented the critical analysis of Empowerment of Women in India. It is noted that **Empowerment** may be described as a process which helps people to assert their control over the factors which affect their lives. Empowerment of women means developing them as more aware individuals, who are politically active, economically productive and independent and are able to make intelligent or rationale decisions in the matters concerned to their all-inclusive development.

Women's empowerment is seen as the process and the result of the process of:

- Challenging the ideology of male domination and women's subordinations.
- Enabling women to gain equal access to and exploring the resources like (material, human and intellectual growth).

It is identified that Women empowerment has five dimensions, viz. Cognitive, psychological, economic, political and physical.

- The cognitive dimension refers to women having an understanding of the conditions and causes of their subordination at the micro and macro levels. It involves making choices that may go against cultural expectations and norms.
- The psychological dimension includes the belief that women can act at personal and societal levels to improve their individual realities and the society in which they live.
- The economic component requires that women have access to, and control over, productive resources, thus ensuring some degree of financial autonomy. However, she notes that changes in the economic balance of power do not necessarily alter traditional gender roles or norms.
- The political element entails that women have the capability to analyse, organise and mobilise for social change.
- There is a physical element of gaining control over one's body and sexuality and the ability to protect oneself against sexual violence

Jatin Pandey (2012) analysed the empowerment of rural women through Self Help Goups. It is observed the empowerment of rural women means eradication of poverty by rasing the economic conditions, to spur entrepreneurship intent and creating awareness of financial services through microcredits and financial services. SHG (Self-Help Group) is defined as a voluntary group valuing personal interactions and mutual aid as a means of altering or ameliorating the problems perceived as alterable, pressing and personal by most of its participants.

There are 3 models of credit linkage of SHGs with banks that exist in India:

Model I: SHGs formed and financed by banks. During last five years almost one-fifth of the total number of SHGs financed were from this category.

Model II: SHGs formed by NGOs and formal agencies but directly financed by banks. This model continues to have the major share, i.e. 72 per cent to 75 per cent of the total number of SHGs financed.

Model III: SHGs financed by banks, using NGOs and other agencies as financial intermediaries. The share of cumulative number of SHGs linked under this model up to March 2006 continued to be relatively small at 6 per cent.

From the study it is found that women empowerment is associated with financial literacy, gender awareness, health care awareness, participation in community activities, political participation, and freedom of movement towards primary and joint roles in decision making in the interest of community well-being and family welfare in particular.

Research Gap: The earlier studies on women empowerment have focused on societal aspects of empowerment giving more focus on the economical dimension. The majority of the studies reported so far are primarily from northern states of the country. Except few studies from Tamil Nadu, not enough amount of research is reported with regard to the women empowerment in general and political empowerment in particular from Coorg District.

The study is a minuscule attempt to report empirical research on political empowerment of women in the Kodagu District of Karnataka. The district Coorg or Kodagu is a niche geographical segment which needs to be explored in terms of several aspects of modern infrastructure and development including the research studies on women empowerment, SHG initiatives and participation of womenfolk in the process of holistic development of the district.

Statement of the Problem

India's journey on women empowerment and gender equality started when it became a sovereign state in 1947. While visible gains have been made through legal reforms, human development and grassroots initiatives, New Delhi still has a long way to go in many areas of women empowerment. A more concerted effort is needed to close the urban-rural divide and ensure that women in rural areas enjoy the same access to education, employment, healthcare and decision-making as their urban counterparts.

The hardest challenge will be to change attitudes, given that many barriers to women empowerment are attributed to patriarchal and patrilineal traditions that are deeply entrenched in many South Asian societies, including India.

The very goal of SHG is to alleviate poverty by creating more revenue by creating effective work. The administration of India currently offers ample scope for SHGs, especially female SHGs, Providing micro credit facilities to pave the way for small investment projects, this attempt increases the standard of life, self-reliance, freedom, independence and political participation of women in society.

As no such studies have been reported on women empowerment from Coorg District of Karnataka state, the present study is undertaken to address the various issues relating to the political empowerment, as a major dimension in the backdrop of Self Help Groups and their emerging trends in empowering the local women members.

Objectives of the Study

1. To evaluate the demographic features of SHG members in the study area.
2. To assess the state of nature of political empowerment among the SHG members.

Hypothesis of the Study

Hypotheses

H (0): There is no significant difference in the state of nature of political empowerment among the SHG members.

H (1): There is a significant difference in the state of nature of political empowerment among the SHG members.

Research Methodology

The present study is based on primary data. The primary data collected from 100 SHG women members through the interview schedule/questionnaire. Both descriptive analysis and inferential statistical analysis have been attempted to throw more light on the study. Convenient sampling technique is adopted for the study, due to the constraint of COVID-19 pandemic, time schedule nature of respondents and their availability for administering the questionnaire.The set parameters of political empowerment (Table 16.7) are measured on 5 point Likert scale (5 = strongly agree, 1 = strongly disagree).

The study is cross-sectional in nature and the primary data are collected during the past three months (October, November and December of the Financial Year 2021).

Data Analysis and Interpretation

Section A—Demographic Profile

Objective 1: To evaluate the demographic features of SHG members in the study area.

The objective 1 is analysed by using frequency and per cent analysis techniques as mentioned in Tables 16.1 to 16.7.

Table 16.1: Age Categorization of SHG Members

Age in Years	Frequency
20-25 years	5
25-30 years	8
30-35 years	9
35-40 years	9
40-45 years	41

(Contd.)

Age in Years	Frequency
45-50 years	4
50 years and above	24
Total	**100**

Source: Primary data.

Table 16.2: Occupational Status of SHG Members

Occupation	Frequency
House wife	53
Daily Wages	13
Self-employed	29
Social helper	5
Total	**100**

Source: Primary data.

Table 16.3: Educational Background of SHG Members

Education	Frequency
Illiterate	4
Up to 4th standard	5
Up to 7th - SSLC	25
PUC or + 2	22
Graduation and above	44
Total	**100**

Source: Primary data.

Table 16.4: Social Background of SHG Members

Social Background	Frequency
SC	23
ST	4
OBC	73
Total	**100**

Source: Primary data.

Table 16.5: Family Status of SHG Members

Family Status	Frequency
Nucleus Family	72
Joint Family	28
Total	**100**

Source: Primary data.

Table 16.6: Periodicity of Elections held

How frequently elections are conducted	Frequency
Once in every year	57
Once in every two years	20
Once in every three years	23
Total	**100**

Source: Primary data.

The above table numbers 16.1, 16.2, 16.3, 16.4, 16.5 and 16.6 show demographic profile of the women SHG members of Coorg District. From the frequency Table 16.1 it is found that 41 per cent of the members are of the age group 40-45 years, which is followed by 24 per cent of the members of age group 50 years and above.

Tables 16.2 and 16.3 reveal that 53 per cent of the SHG members are housewives and 47 per cent of the respondents are literates of minimum 7th standard to maximum PUC or + 2 qualification. Further it is found that 73 per cent of the respondents belongs to OBC category and 23 per cent of Scheduled Castes. The SHG office bearers are found to be selected by formal elections of democratic in nature. Table 16.6 show that 57 per cent of the SHG office bearers do conduct elections once in every year, which is followed by 23 per cent of once in every three years and 20 per cent of the office bearers are elected once in every two years.

Section B: Objective 2 & Testing of Hypothesis

To assess the state of nature of political empowerment among the SHG members.

Hypotheses

H (0): There is no significant difference in the state of nature of political empowerment among the SHG members.
H (1): There is a significant difference in the state of nature of political empowerment among the SHG members.

Table 16.7: One Sample Test

Parameters of Political Empowerment (N =100)	**Mean**	**SD**	**P value**
The association with SHGs helps women to realize their leadership ability	4.69	0.46	0.000
The association with SHGs made to me realize my constitutional rights of justice and equality	4.39	0.82	
The association with SHGs made me to realize my potential to participate in public gatherings and meetings	4.57	0.71	
The association with SHGs made me improve Self-reliance and sense of dignity	4.54	0.70	
I can express my views and ideas without any fear of inferiority	4.71	0.46	
The association with SHGs has influenced to contest for local elections at Village Panchayats/ Taluk panchayats/Zilla panchayaths	4.62	0.75	
I am better informed about the concept of Social Inclusion of community	3.68	0.79	

Source: Primary data.

Table 16.8: ANOVA—Analysis of Variance

Variance	**SS**	**DF**	**MS**	**F**	**p**	**Result**
Between:	77.274	6	12.879	27.517	0.000	H (0): Rejected H (1): Accepted
Within:	324.354	693	0.468			
Total:	**401.628**	**699**				

Source: Primary data.

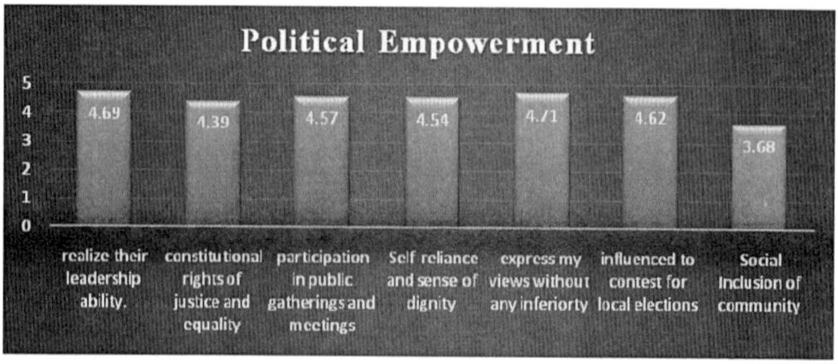

In order to assess the state of nature of political empowerment among the SHG members of the study One Sample Test is used so that the mean values taken into consideration and the respective P values at 99 per cent of level of confidence. From the study, it is found that SHGs are playing a dominant role in the political empowerment of women of the study area. The parameters like enhancement of leadership ability, facilitating the participation in public gatherings and meetings, expression of free and fair ideas without any fear of inferiority, improvement of self-reliance and sense of dignity, motivation to contest for local elections at Village Panchayats/Taluk panchayats/Zilla panchayats are the major determinants of political empowerment. However, the sharing of information is not better informed with regard to the concept of Social Inclusion of the community is not well encouraged among the women SHG members of the study.

The one way ANOVA as well as One Sample Test both reveals that there is a significant difference in the state of nature of political empowerment among the SHG members. **H (0): Rejected, H (1): Accepted)**. Therefore, it may be concluded that SHGs are adding to the political empowerment, but with varied levels of its impact on the set parameters of political empowerment as mentioned in the Tables 16.7 and 16.8 respectively.

The parameters like enhancement of leadership ability, express ideas/views without any fear of inferiority and the motivation to participate in local elections including Village Panchayats/ Taluk panchayats/Zilla panchayats are the most important determinants of political empowerment of with the help of SHGs intervention.

Summary of Findings and Conclusion

From the study it is found that SHGs are playing the role of catalyst agents to politically empower women SHG members. The women SHG members of middle age group of 40-45 years and Nucleus Family members constitute the major demographic profile of the study area.

References

Jatin Pandey, Rini Roberts (2012). "A study on empowerment of rural women through Self Help Groups." *National Monthly Referred Journal of Reasearch in Commerce & Management*, 1-10.

Mamta Mokta (2014). "Empowerment of Women in India: A Critical Analysis." *Indian Journal of Public Administration.*

Mrs. Farha Khan, G.S. Lodhi (2018). "The Role of SHG and NGOs for Promoting Living Standard of Poor and Slum Area People." *International Conference on Contemporary Technological Solutions towards fulfilment of Social Needs*, pp. 58-64, Bhopal.

Naresh Rout. (2016). "Role of Women in Ancient India." In N. Rout, *Role of Women in Ancient India*, pp. 42-47, Odisha.

Prof Seems Singh, Antra Singh (2020). "Women Empowerment in India: A Critical Analysis." *Tathapi—UGC Care List Journal, 19*(44).

Runi Datta (2019). "Emancipating and Strengthening Indian Women: An Analysis of B.R. Ambedkar's Contribution." *Contemporary Voice of Dalit*, 25-32.

Tam O'Neil, Pilar Domingo (2014). *Progress on Women Empowerment—From technical fixes to ploitical action.*

Women's Movement and Internationalisation—Engendering the Global Agenda, A Success Story of Women and the United Nations (1999).

Index